IMAGES
of America

MEXICAN AMERICANS IN REDONDO BEACH AND HERMOSA BEACH

ON THE COVER: Fiesta Days, sponsored by the City of Redondo Beach, started in 1940 and continued until 1950. Parades included floats, horse-drawn wagons, and equestrian units, and food booths, offering Mexican specialties, were set up on El Paseo Avenue. In this 1942 image, Delfina Gonzalez Reynaga and a military friend dance in the middle of Pacific Avenue in old downtown Redondo Beach in celebration of the event. (Photograph by Senaida "Sadie" Lopez; courtesy Alice Lopez Buffington.)

IMAGES
of America

MEXICAN AMERICANS IN REDONDO BEACH AND HERMOSA BEACH

Alex Moreno Areyan

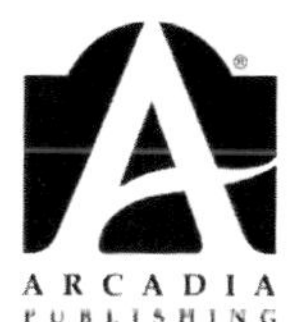
ARCADIA PUBLISHING

ISBN 978-0-7385-4699-5

Published by Arcadia Publishing
Charleston, South Carolina

Printed in the United States of America

Library of Congress Catalog Card Number: 2006933256

For all general information contact Arcadia Publishing at:
Telephone 843-853-2070
Fax 843-853-0044
E-mail sales@arcadiapublishing.com
For customer service and orders:
Toll-Free 1-888-313-2665

Visit us on the Internet at www.arcadiapublishing.com

To Rudy Moreno Areyan for the lesson regarding the streets of life; Cesar Chavez for allowing me to understand the meaning of "Si Se Puede;" Domingo Moreno for exemplifying dignity and leadership; John Luna Moreno for reminding me to stop talking and start doing; and Damian, Analisa, and Ryan for trying to understand my cultural passion.

Contents

ACKNOWLEDGMENTS

This pictorial history would not have been possible without generous assistance of many people in the Mexican American communities now living in Redondo and Hermosa Beaches, Carson, Gardena, and Grover Beach. Heartfelt gratitude is extended to the oral historians whose patience and cooperation were critical to producing this book. They are Carmen Hernandez, Nieves and "Cal" Gonzalez, "Chuey" and Lupe Hernandez, and Senaido and Irma Vargas. They also produced some priceless photographs. For the lengthy interviews and the treasured photographs, my deep appreciation to Andrea Adame; Ray Adame; Victoria Arendain; Junior Anaya; Porfiria Banda; Herminda Banda; Alice Buffington; Albert and Emma Castillon; Margaret Carillo; Richard Castillon; Sally Chavez; Luis and Chavela Cordova; Irene Cota; Carmen Daugherty; Robin Duarte; Amador Espinosa; Danny Espinoza; John Fernandez; Ordie Fernandez; "Buzzy" Garcia; Dona Berta Gomez; "Ponche" Gonzalez; Minerva Heredia; Natalie Herrera; Fr. Raymond Mallett, OFM, Conv.; Josie Mendez; David Mendoza; Ismael Mendoza; Julian Mendoza; Candy Millan; Diana Millan; John and Willa Moreno; Mary Lou and "Rom" Ordaz; Rachel Ortiz; Lionel Preciado; Ricardo and Betty Real; John "Jack" and Jane Renke; Rosie Salazar; Louis Saldana; Jody Scully; Diana Swarz; Pearl Vidal; and Nick Vargas. I would also like to express my thanks to John Bogert, columnist for the *Daily Breeze* newspaper, for his story on Berta Gomez; Patricia Dreizler for her encouragement; Mary Ann Keating also for her encouragement; "Tike" Karavas for the sports information; Don Lechman for his friendship and technical support; Rol Rogers for his support; and the Redondo Beach Historical Museum.

Last but not least, to my wonderful wife, Linda, whose infinite patience, love, and unconditional support carried me through this book's journey of twists and turns.

INTRODUCTION

Beginning with the arrival in 1905 of Mauro Gonzalez, who unloaded lumber ships at the old Redondo Beach wooden pier, to 1960, a 50-year period, the lives of Mexican Americans are told for the first time in print. The Mexican Americans who make Redondo and Hermosa Beach home consider the beach cities a superb place to live, and the photographs and oral history collected for this book provides a view of their lives for the first time from the inside.

The first Mexican Americans labored primarily in agriculture, later turning to harvesting crops in the valleys of Northern California and the San Fernando Valley. Prior to World War II, they sustained Japanese American and Greek American farmers in growing and harvesting flowers in southern Redondo Beach, Hermosa Beach, Manhattan Beach, and Torrance, and they later grew vegetables on the Palos Verdes Peninsula, near land that later became Marineland of the Pacific Aquarium, which closed in the 1970s.

During this period, the flowers and vegetables harvested by Mexican American labor contributed to the economic growth of the Los Angeles produce market until the mid-1950s. In the beach cities in the early 1930s and early 1940s, entrepreneurs began operating restaurants, delicatessens, grocery stores, beauty shops, excavation, land grading, demolition, and construction businesses. In 1934, Bill Valenzuela operated a service station on the corner of Ford and Pier Avenue, in northern Redondo Beach. Albert Castillon owned a successful brake supply business in Hermosa Beach for over 20 years. In later years, Mexican Americans were politically active in Redondo Beach where Steve Colin, an attorney, and Ronald Cawdrey, a union representative, served on the Redondo Beach City Council.

This book begins to document the history of Mexican Americans in southwest Los Angeles County. It is based largely on oral history provided by many senior Mexican American residents of both cities, since no prior recorded history of this community existed outside of a few photographs found at the Redondo Beach Historical Society museum in northern Redondo Beach. Regrettably, due to time and other constraints, it was not possible to do as comprehensive a treatment of the topic as originally intended. In some cases, certain photographs could not be included due to space, and some important interviews could not be conducted due to time constraints. It is hoped, however, that future publications will document with greater depth the presence, achievements, and contributions of Mexican Americans in southwest Los Angeles County. Any factual errors in this publication are the sole responsibility of the author.

FOREWORD

My family moved to Carlson Lane in northern Redondo Beach when I was five years old. In a short time, looking for other boys to play with, I became aware that everyone had dark hair and brown eyes and spoke a language I did not understand. I was blond and blue eyed and spoke English. In time, with the help of the Solis and Torres families, I learned to speak Spanish, which to this day has served me well. I was always treated as just another one of the children in the neighborhood, and looking back, I realize how fortunate I was to be assimilated into the community. Thank you to the Mexican American mothers who treated me as family. I would not trade my experience or the values they passed on to me for anything.

My mother often spoke of being a part of the community and remembered acting as a midwife for several neighborhood families. For some time, she had the only telephone in the neighborhood and was always ready to loan it to our neighbors in time of need.

As a child, I noticed that Sundays were very special to my new neighbors because they all dressed up and went to church! As time went by, I realized Our Lady of Guadalupe Church was the main focal point of the community, with weddings, funerals, cultural events, and many other activities always going on there.

As I grew older, I began to realize that the members of the Mexican American community were no different from anyone else; they were honest, had a very strong work ethic, and extremely close family ties. Many of the descendants of the families I grew up with have gone on to become professionals in their fields—doctors, lawyers, and nurses. Two of the community's descendants went on to become members of the city council. I am sure the descendants of these early families thank their forbearers for instilling in them a strong set of values, which included the desire to achieve and excel as they grew up.

I congratulate the Mexican American families of Redondo Beach and Hermosa Beach for their contributions and achievements to our community over the years.

—John "Jack" Renke

One

Coming to Redondo Beach and Hermosa Beach

The settlement of Mexican Americans in Redondo Beach and Hermosa Beach occurred in three stages between 1905 and 1960. Stage one began with the arrival of Mauro and Maria Gonzalez in central Redondo. The family, who lived on Elena Street, had eight children and 23 grandchildren. Around 1915, Domingo and Maria Moreno and Mauricio and Catarina Colin left Mexico to escape the ravages of the revolution and settled in the Villa Tract. Eventually, they purchased properties, passing them on to their children. Domingo Moreno had 12 children and 54 grandchildren; Mauricio Colin had 13 children and 65 grandchildren. Mauro, Domingo, and Mauricio began the three largest groups of Mexican Americans in Redondo Beach during this phase.

Stage two occurred between 1930 and 1936, when a group of about 15 families moved to Redondo Beach from Lompoc in central California after the Celite diatomaceous earth mine in Lompoc closed in 1930. As a new mine, named Dicalite, opened in Walteria, families followed the work, buying homes in central, and later, in northern Redondo Beach and Hermosa Beach. The mine's workers were mainly Mexican Americans, who were instrumental in helping Dicalite become the world's largest provider of filtering material.

The third stage of settlement, starting around 1933 and continuing until about 1960, involved the alignment of economic and social forces. The Dicalite Mine and the Columbia Steel foundry in neighboring Torrance brought together the original Mexican American settlers, the relocated families from Lompoc and the Torrance colony of "La Rana" (Spanish for frog). These groups intermarried and joined with Mexican Americans from Gardena, Lomita, Harbor City, and San Pedro, gathering at large *jamaicas* (fiestas) at Our Lady of Guadalupe Church, which served as the central religious and social meeting point for the community. After World War II, Mexican American soldiers returned to Redondo and Hermosa Beaches, marrying and raising their children there. Between 1945 and 1960, companies such as General Telephone, Redondo Tile, American Standard, Harvey Aluminum, and the emerging aircraft companies attracted additional Mexican American families from other areas.

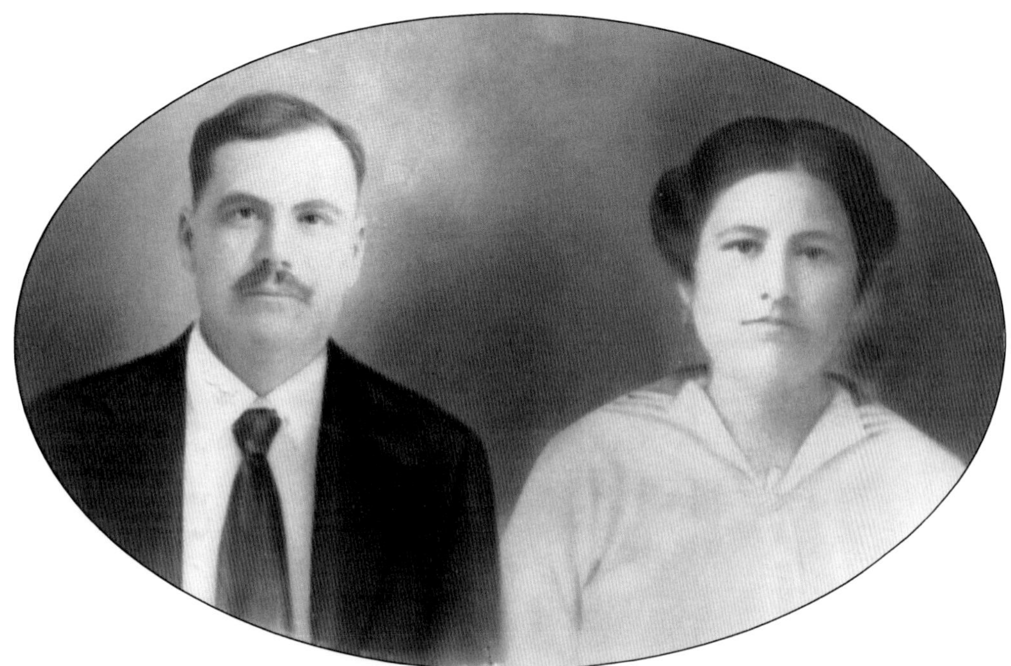

Mauro Gonzalez was the first Mexican American to settle in Redondo Beach, in 1905. In this rare 1920s image, he is pictured with his wife, Maria. They raised eight children in central Redondo near what is now city hall. He installed the early electrical lines for the operation of the old Pacific Electric cars. (Courtesy Darlene Swarz.)

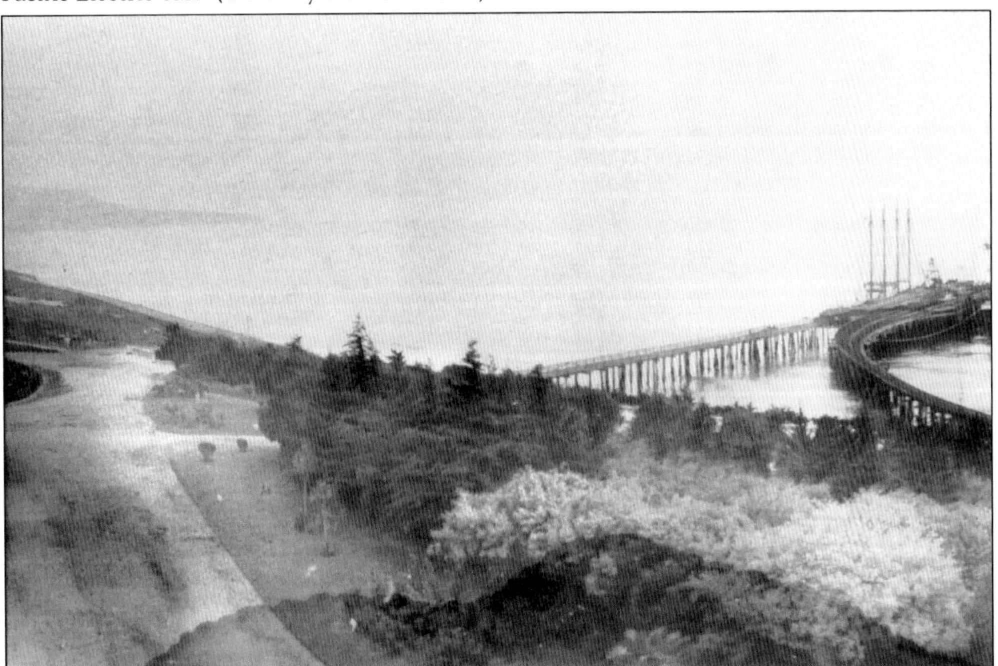

This 1900 image of the old wooden wharf in Redondo Beach is what Mauro Gonzalez saw while he unloaded lumber ships coming to Redondo from the Oregon coast. Note the hazy Palos Verdes Peninsula in the upper left. (Courtesy Katie Aguilar Bopp.)

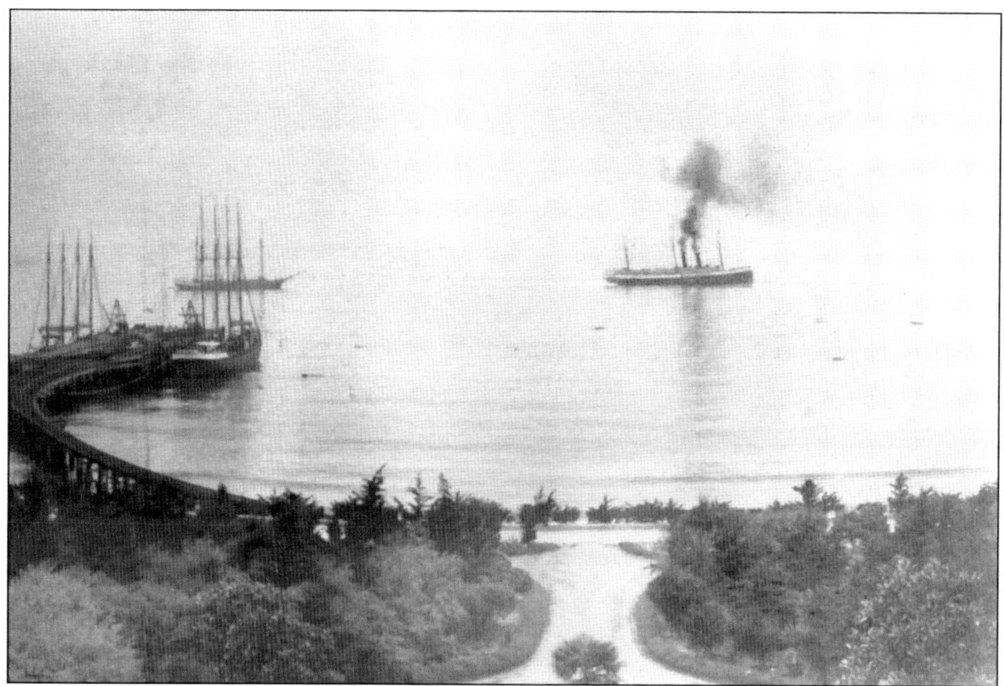

This 1900 photograph of the Redondo Beach wharf shows two types of ships that brought in cargo to the old pier. On the left are two four-masted sailing ships. On the right, a coal-burning steamship reveals the transition from sailing ships to steam. The street in the center would later become Coral Way. (Courtesy Katie Aguilar Bopp.)

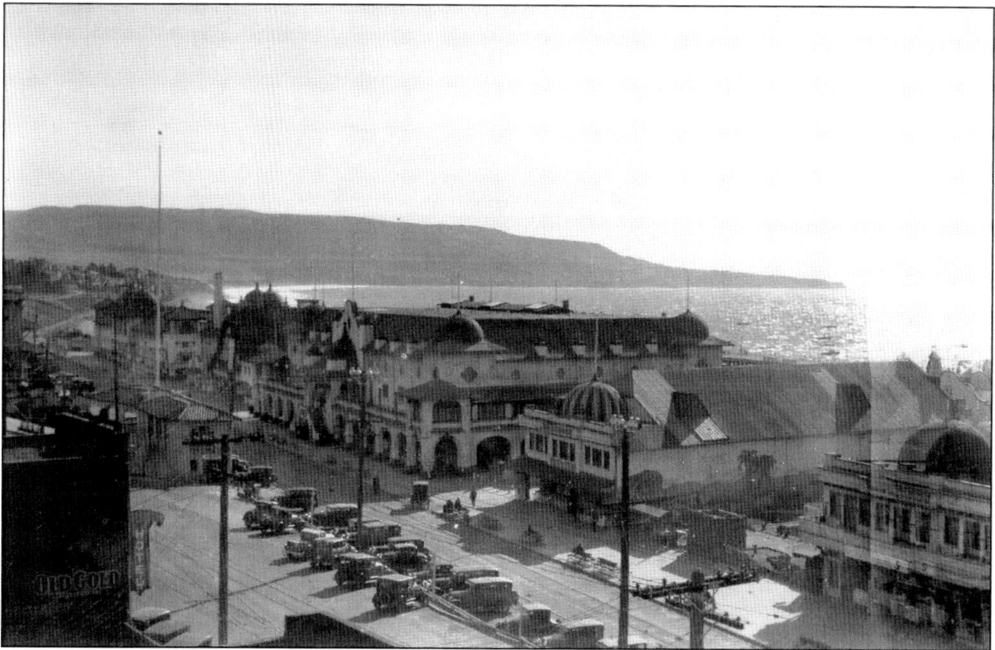

In this photograph from around 1920, the buildings in downtown Redondo Beach, with domes and spires, reflected the architecture of that period. The old Redondo Pavilion, which later became the Old Redondo Barn Dance Hall, is seen in the center. (Courtesy Caroline Villa.)

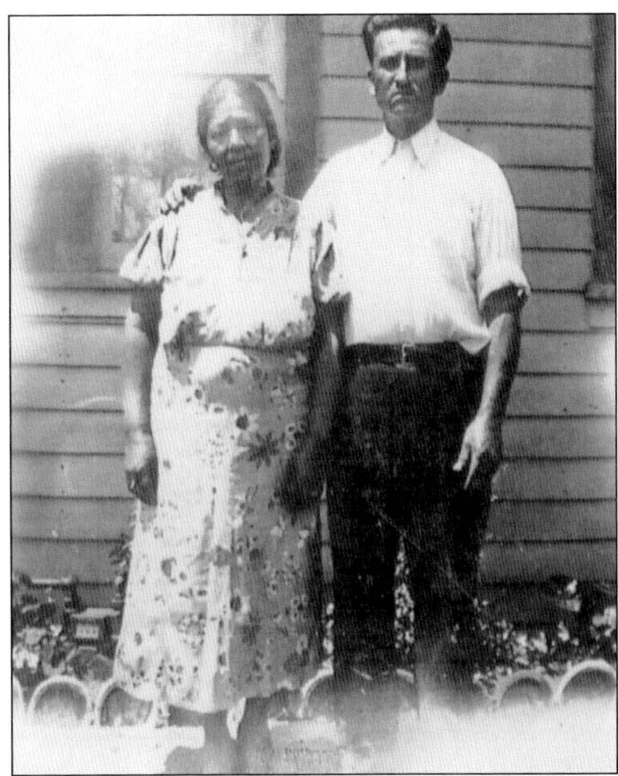

In 1915, Domingo and Maria Moreno settled in northern Redondo Beach. In 1939, they purchased this home on Carmelita Avenue, where they raised 12 children. Domingo led the group of community leaders who built Our Lady of Guadalupe Church in Hermosa Beach in 1923. The abalone shells in the flower bed came from the Palos Verdes Peninsula, when abalone hunting was unrestricted. (Courtesy John Luna Moreno.)

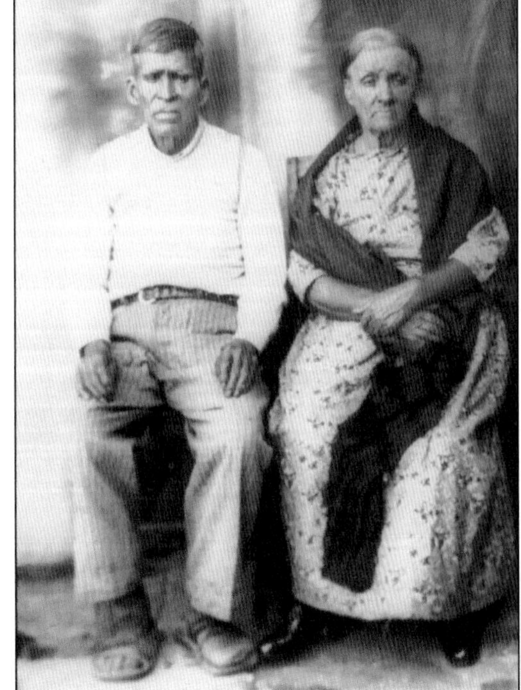

Iginio Moreno and his wife, Martina Vasquez, parents of Domingo Moreno, are seen in this image taken in Mexico in 1900. Martina came to Redondo Beach in 1940 to join Domingo, their only son, after her husband passed away in Mexico. (Courtesy Inez Moreno Areyan.)

Domingo & Mary Moreno 8.4% July 5 1938

PAYMENT DUE MONTHLY ON THE 15th

AMOUNT 750.00

TERMS { Payable $20.00 on 15th each month interest included or more

DATE PAID	TOTAL AMOUNT PAID	INTEREST	INTEREST PAID TO	PAID ACCT. PRINCIPAL	BALANCE PRINCIPAL DUE	TELLER'S INITIALS
July 5/38	Note secured by Deed of Trust against Lots 4-5-6-7 & 8 of Block 135 Redondo Villa Tract				750.00	
Oct 22/38	Cash advanced to pay exp of Foreclosure				94.90	
" "	" Geo [illegible] a/c " 2 trips Santa Ana				2.00	
					846.90	
Dec 13/38	Cash returned by Bank of Am a/c Foreclosure 94.90					
" "	" Cash paid by Mrs Hagerman 80.00					

This mortgage payment record book issued to Domingo and Mary Moreno in 1938 shows they paid $750 for five residential lots in rural northern Redondo's Villa Tract, as the area was known at that time. Affordable land such as this was a strong draw for the early settlers. (Courtesy John Luna Moreno.)

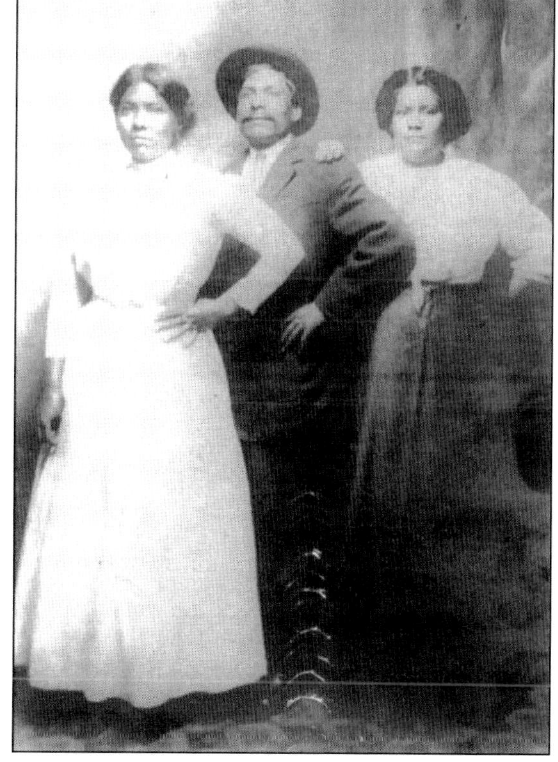

Maria Bravo Moreno (left), Mauricio Colin, and his wife, Catarina Bravo Colin, are pictured in 1915 shortly after coming to Redondo Beach with Maria's husband, Domingo. Both of these families first settled on Morgan Lane in northern Redondo Beach. (Courtesy Victoria Arendain.)

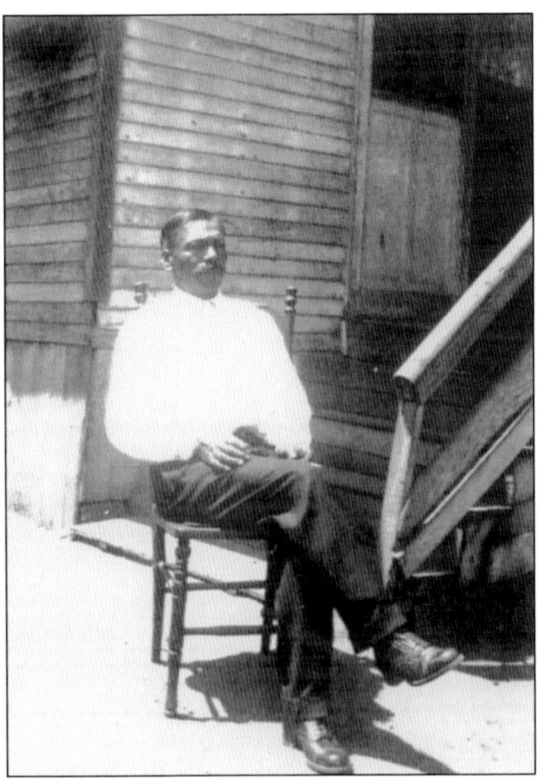

Mauricio Colin is pictured here in the 1920s in front of his home on Morgan Lane. He farmed cornfields near Harkness and Morgan Lanes from the late 1930s to the early 1950s. He and his wife, Catarina, raised 13 children who then bore them 65 grandchildren. (Courtesy Victoria Arendain.)

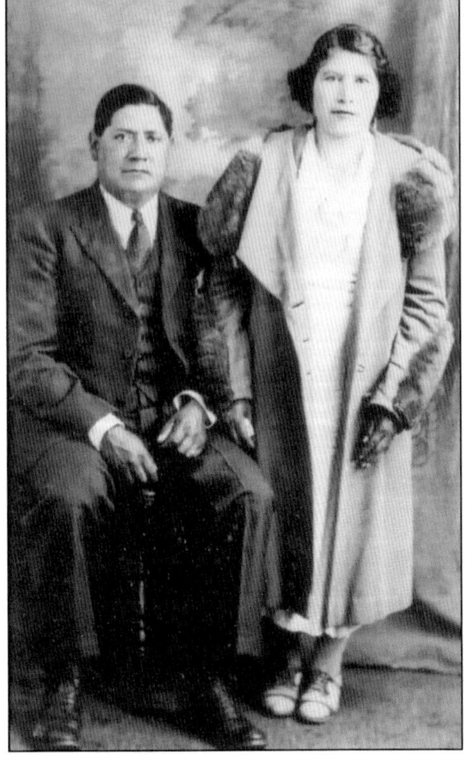

The Feliciano and Catarina Vallejo family came to Redondo Beach from Kansas City, Missouri, in early 1920, after Feliciano's retirement from railroad work. He was one of the workers who helped Domingo Moreno and a team of approximately 11 other community leaders in constructing Our Lady of Guadalupe Church in Hermosa Beach. (Courtesy Ray Adame.)

This 1923 photograph shows Ignacio Hernandez and his wife, Maria Hurtado Hernandez, with their infant daughter Grace, who came to Redondo Beach during this period. In the 1940s, Ignacio Hernandez was a flower grower, with fields on Knob Hill Avenue in southern Redondo Beach and Beryl Street in northern Redondo. Their daughter Mary Lou was born in their ranch house on the Knob Hill property. (Courtesy Mary Lou Ordaz.)

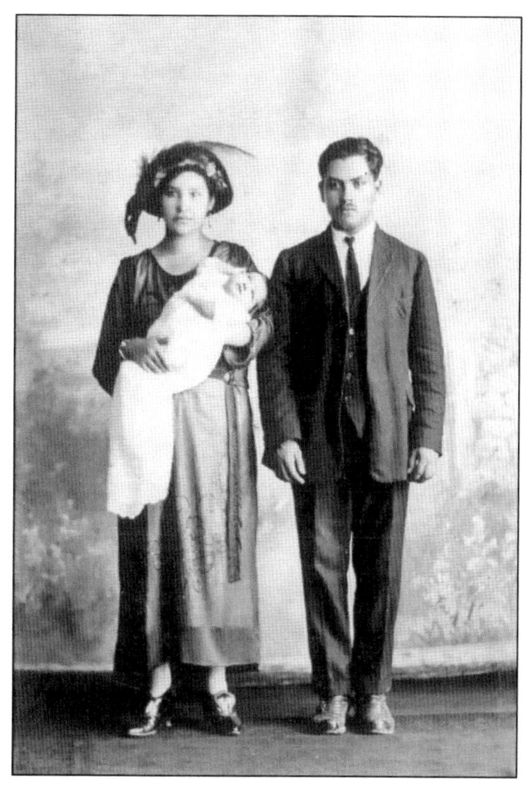

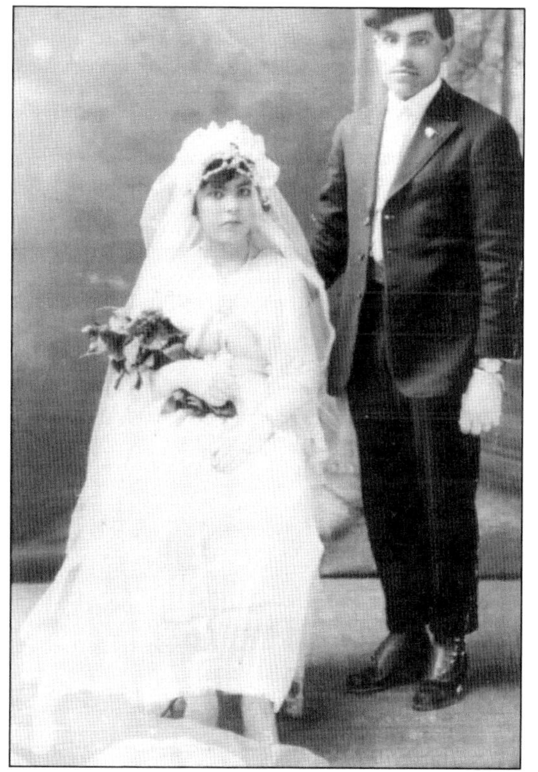

Enrique Espinoza and Wilfrida Contreras met on a 90-mile Model T Ford ride from Bakersfield to Lompoc, California, around 1913. Danny Espinoza, their son, explains that Enrique rode on the running board while company representatives and family members transported Wilfrida and her mother to Lompoc, where the mother had been hired to be the cook for the Dicalite Corporation mine workers. They were married in 1914; she was 14 at that time. (Courtesy Danny Espinoza.)

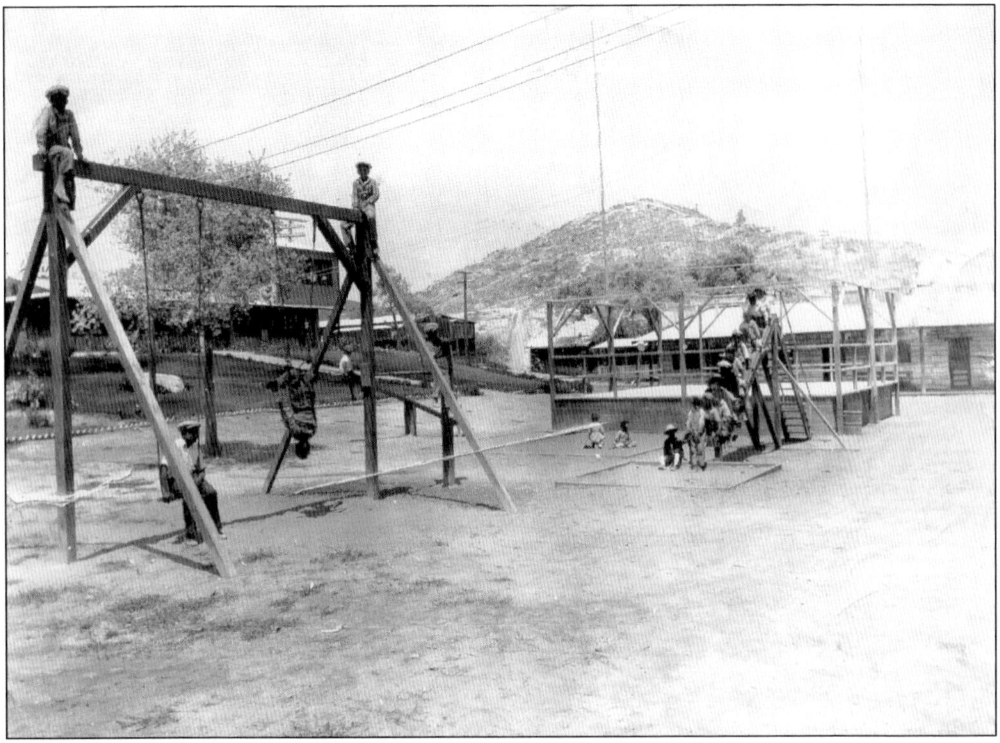

Dicalite Corporation mine workers were provided company housing and recreation near the mine in Lompoc, California. This *c.* 1927 photograph shows children on playground equipment in front of the billiard hall, located behind the swing set. Note the boxing ring behind the slide. One of the two girls in the sandbox is believed to be Laura Luna, who later married Gonzalo Moreno of Redondo Beach. (Courtesy John Luna Moreno.)

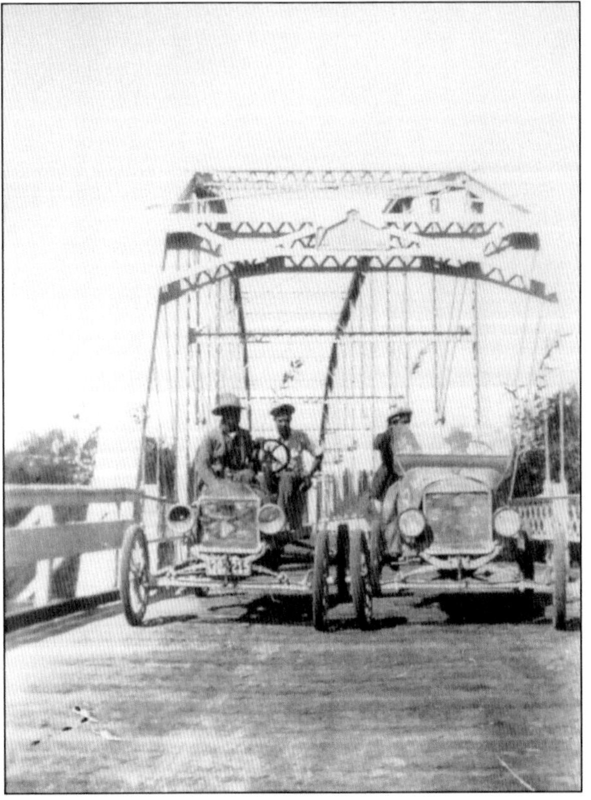

Men of the Flores and Mendoza families cross a bridge in Lompoc, California, in the early 1920s in their 1915 and 1925 Model T Ford sedans. These vehicles sold for about $200 each when new. Both families relocated to Redondo Beach around 1930. (Courtesy Mendoza brothers.)

The Dicalite Mine in Walteria, California, was the background for this 1926 photograph. At far right is Antonio Castillon, and Jesus Castillon is in the middle with two unidentified workers. The steam shovel loaded Dicalite material, used extensively for all types of industrial filtration all over the world, into the grinders for processing and shipment. (Courtesy Albert Castillon.)

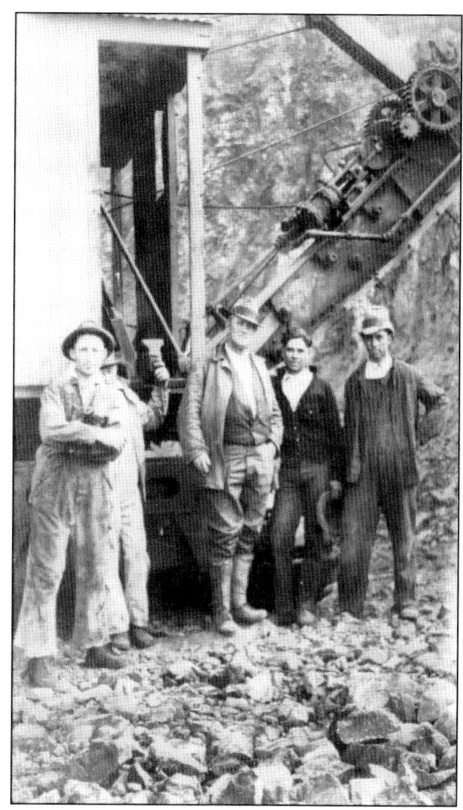

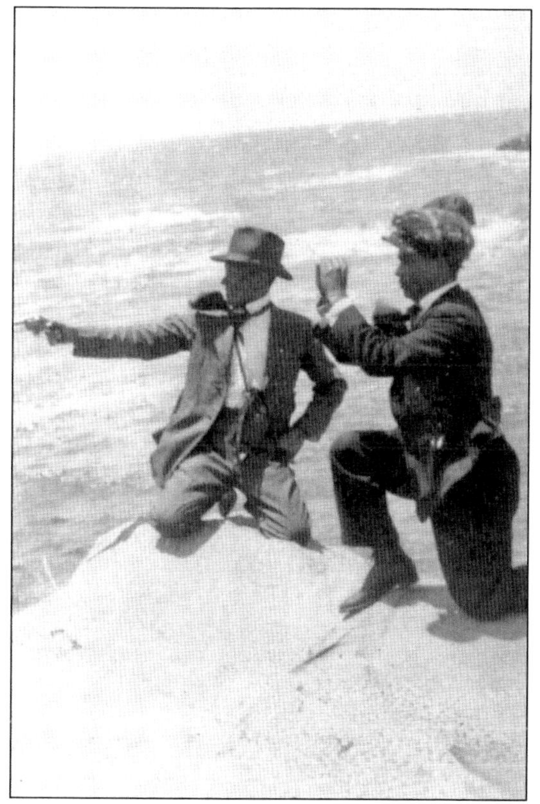

In this rare photograph, Pablo Mendoza, right, and an unidentified friend engage in target practice on a beach near Lompoc, California, around 1927. Note the holster on Pablo's hip and the friend's holster around his neck. Pablo relocated to Redondo Beach in the late 1920s along with other families when the Dicalite Mine in Lompoc closed. (Courtesy Mendoza brothers.)

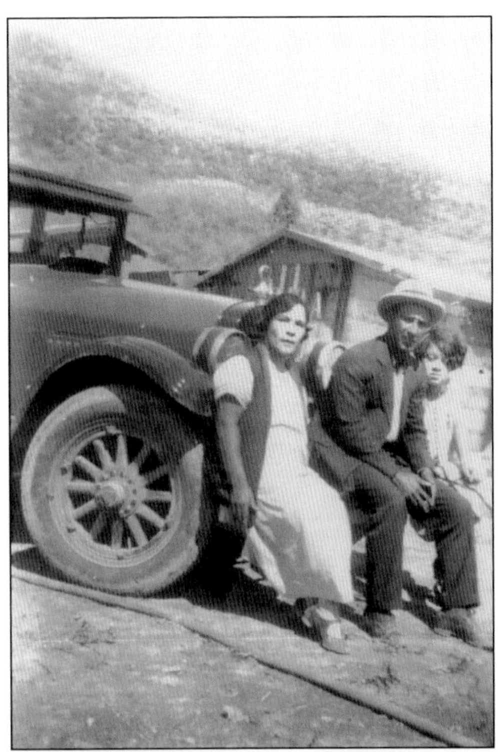

This photograph, taken before 1920, shows Eugenia and Vicente Lopez and young Dolores posing with their 1925 Packard at Dicalite's employee housing in Lompoc. Dolores married Pablo Mendoza around 1929. (Courtesy Mendoza brothers.)

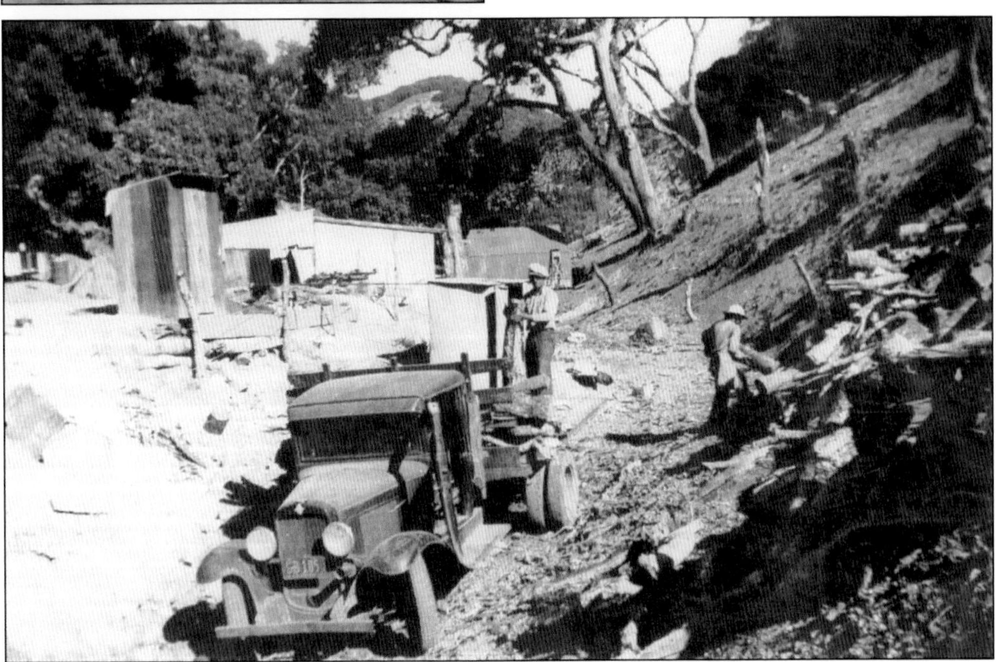

In the early 1920s, in Lompoc, California, Joe Ybarra and his helper gather wood for charcoal making. Ybarra sold charcoal to stores in Lompoc before coming to Redondo Beach in the early 1930s. Note the two-letter, three-number license plate on the old Ford truck that denotes the low number of commercial trucks that were registered in California at that time. (Courtesy Caroline Villa.)

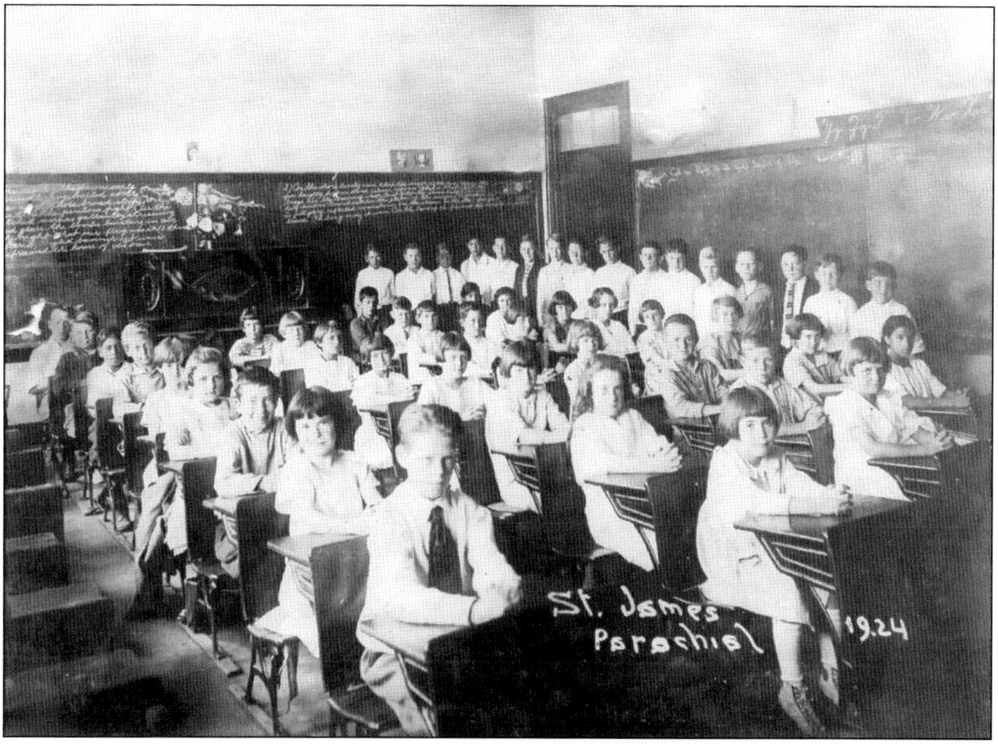

This is a 1924 class picture at St. James Catholic School in Redondo Beach. Salvador Ortiz is shown in the left row, third from the rear. Ortiz's children, fraternal twins Rachel and David, graduated from St. James 39 years later. (Courtesy Rachel Ortiz.)

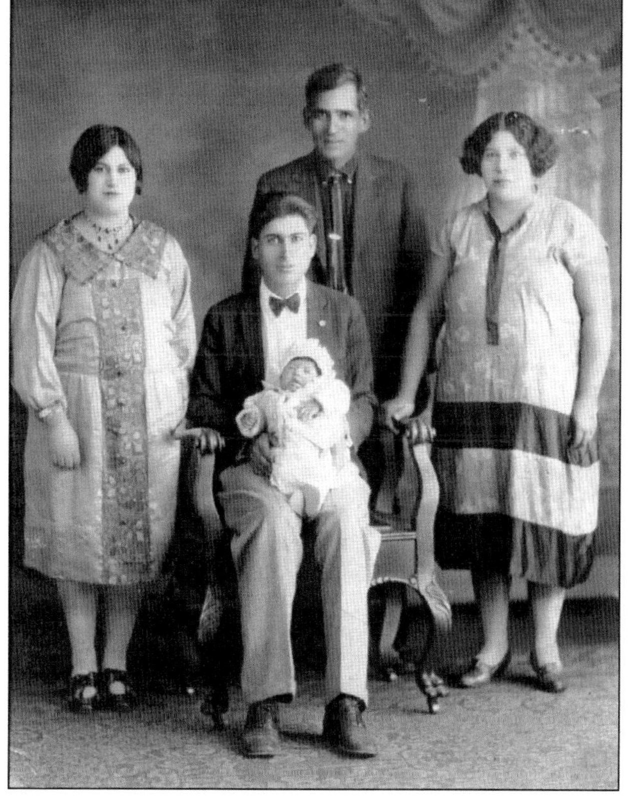

In 1926, after the baptism of their daughter Alice, Joe Lopez (center) and his wife, Senaida "Sadie" Lopez (right), proudly pose for the child's first photograph taken at a studio near the Dolores Mission on Olvera Street, in old downtown Los Angeles. The Lopez family was originally from Culver City, California, before moving to Redondo Beach in 1935. The godparents of the child are unidentified. (Courtesy Alice Buffington.)

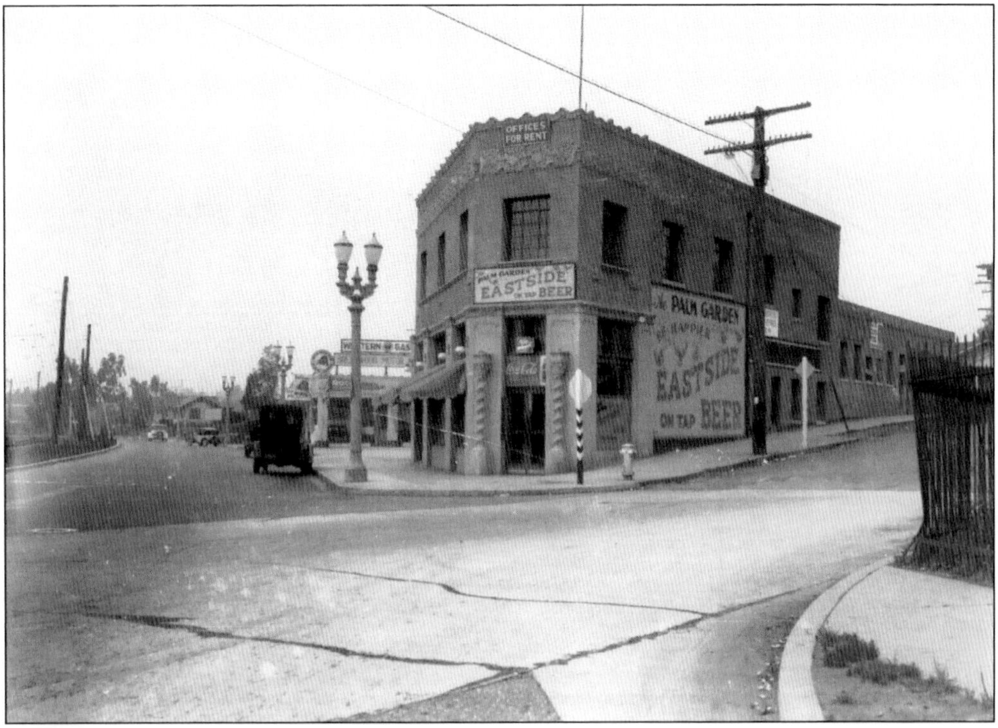

This is how downtown Redondo Beach appeared to some of the early Mexican American settlers a few years after arriving. This building was at the corner of Emerald Avenue and Pacific Avenue. Behind the building to the right were the old city hall and fire and police departments. (Courtesy Caroline Villa.)

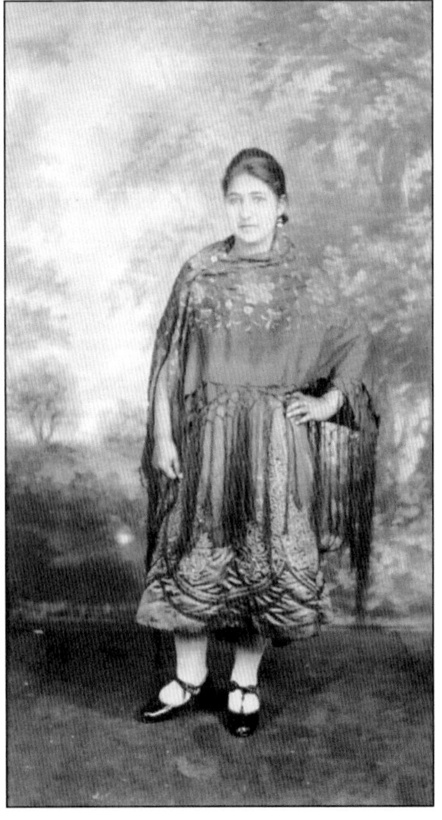

This 1928 photograph shows Inez Moreno at the age of 15. She and her brothers, Frank and Gonzalo, attended catechism classes in their father Domingo's garage on Carmelita Avenue with other neighborhood children. Overcrowding prompted Domingo to seek out others to help him build Our Lady of Guadalupe Church in Hermosa Beach. Inez married Alejo Areyan in 1929, at the age of 16. They raised seven children, including the author, at 1718 Morgan Lane in Redondo Beach. (Courtesy Alex Moreno Areyan.)

This June 1929 photograph celebrates the marriage of Alejo Areyan and Inez Moreno, who married at the beginning of the Depression. Alejo worked on Japanese American truck farms during the Depression years, and the vegetables the farmers shared with him helped to support his family. Alejo spoke some Japanese and sang Japanese lullabies to his children. (Courtesy Inez Areyan.)

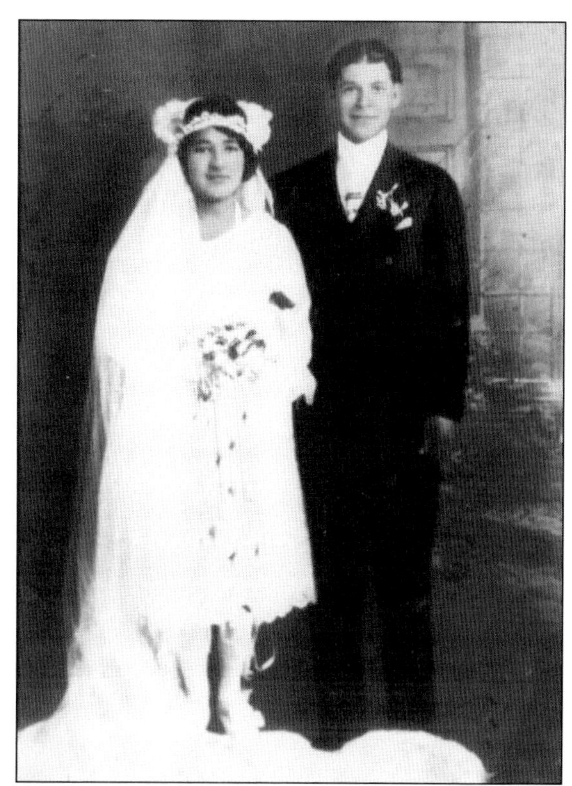

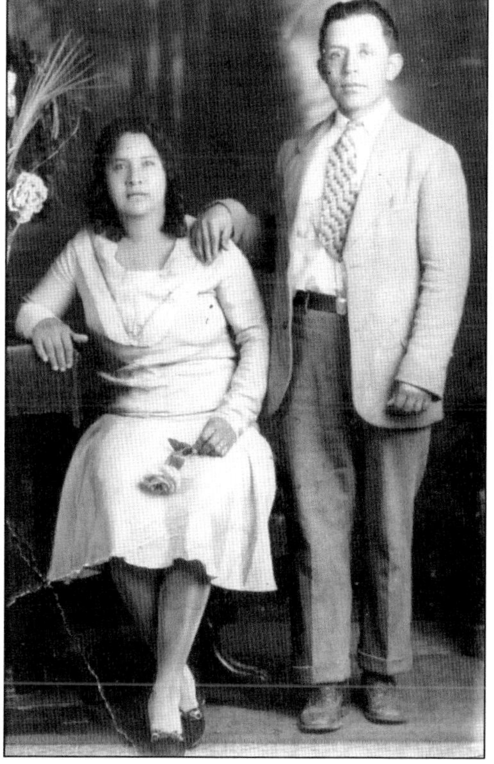

Romaldo and Pascuala Saldana are seen in this 1920s photograph. In 1924, they came to Redondo Beach from Columbine, Colorado, where he had worked at the Columbine Mine. After moving to northern Redondo Beach, he continued to do mine work at the Dicalite Mine in Walteria, California. He was another community leader who helped build Our Lady of Guadalupe Church, and he served as a church usher there for many years. (Courtesy Carmen Daugherty.)

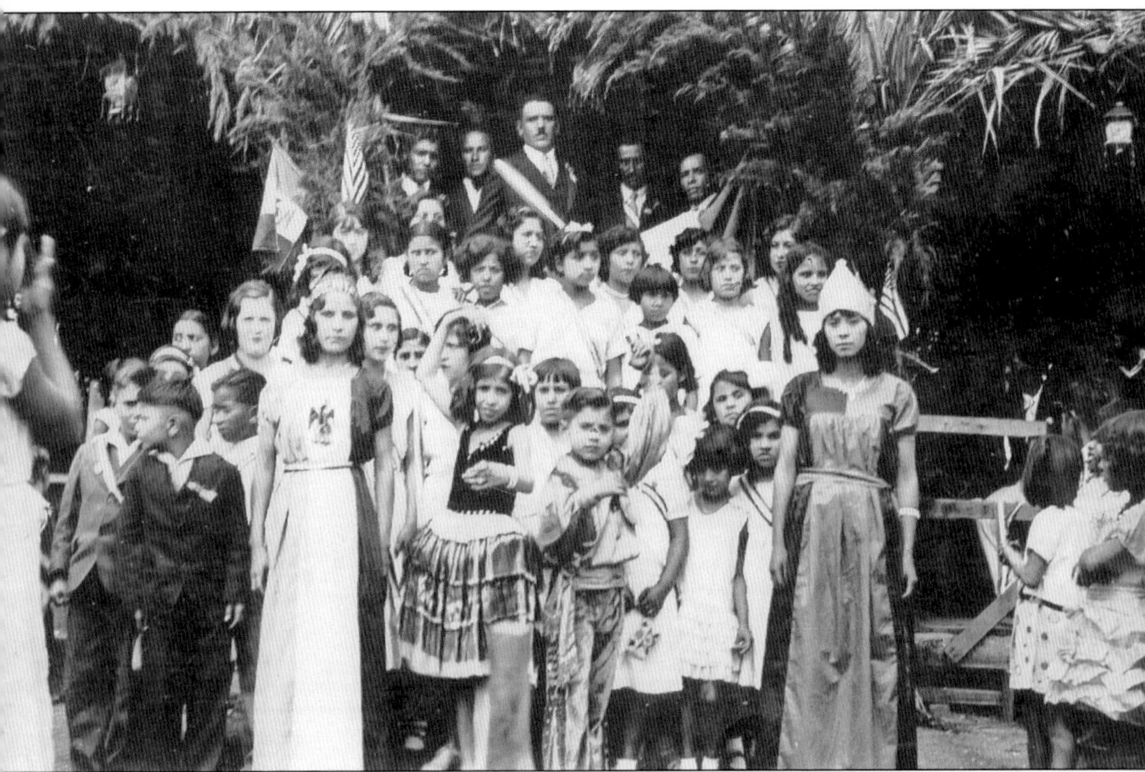

Nearly 50 children, descendants of the early Mexican American settlers of Redondo and Hermosa Beach, were brought together to celebrate Mexican Independence Day at Clark Stadium in Hermosa Beach on September 16, 1932. Standing in the background are some of the community leaders, including Alfredo Flores, Domingo Moreno, and Romaldo Saldana. Note the American and Mexican flags behind the children at the top far left and the American flag at the far right. (Courtesy Inez Areyan.)

Two

FAMILY LIFE

For Mexican Americans, the concept of family unity is a belief that is usually more important than economic success, status, or prestige. Values that are stressed are respect for elders and family members, honesty, sharing, kindness, collaboration, and hospitality. Public respect toward women such as sisters, wives, and mothers is expected at all times, since they are considered the center of home life. A high level of respect toward one's parents is of paramount importance, as is respect toward one's godparents, who in Spanish are known as *padrinos*. When godparents agree to become sponsors for a child, a religious and social contract is formed between the sponsors and the child's parents, who refer to the relationship between them as *compadres* (co-parents).

Compadres agree to become patrons and protectors of the child, assuring that the child will be raised in the Catholic faith if the parents die. Mexican Americans also become *compadres* when couples agree to become best man or maid of honor at a wedding. As *compadre* relationships are entered into, strong bonds are formed among families. When viewing Mexican American wedding photographs, frequently members of the wedding party are related through intermarriage or by *compadre* relationships. A popular wedding custom is the money dance, where guests pin large bills on the bride's veil or place them in the groom's handkerchief pocket or hand. The dance symbolizes the guests' wishes for a prosperous future.

Family gatherings always include abundant and appetizing food, particularly at baptisms, confirmations, and weddings. Thanksgiving and Christmas involve the ritual of tamale making. Making of these delicacies provide an occasion for families, friends, and neighbors to gather to exchange family stories and *chismes* (friendly gossip). Mexican American family life values are strongly connected to those of the Catholic faith; they are nearly identical and mutually supportive of family life.

STATE OF CALIFORNIA
DEPARTMENT OF PUBLIC HEALTH
VITAL STATISTICS

CERTIFIED COPY OF BIRTH RECORD

DISTRICT NO. 1909 REGISTRAR'S NO. 28

Maria Hernandez
FULL NAME OF CHILD

DATE IF NAME ADDED BY SUPPLEMENTAL REPORT

PLACE OF BIRTH: COUNTY Los Angeles
CITY OR TOWN Redondo Beach
IF OUTSIDE CITY OR TOWN LIMITS, WRITE RURAL

NAME OF HOSPITAL OR INSTITUTION Knob Hill near Sepulveda Blvd.
IF NOT IN HOSPITAL OR INSTITUTION, GIVE STREET NUMBER OR LOCATION

SEX F

TWIN OR TRIPLET ____ IF SO—BORN 1ST ____ 2D ____ 3D ____

DATE OF BIRTH May 13, 1932 10 P. M.
MONTH BY NAME DAY YEAR HOUR

FATHER OF CHILD

FULL NAME Ignacio Hernandez
COLOR OR RACE Mexican
BIRTHPLACE Mexico

MOTHER OF CHILD

FULL MAIDEN NAME Maria Hurtado
COLOR OR RACE Mexican
BIRTHPLACE Mexico

DATE RECEIVED BY LOCAL REGISTRAR May 16 1932

REGISTRAR'S SIGNATURE J. L. POMEROY, M. D.

BY By Louise Sturges

I hereby certify that I attended the birth of this child, on the date above stated.

ATTENDANT'S OWN SIGNATURE J. F. Spencer, M. D.

ADDRESS Redondo Beach DATE SIGNED 5/15/32

CERTIFICATION BY LOCAL REGISTRAR OR COUNTY RECORDER

THIS IS TO CERTIFY, That the foregoing is a true and correct copy of statements appearing on the recorded birth of the above named child, as filed in the local or county records and is issued under the provisions of Section 10202, Health and Safety Code.

IN TESTIMONY WHEREOF, *Witness my hand and seal this* 21st *day of* May 1948

at Torrance, *California.*

FEE $1.00

[SEAL]

Los Angeles County Health Department
Roy O. Gilbert, M.D., County Health Officer
and Registrar of Vital Statistics
By Margaret W. Patrigan
Deputy Registrar

FORM XI

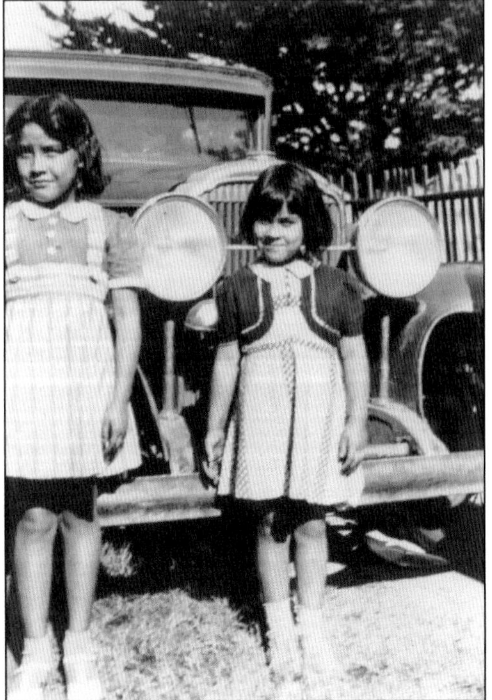

Mary Lou Hernandez Ordaz's birth certificate attests to the rural nature of southern Redondo Beach in 1932. Her place of birth is stated as "Knob Hill near Sepulveda Blvd." because street addresses were not used at that time. Her father, Ignacio, together with other Mexican American nursery and flower growers, such as Amador Fernandez and Peter Serrato, had flower fields throughout the cities of Redondo, Hermosa, and Torrance, and on the Palos Verdes Peninsula.

This photograph, taken around 1939, shows the 1937 Buick limousine that provided ample transportation for Ignacio Hernandez and his family for periodic trips to Watts, in south central Los Angeles, to purchase bulk groceries. On the return trip, Mary Lou Hernandez (left) and her sister Natalie happily recall eating much of the fresh fruit while sitting on the spacious back seat. (Courtesy Mary Lou Ordaz.)

This early 1930s image shows Ramon "Ray" Millan and his bride, Laura, as newlyweds. They married in Santa Ana, California, in 1931 and subsequently moved to Hermosa Beach. After living in several locations, they finally settled in a two-story home located at Prospect Avenue and First Street in Hermosa. Before serving in World War II, Ray served as a block warden during wartime blackouts. (Courtesy Candy Millan.)

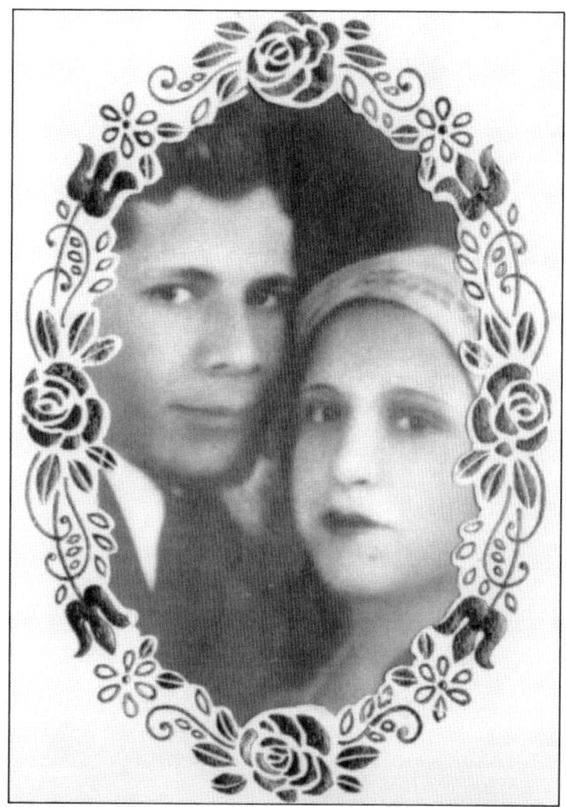

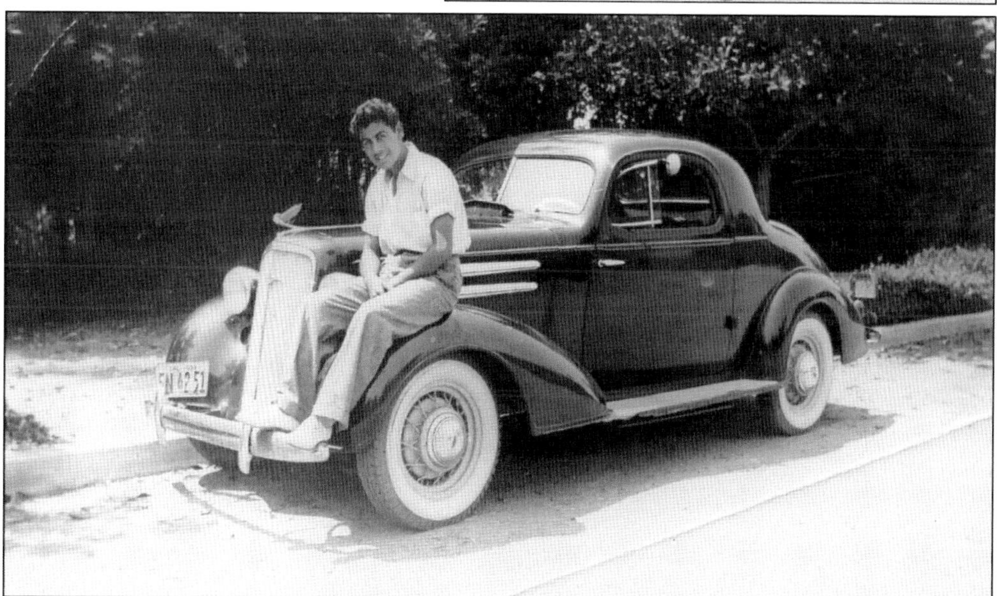

Francisco "Kiko" Gomez poses on the fender of his 1935 Chevrolet coupe in front of the entrance to Palos Verdes Estates in California. This photograph was taken after his graduation from Redondo High School, where he excelled as an artist. After his discharge from World War II, he studied art in Europe and Los Angeles and was frequently commissioned to paint portraits of Hollywood celebrities. (Courtesy Robin Duarte.)

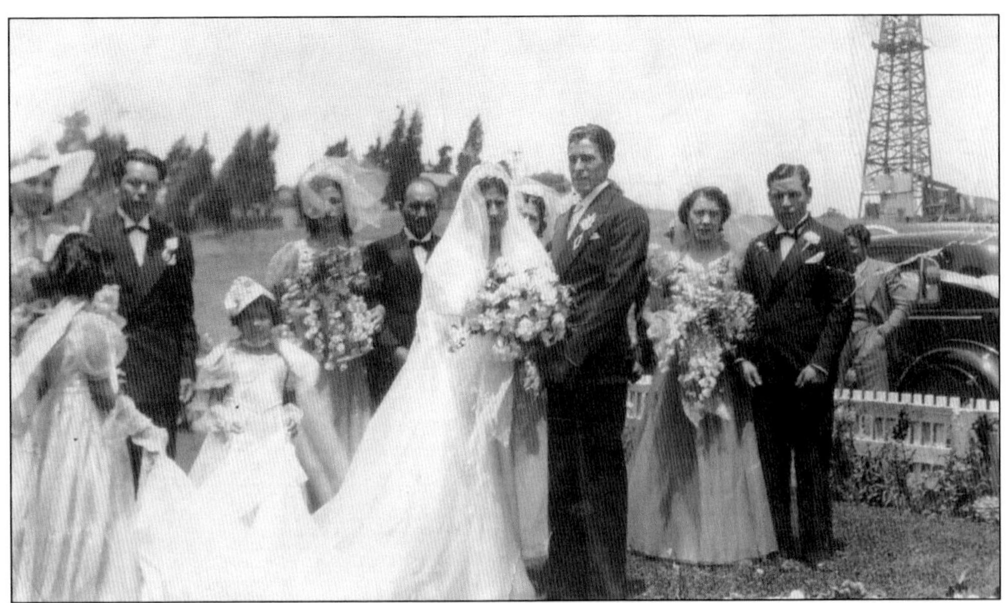

Rural northern Redondo was the setting for this June 1939 wedding photograph of Jose Savedra and Irene Moreno at Domingo Moreno's home on Carmelita Avenue. From left to right are Louie Lara, Bobbie Vail, and Calero Yniguez. At the far right is Rafaela "R. C." Colin with an unidentified partner. The flower girl at left front is Lupe Granados, who became the first Mexican American song leader at Redondo High School. (Courtesy Herminda Banda.)

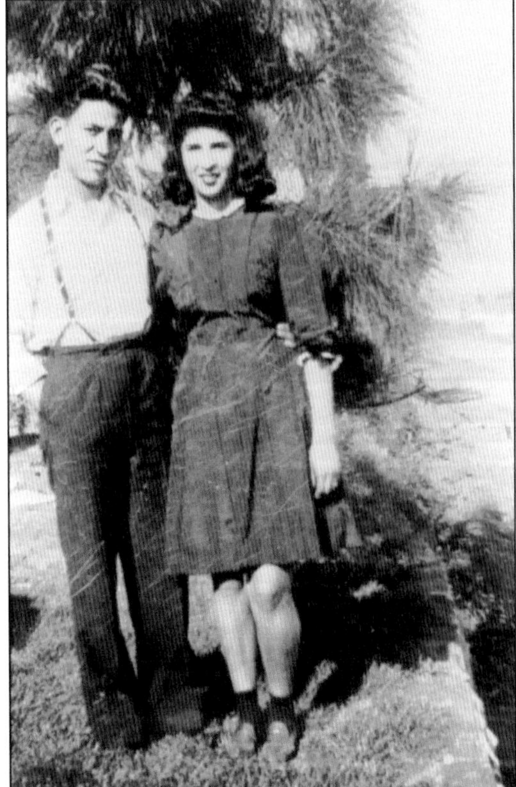

Newlyweds Isaias "Chayo" Moreno and Rose Camereno were in Manhattan Beach in 1940 when this photograph was taken. Shortly after, "Chayo" enlisted in the U.S. Army, leaving his new bride at her parent's home during World War II. He would later capture a large German flag at the invasion of Normandy, France.

Artemio Adame and his wife, Delfina, the daughter of Feliciano and Catarina Vallejo, pioneer residents of northern Redondo, pose with their children—(from left to right) Anita, Ray, and Artemio Jr.—in front of their home on Dewey Avenue. Seated in the stroller is Yolanda. Later the family moved to Carlson Avenue, where the old Coca Cola ballroom was located in the 1930s. (Courtesy Ray Adame.)

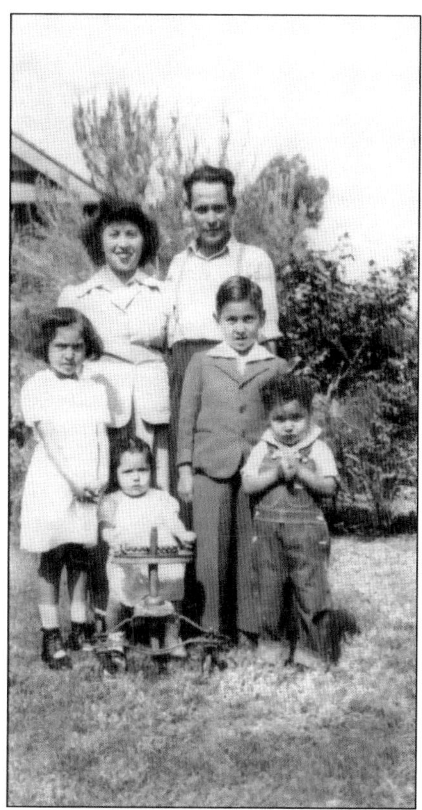

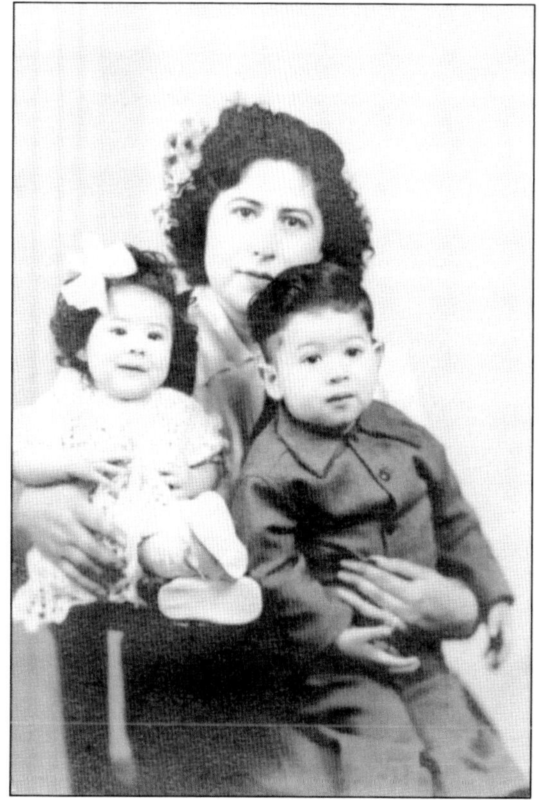

This 1943 photograph shows Rebecca Duarte with her two children, Margaret, left, and Richard. Rebecca cared for the children while her husband, Alfonso, served overseas during World War II. Alfonso operated amphibious landing craft with the U.S. Marines. (Courtesy Margaret Carillo.)

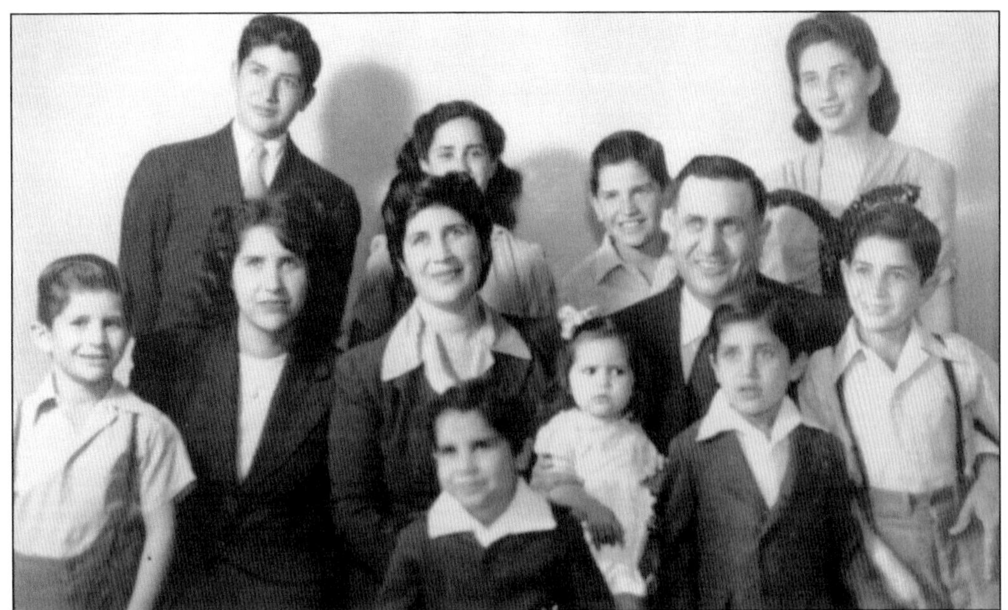

The Trujillo family, who lived near the New Mexico atomic proving grounds and were concerned for their safety, moved to Redondo Beach in 1944. They lived on Goodman Avenue. Anastacio had published a newspaper in Mora, New Mexico; his wife, Eloisa, taught elementary school. Family members from left to right are (first row) Carlos, Stella (in arms), and Peter; (second row) Manuel, Tillie, Eloisa, Anastacio, and Leroy; (third row) Ted, Ralphie, Phillip, and Margaret. (Courtesy Leroy Trujillo.)

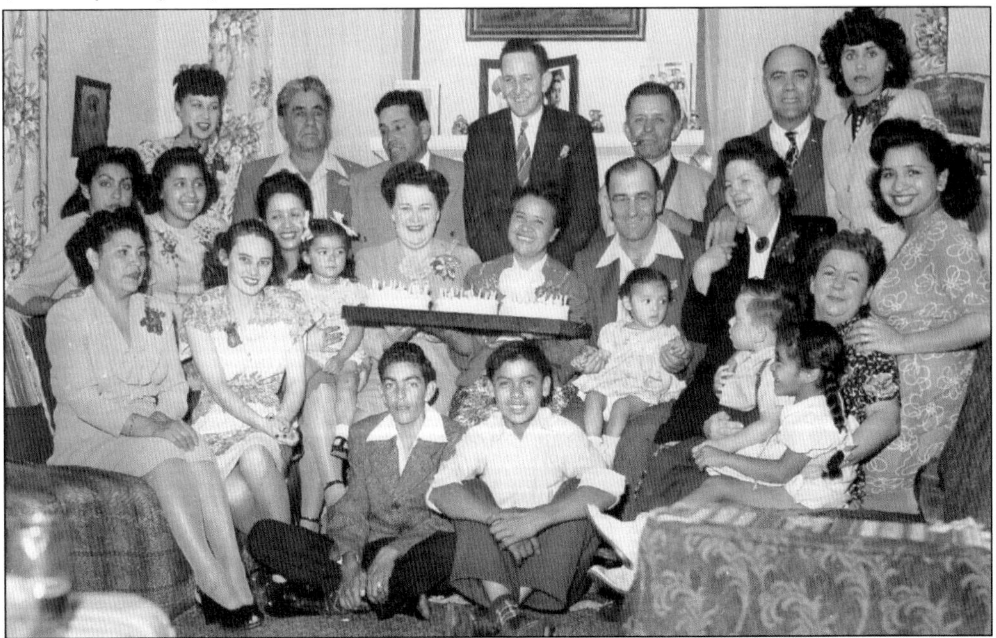

In May 1945, the birthday celebration of Pascuala and Lina Saldana and family friend Betty Lou Parks brought together the Saldana, Espinoza, Valenzuela, Herrera, and Parks families at the Saldana home on Marshallfield Lane in northern Redondo Beach. The Saldana family came to Redondo Beach from Colorado. (Courtesy Carmen Daugherty.)

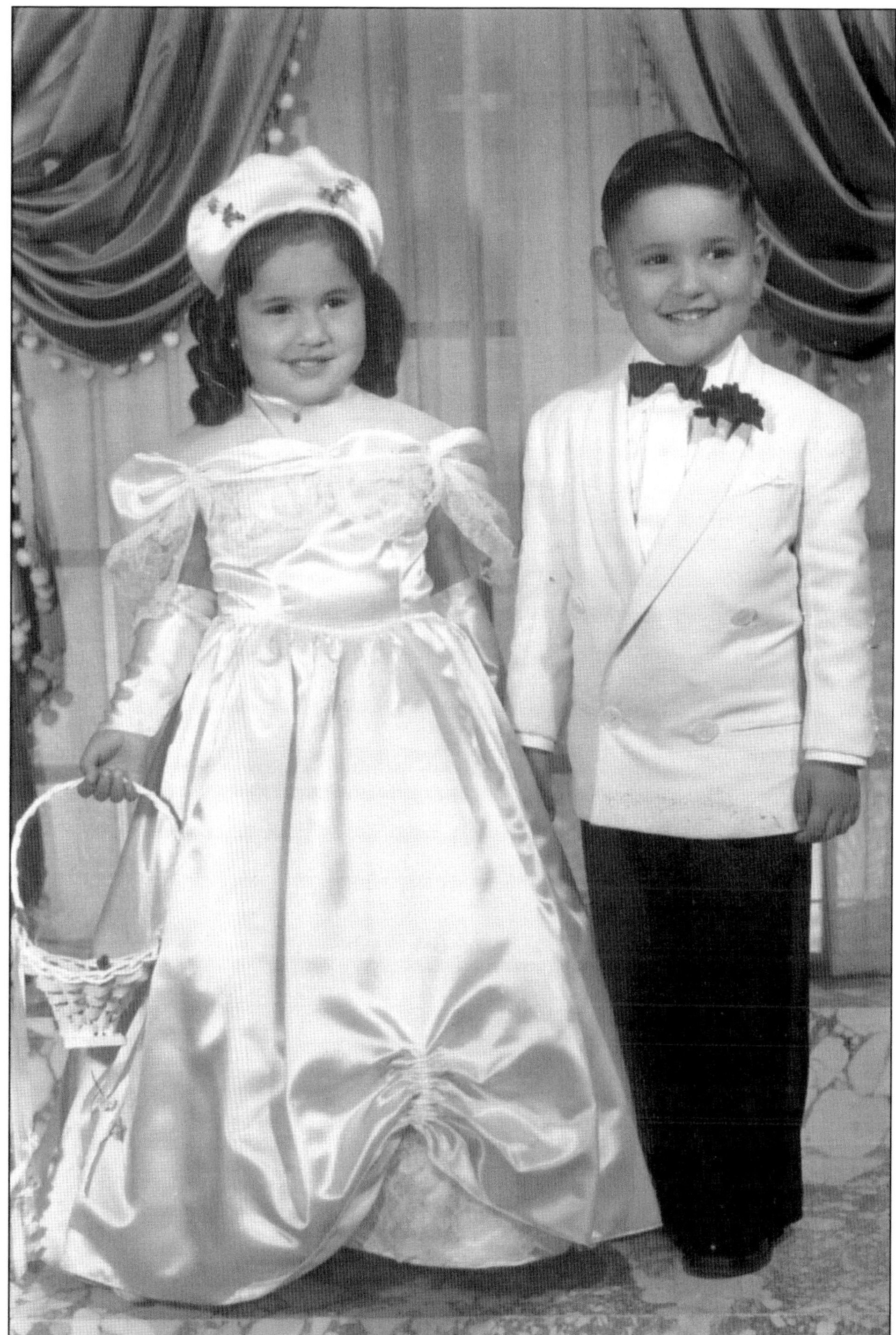

Fraternal twins David and Rachel Ortiz were ring bearer and flower girl in their Aunt Chavela's marriage to Luis Cordova in 1951. Like many descendants of early Mexican American families, they were born and remain South Bay residents. They attended Bishop Montgomery High School in Torrance, California, with David later earning a master's degree.

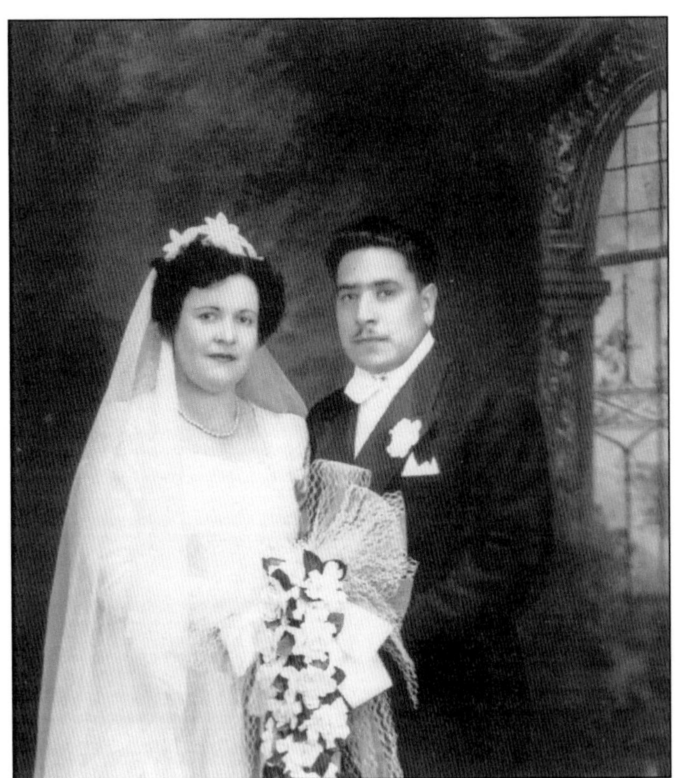

Salvador and Socorro Ortiz married in 1946 and settled on Morgan Lane in northern Redondo. Salvador was a student at St. James Catholic School in central Redondo in the early 1920s. The Ortiz family was one of 10 families living on Morgan Lane in the 1940s. Morgan Lane was named for American banker J. P. Morgan. Other streets, such as Marshallfield and Rockefeller Lanes, were named after American captains of industry by the land developers in northern Redondo. (Courtesy Rachel Ortiz.)

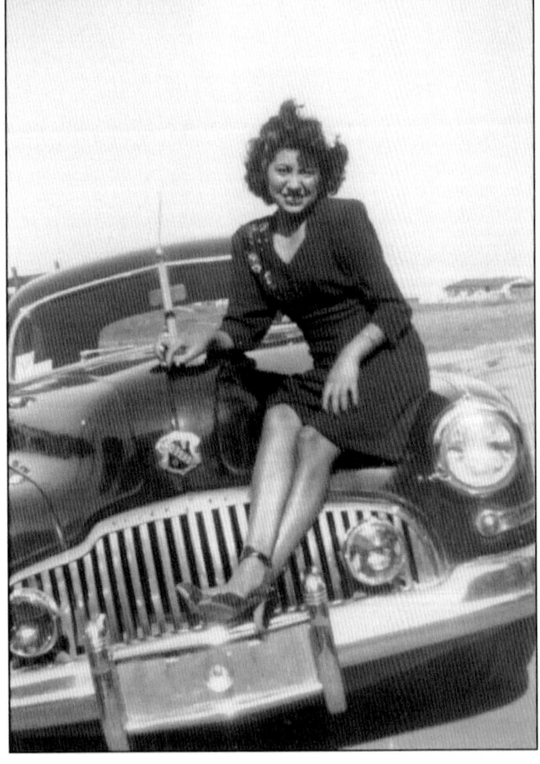

Seated on the Colin family's 1946 Buick Roadmaster sedan, Antonia Colin strikes an attractive pose at their home in northern Redondo. Antonia's parents, Mauricio and Catarina Colin, came to Redondo with the family of Domingo and Maria Moreno. Maria and Catarina were sisters. Between the Moreno and Colin families, who were cousins, the two sisters raised 26 children. (Courtesy Katie Aguilar Bopp.)

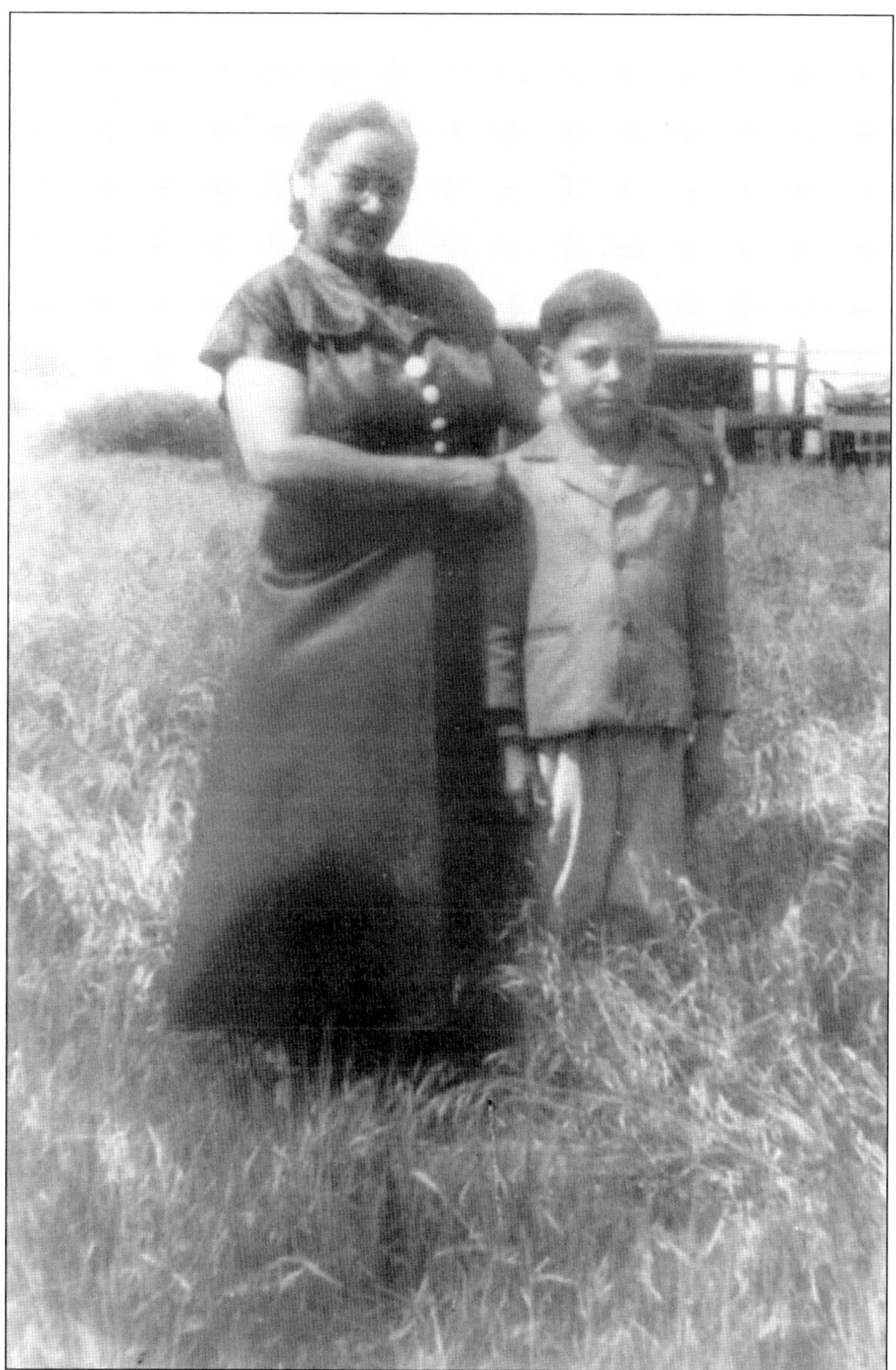

Another Morgan Lane family was the Ledesmas. Pictured is Frances Ledesma and son Emilio. Early in her nursing career, Frances was a nurse at White Memorial Hospital in Los Angeles before coming to Redondo Beach. Old Morgan Lane residents will remember their famous dog Barbas (Beards), who chased anyone that came near the home. (Courtesy Margaret Carillo.)

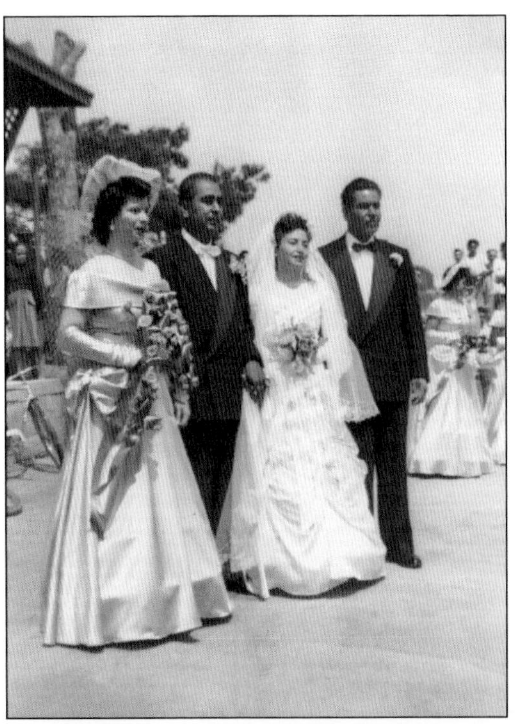

One of the many weddings at Our Lady of Guadalupe Church in Hermosa united Lupe and Emma Aguirre, around 1950. Sara Cerda, left, was Emma's sister and maid of honor. Louie Pina, right, was best man. This photograph was taken in the church parking lot. (Courtesy Luis Cordova.)

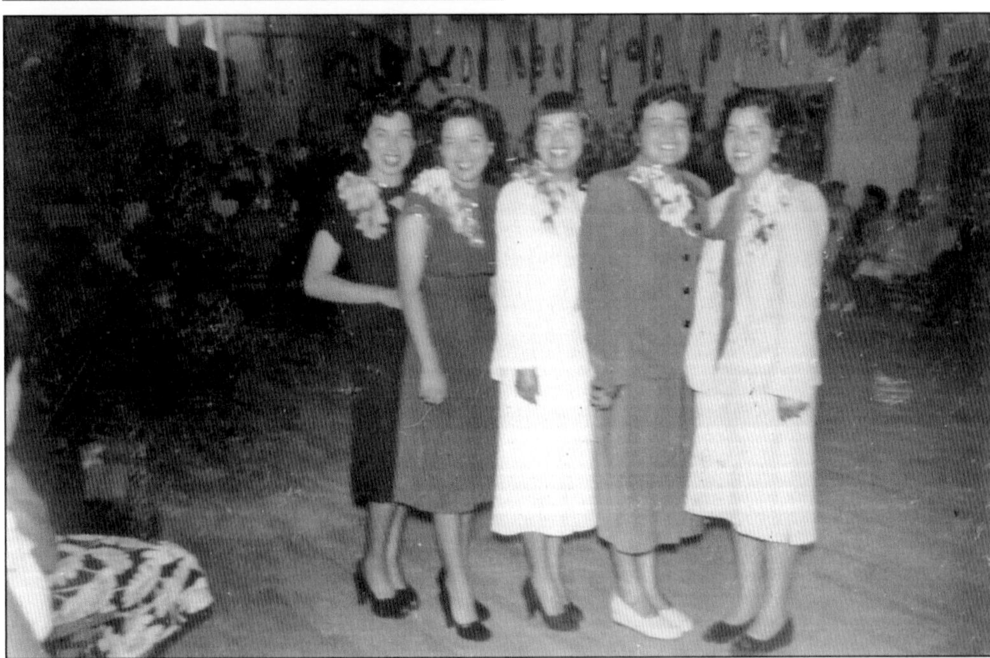

Congratulations were in order in this 1948 high school graduation photograph taken at Carpenter's Hall on Aviation Boulevard in northern Redondo Beach, which brought together five graduates of early Redondo settlers. From left to right are Ophelia and Emma Saucedo, Jenny Gomez, Celia "Sally" Hernandez, and Carmen Contreras. The special corsages were made especially for this occasion by "Sadie" Lopez of Hermosa Beach, who owned Sadie's Hat Nursery. (Courtesy Carmen Hernandez.)

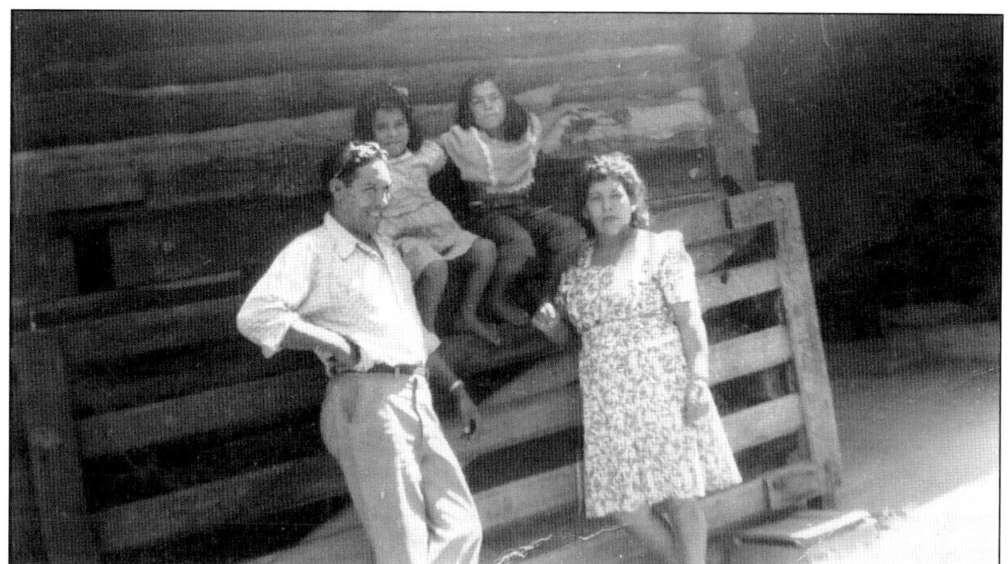

Ernie Chavez and his wife, Guadalupe, are pictured here around 1950 with daughters Gloria and Sally. The Chavez family owned a nursery on Plant Avenue and Aviation Boulevard in northern Redondo that opened in 1943. The nursery carried most traditional plant-care items but was well known for Ernie's specialization in raising hard-to-grow azaleas. The Redondo Beach Historical Museum in northern Redondo placed the historic Chavez nursery sign in its collection. (Courtesy Sally Chavez.)

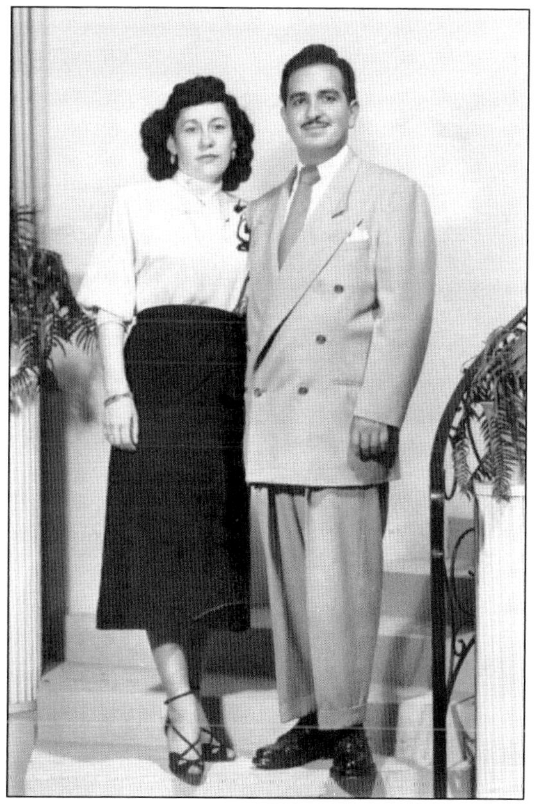

Pictured is Luis and Chavela Cordova. Luis, born in Kansas City, Missouri, moved to Mexico to live with his uncle, a government official, who saw that he was trained as a banker. In 1947, he returned to the United States and joined the U.S. Army. Luis and Chavela raised three sons who all earned university degrees. One son is a Superior Court judge, and another is a lawyer. (Courtesy Chavela Cordova.)

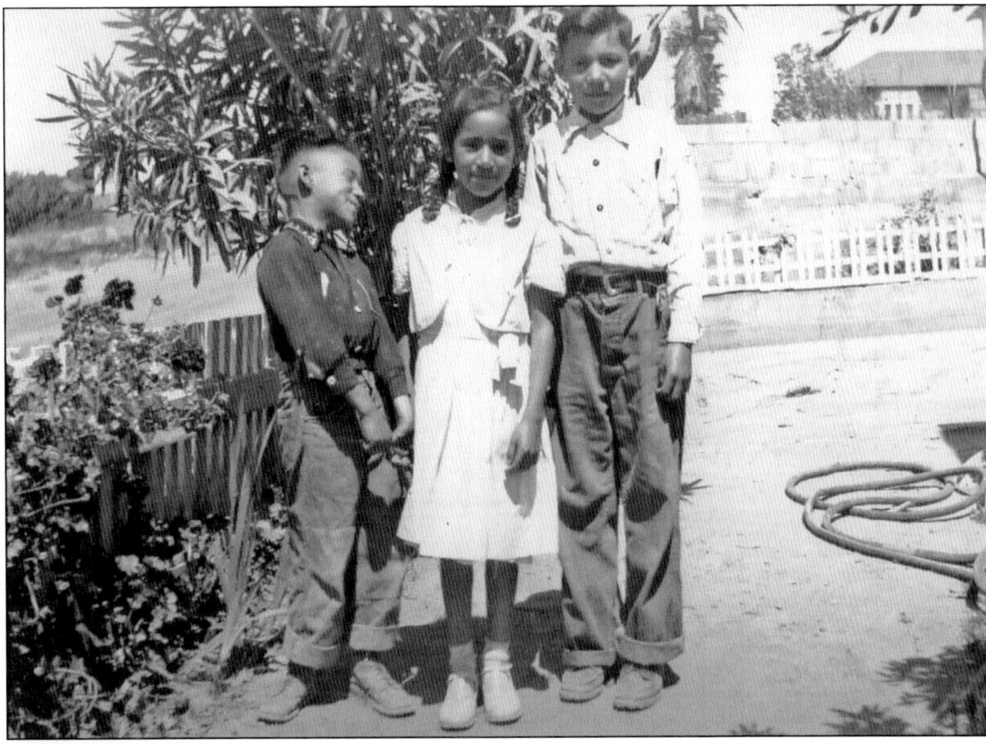

This 1950s photograph of the Aguilar children was taken at 1710 Morgan Lane while they visited their grandparents Mauricio and Catarina Colin. At left is Guadalupe "Lou," Dolores, and older brother Antonio "Tony." The Aguilar's home was located half a block up the street, beyond the large house on the right. (Courtesy Katie Aguilar Bopp.)

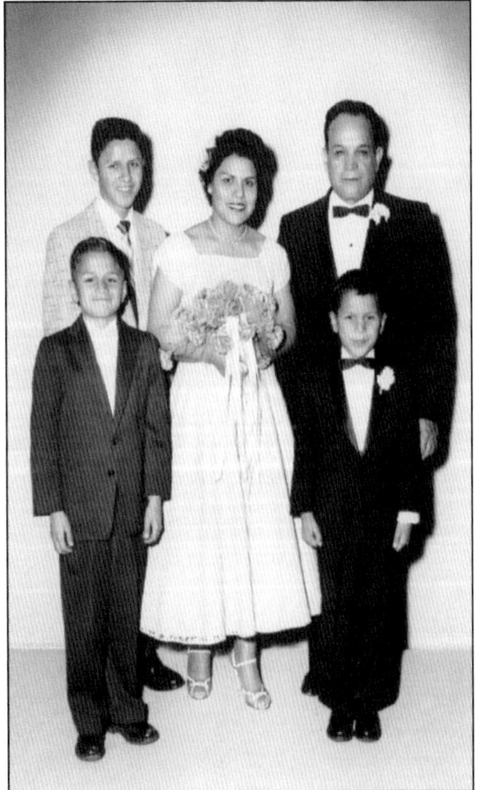

Constantino and Andrea Adame and their three sons lived on Carlson Lane in Redondo. At left front is Arthur, right front is Rudy, and at left rear is Gilbert. Arthur attended the Franciscan Seminary in Crystal Lake, Illinois, before returning to California to earn a university degree. Rudy completed his degree shortly after Arthur completed his. Gilbert was a varsity basketball player at Redondo High School. (Courtesy Andrea Adame.)

Near Redondo High School, Antonio and Senaida Saucedo's family settled in a stately two-story home where they raised five children—Ophelia, Emma, Gloria, Antonio "Tony" Jr., and Lupe. In the mid-1950s, they owned a bakery at the corner of Diamond Street and Catalina Avenue in central Redondo. Their daughters were often selected as candidates for fiesta queen at Our Lady of Guadalupe Church during the early 1950s.

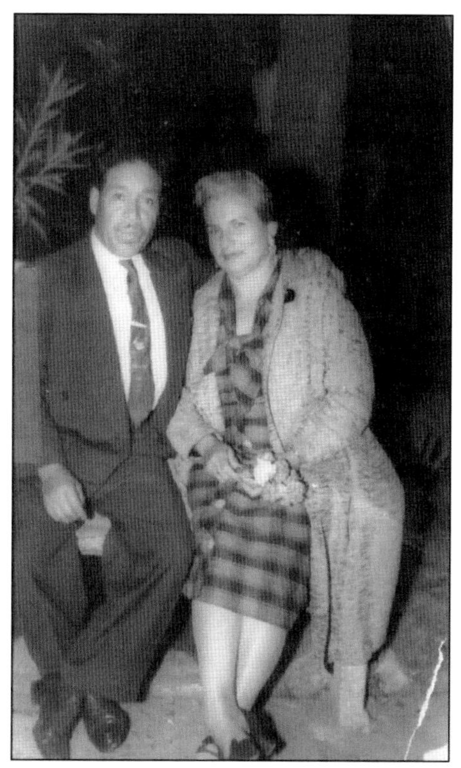

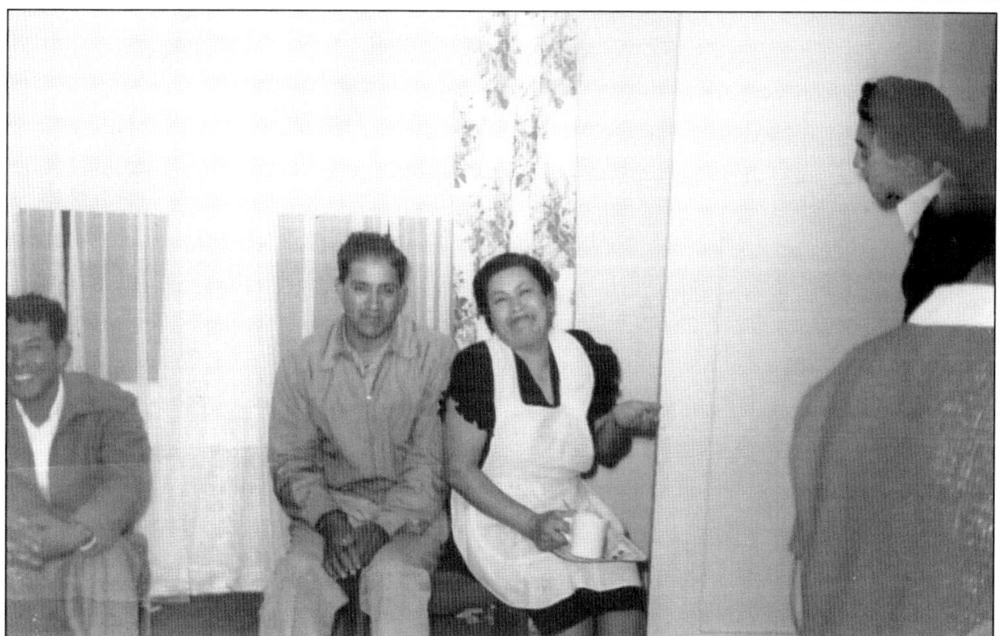

Calistro and Ramona Gomez are pictured at their home on Irena Street, where they raised two children, Lorenzo "Lencho" and Jenny Gomez. The Gomez's were one of several families that relocated to Redondo Beach from Lompoc, California, in the 1930s. They were neighbors of the Saucedo family. Lencho married one of the Saucedo's daughters, Emma, in the early 1950s. He literally married the girl next door. (Courtesy Lencho Gomez.)

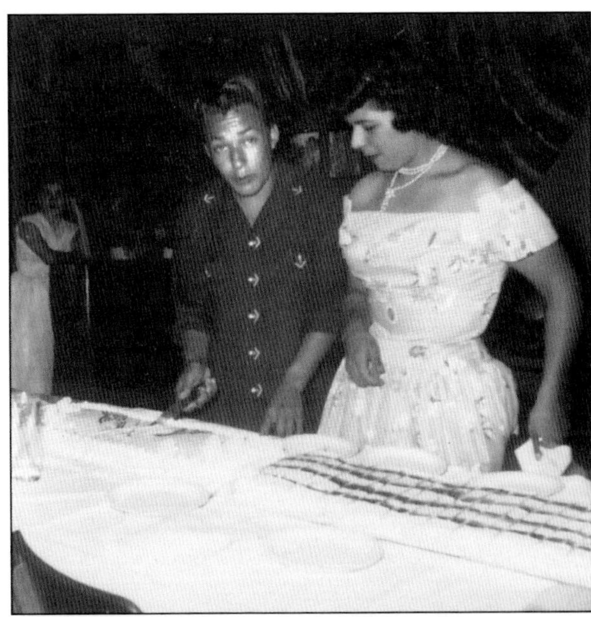

In September 1955, Julia Areyan honors her cousin John Luna Moreno, left, at his U.S. Navy going away party. John was a skilled game hunter for many years, leading hunting parties for friends and family in central California, Colorado, and Utah. After graduating from California Polytechnic University San Luis Obispo, he returned to teach Chicano studies classes in the mid-1970s.

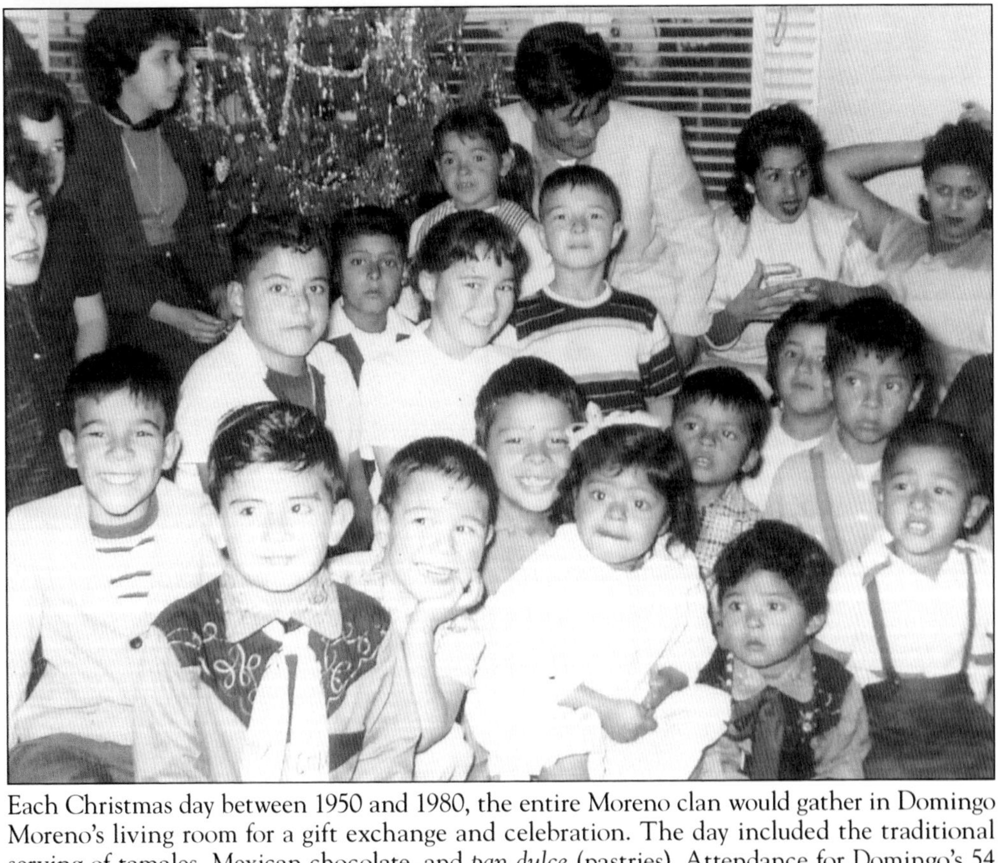

Each Christmas day between 1950 and 1980, the entire Moreno clan would gather in Domingo Moreno's living room for a gift exchange and celebration. The day included the traditional serving of tamales, Mexican chocolate, and *pan dulce* (pastries). Attendance for Domingo's 54 grandchildren posed some interesting space problems for his living and dining rooms. Domingo lived to the age of 95. (Courtesy Roberta Moreno.)

Jesus and Angela Enriquez are seen here with their oldest daughter, Minerva, and their youngest daughter, Angie. This image was taken in the parking lot of Our Lady of Guadalupe Church in 1956, before the Cinco de Mayo (May 5) celebration. The palm fronds were obtained from city of Redondo tree-trimming crews. Minerva was another frequent candidate for the queen of the church fiesta. (Courtesy Minerva Heredia.)

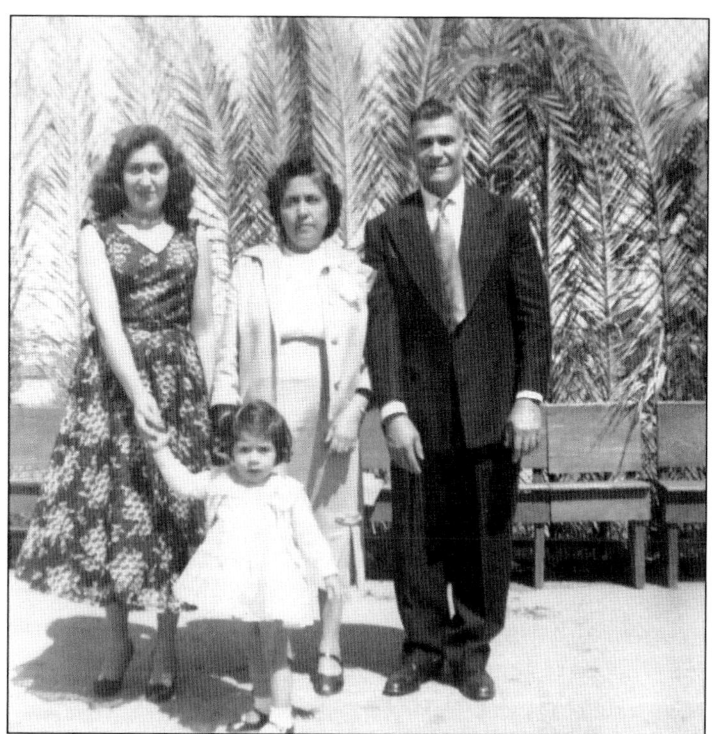

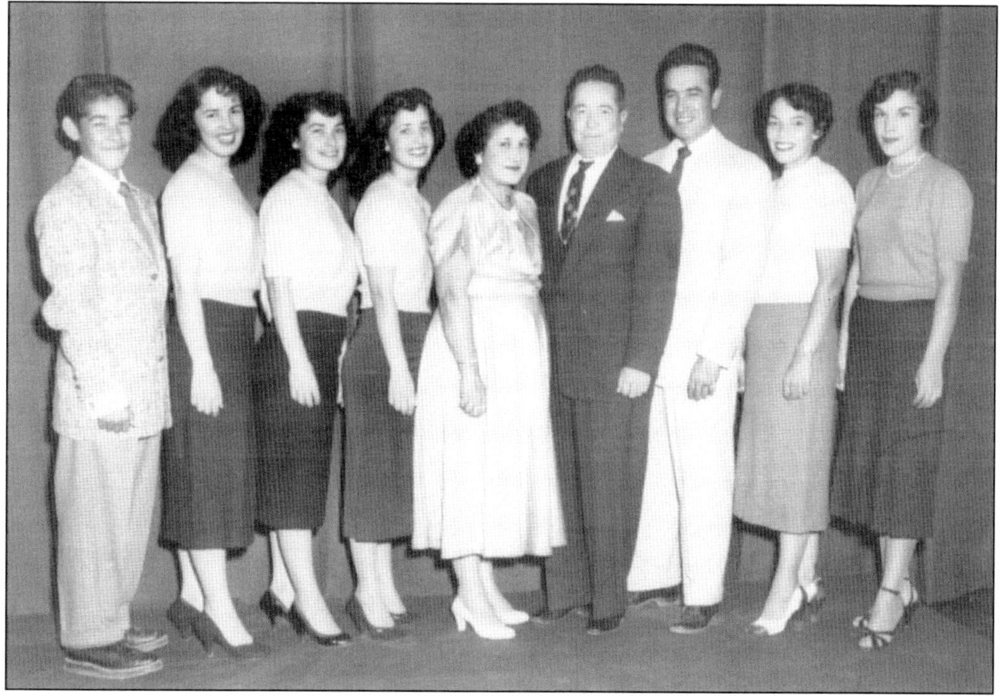

The Salinas family gathered for this photograph in 1956. From left to right are Lorenzo "Gordo," Evelyn, Caroline, Gloria, mother Erlinda, father Lorenzo Sr., Eddie, Carmen, and Dolores Chaidez. The family lived on Marshallfield Lane, and Caroline remembers hearing the explosion of the fireworks factory on nearby Inglewood Avenue in 1944. (Courtesy Caroline Villa.)

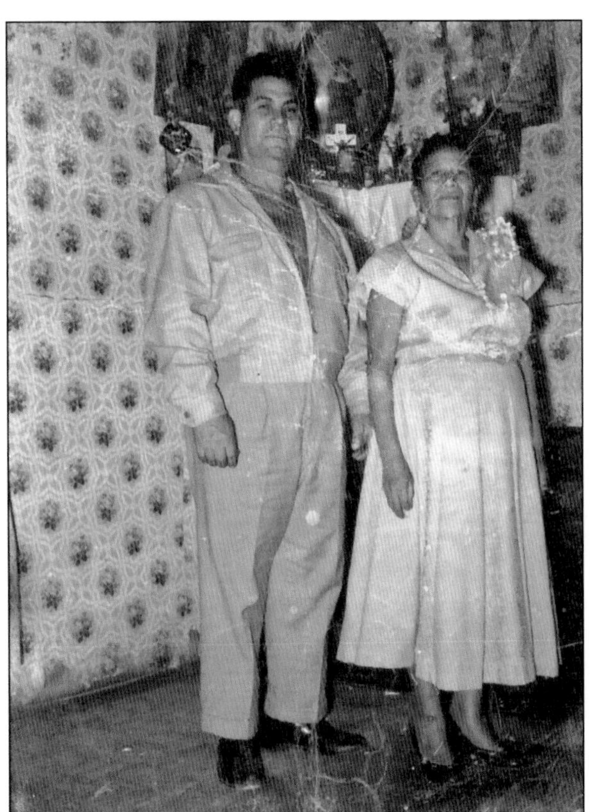

Bernardo and Luz Alvarez raised their nine children on Spreckels Lane in northern Redondo. Luz, a deeply religious person, frequently donated dozens of homemade tamales to Our Lady of Guadalupe Church for fund-raisers. (Courtesy Rosie Salazar.)

The Leon sisters and their mother, Manuela, pose in this 1964 photograph. During the 1930s, under President Hoover's Depression repatriation plan, the family was sent to Mexico because their father, Ramon, was a Mexican citizen. Although Manuela was a United States citizen, they were not allowed to return until 1949, under an amnesty program. Pictured here are, from left to right, (first row) Hortensia "Ordie;" (second row) Carmen, Jennie, Molly, Manuela, Beatriz, and Piedad. (Courtesy Ordie Fernandez.)

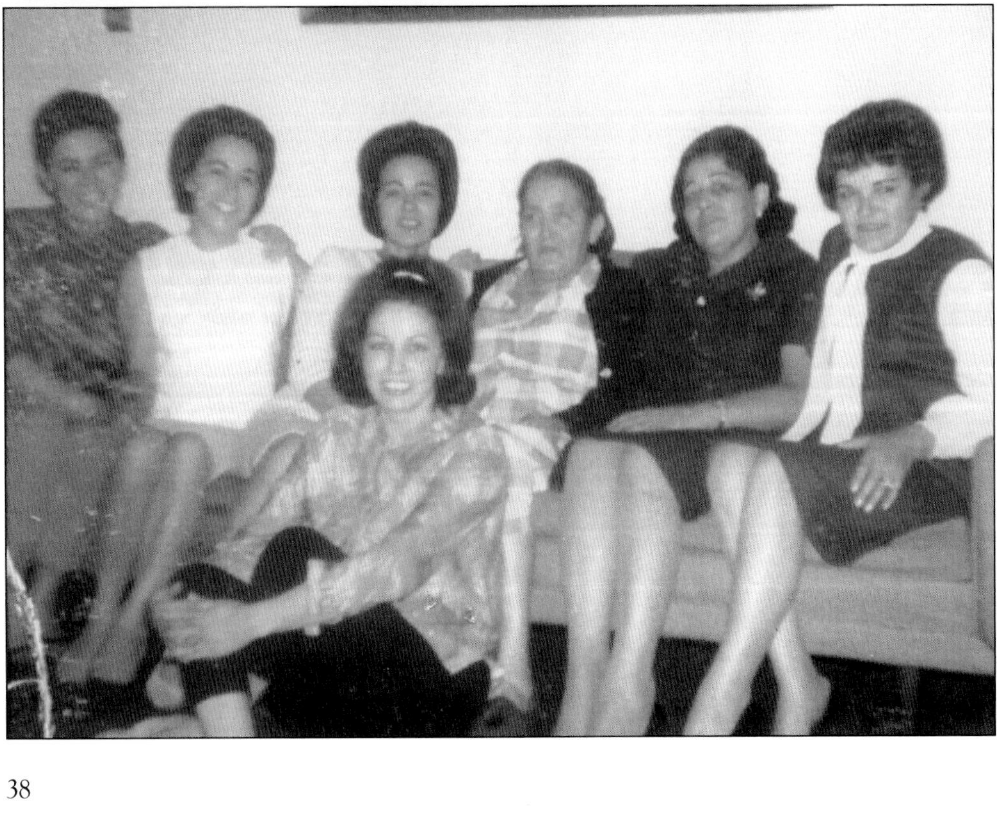

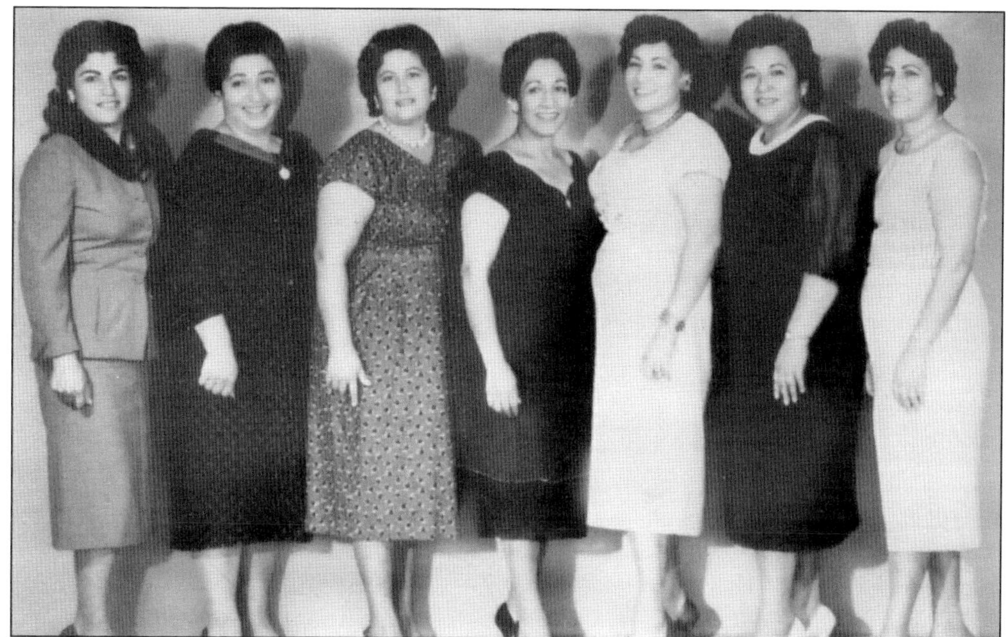

The seven Moreno sisters, daughters of Domingo Moreno, appear in this 1960s photograph. From left to right are Porfiria Banda, Inez Areyan, Dora Segoviano, Anita Savedra, Petra Estrada, Jenny Ortega, and Irene Savedra. (Courtesy Rosie Salazar.)

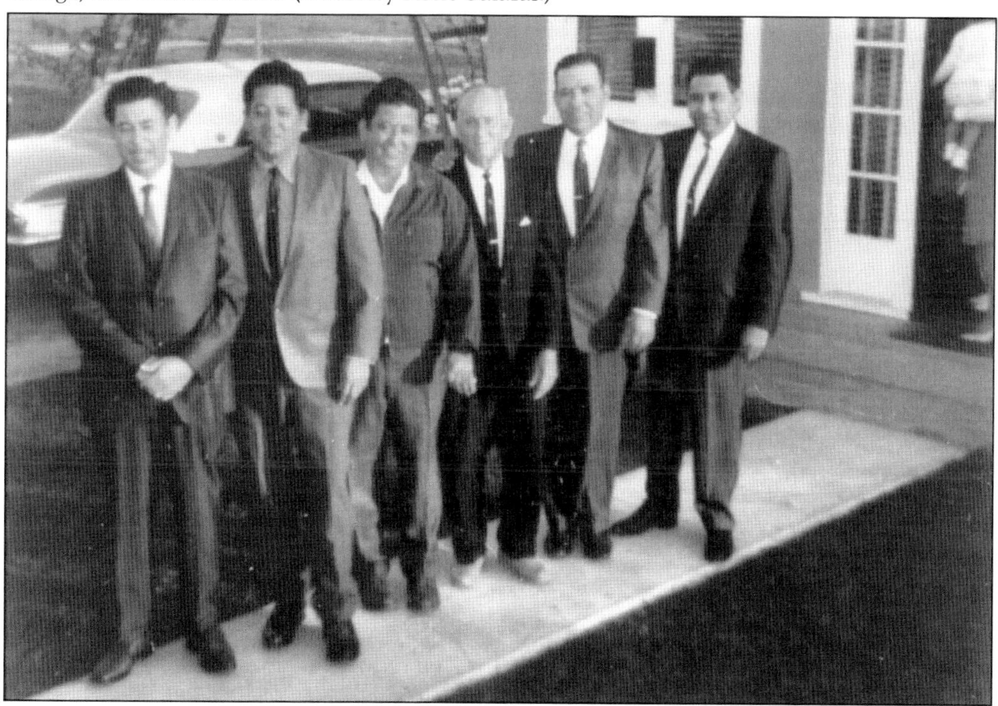

Domingo Moreno and his five sons pose in front of his home for a Christmas photograph in 1962. From left to right are Bonifacio, Vincent, Isaias, Domingo, Gonzalo, and Frank. In the early 1920s, Frank and Gonzalo attended catechism classes in the family's garage along with other neighborhood children. (Courtesy Inez Areyan.)

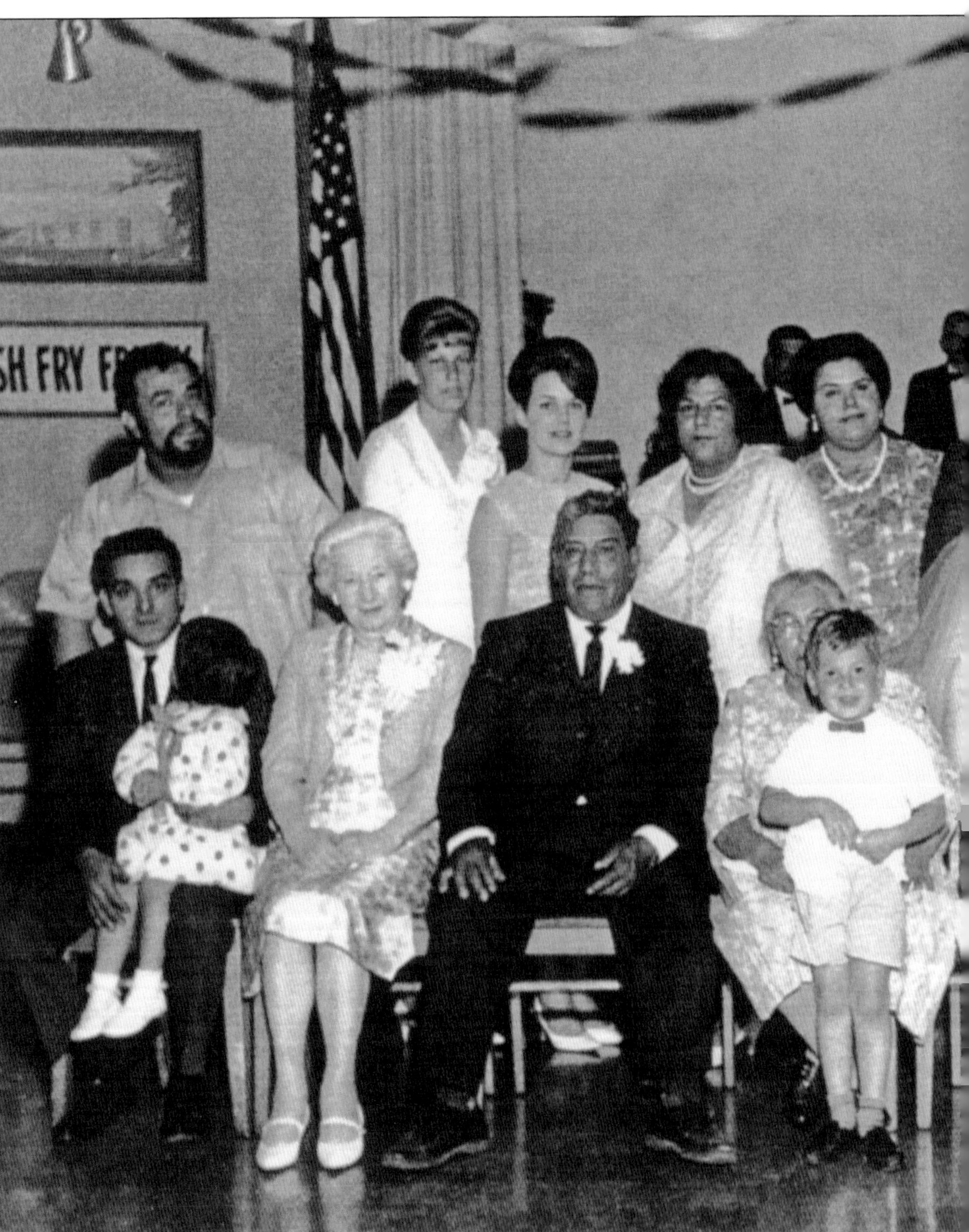

The Torres family was a familiar sight in Redondo Beach. This photograph features the wedding reception of Marcus and Roberta Torres at the Manhattan Beach Moose Lodge in April 1965. Three of the Torres brothers—Marcus, Emo, and "Socko"—excelled in sports at Redondo High

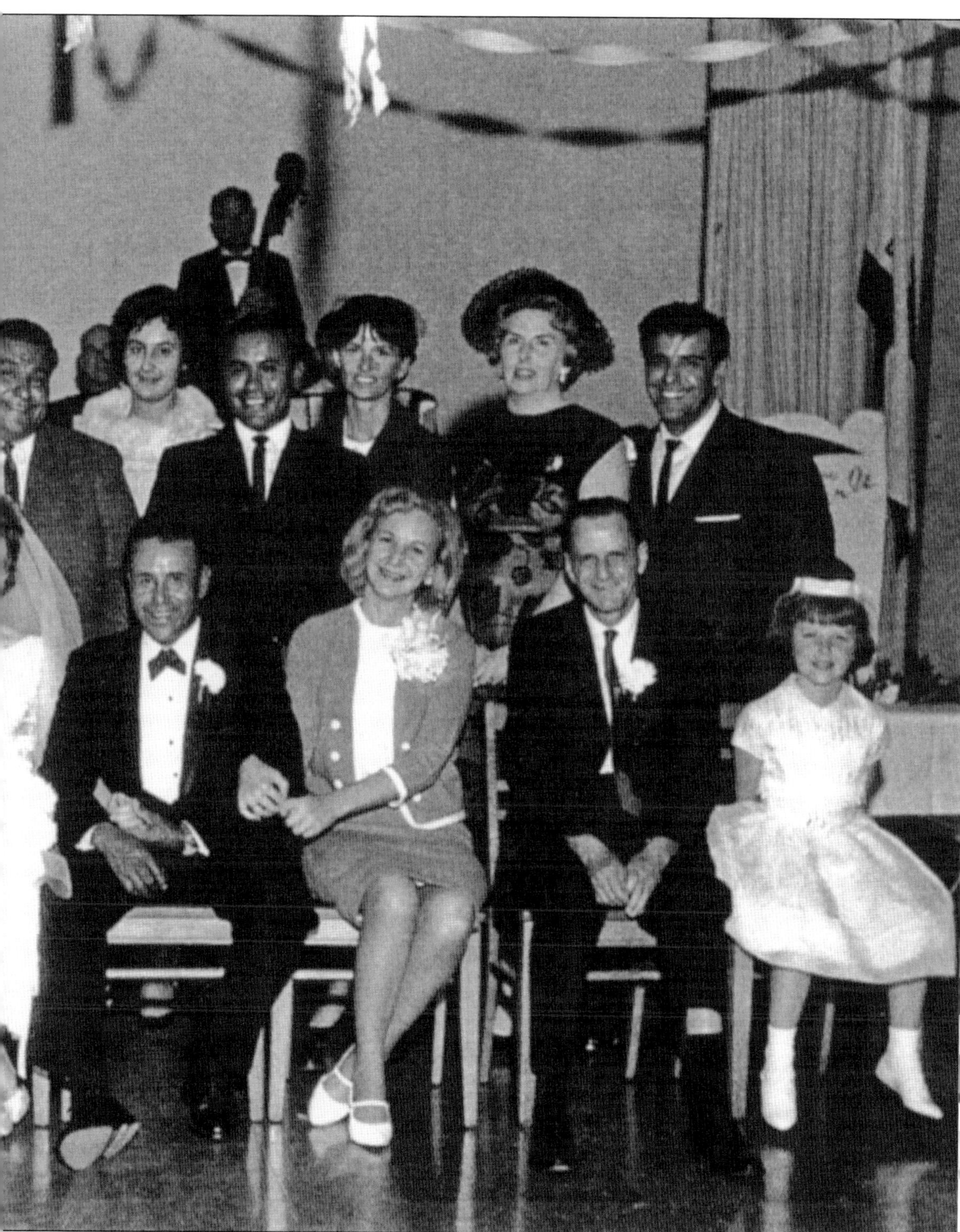

School. Another brother, Clemente, worked as the groundskeeper at the Sweetser Estate for many years. (Courtesy "Socko" Torres.)

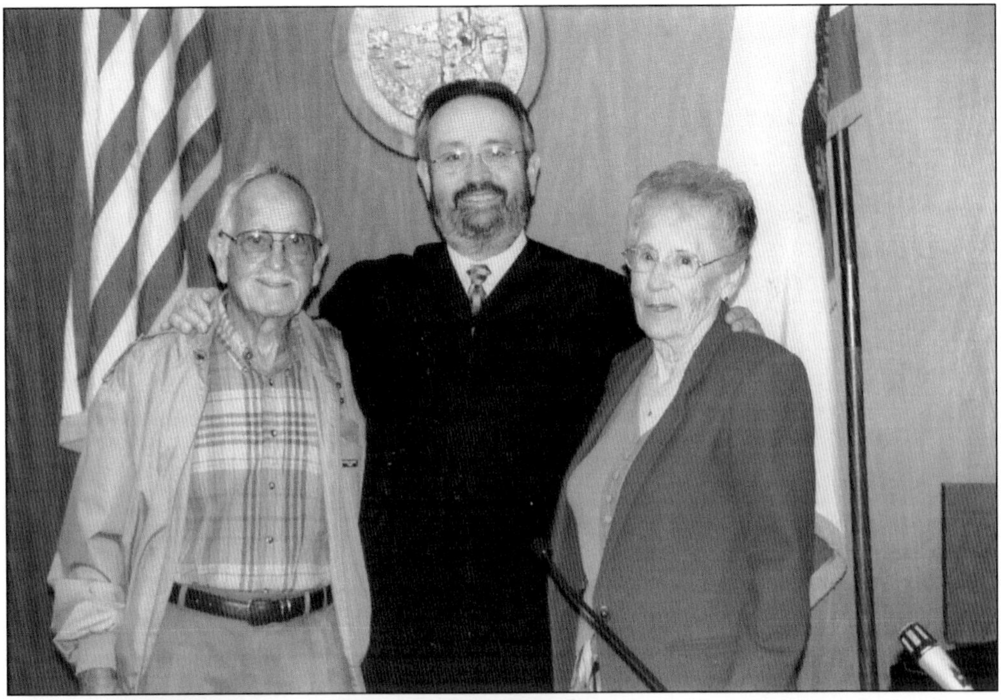

Luis and Chavela Cordova pose in the courtroom with their son Superior Court judge Ricardo Cordova, a graduate of Bishop Montgomery High School in Torrance, California, and the University of California, Davis School of Law. (Courtesy Luis Cordova.)

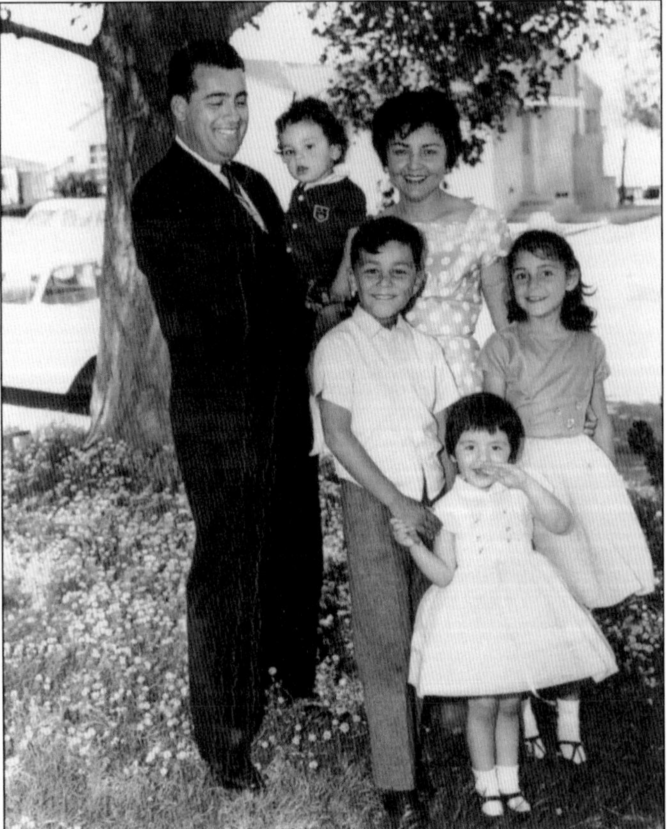

Richard "Dick" Trevino and his wife, Maria, pose in front of their Robinson Street home in northern Redondo with their children Richard Jr., Anna, Diane, and Andrew. A familiar figure in the Mexican American community, Dick and his brother Robert owned Trevino Brothers Plumbing Company. (Courtesy Maria Trevino.)

Ignacio "Nacho" Estrada is seen in this photograph with his wife, Petra, son "J. R.," and daughter Mary Louise. He moved to Hermosa Beach in the 1940s and built his own home on Third Street. He designed the stone grotto at Our Lady of Guadalupe Church in honor of the Estrada and Moreno families. (Courtesy Irene Cota.)

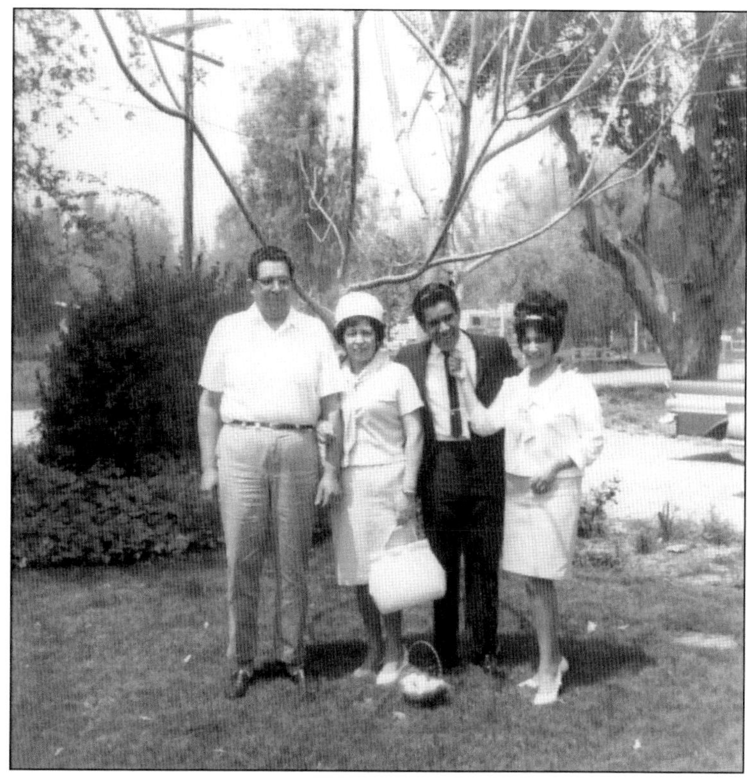

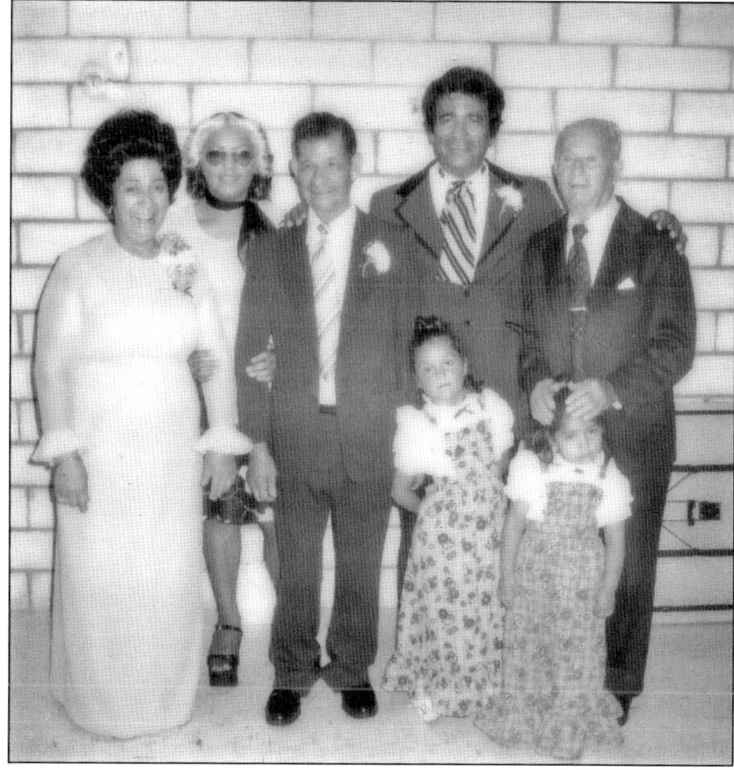

A five-generation photograph depicts the Domingo Moreno family. Pictured from left to right are his daughter Inez, great-granddaughter Theresa, Inez's husband Alejo, grandson Rudy Areyan, and great-great-granddaughters Gina and Trina. At the time of his passing, the Redondo Beach City Council issued a proclamation honoring Domingo as a pioneer resident of the city. (Courtesy Theresa Hobbs.)

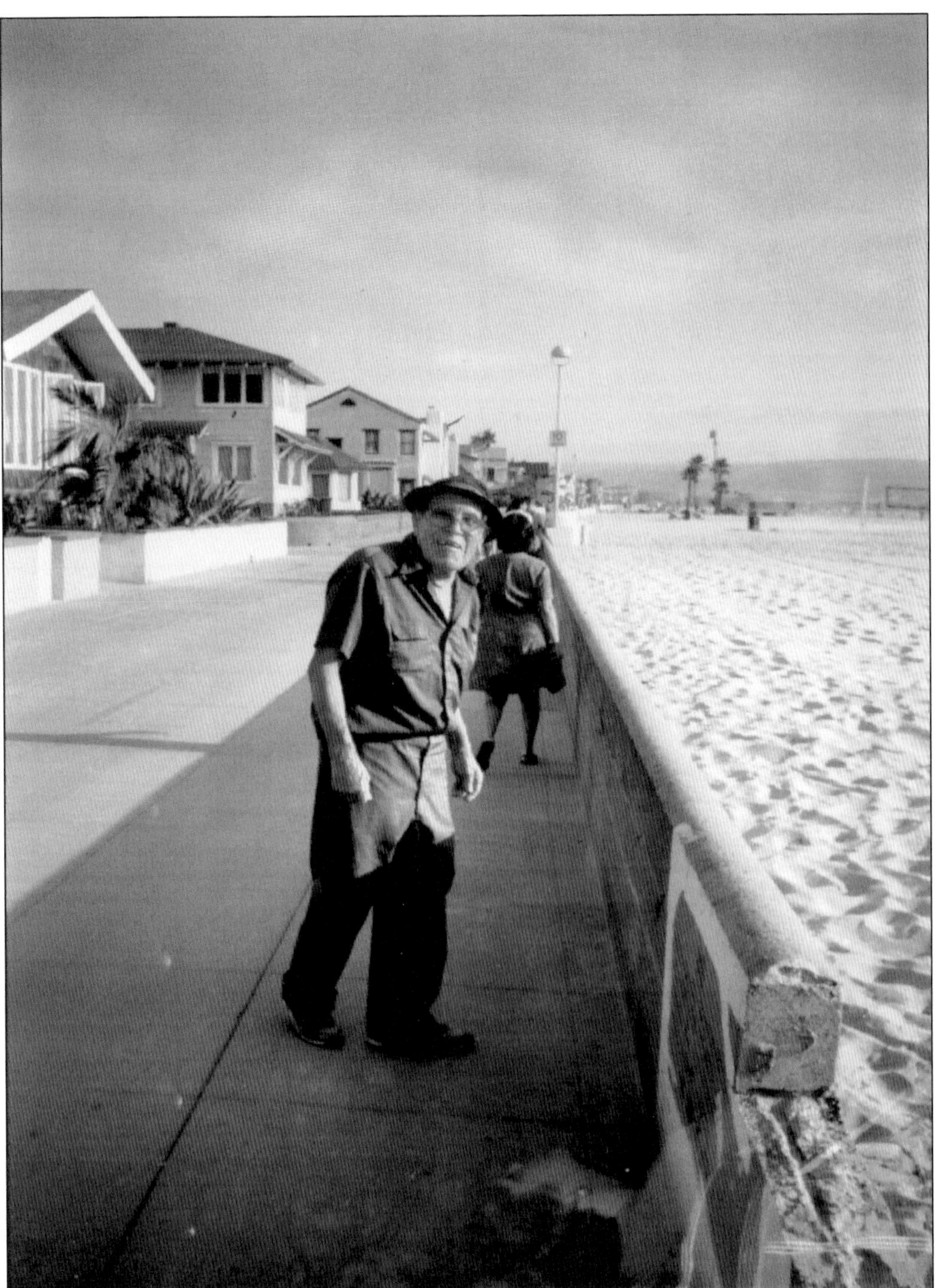

In 1943, Ernie Chavez grew flowers near Mira Costa High School in Manhattan Beach. For several years, he was the groundskeeper at Our Lady of Guadalupe Church in Hermosa. In this photograph, he takes a walk on the Hermosa Strand after celebrating a birthday dinner with his family. (Courtesy Sally Chavez.)

Three

Community Life

Community life has always been strong among Mexican Americans. It is an extension of family and religious life, providing important social and emotional support. In the 1920s, Mexican American community leaders formed cultural and religious clubs such as the *club morelos* at Our Lady of Guadalupe Church. The club sponsored community celebrations called *jamaicas* (fiestas), which lasted three days and commemorated Mexico's independence from Spain. They were important to the community because they provided a link to the traditions left behind in the old country. Fiestas included dances at the Coca Cola ballroom at Goodman and Carlson Lane and piano recitals with Viola Niland, community friend and owner of Niland's Mortuary. Parades went from the ballroom north to Pier Avenue, with a marching color guard displaying the American and Mexican flags. Food booths lined Carlson Lane. The *club morelos*'s president, Domingo Moreno, together with Victoriano Gomez, Mauricio Colin, Cicilio Murillo, Alvino Gonzalez, and others, built the original shell of Our Lady of Guadalupe Church on Labor Day, 1923.

From 1942 to 1949, the church came under the leadership of Fr. Cyril Wood. Before him, the church was staffed by Mexican clergy fleeing religious persecution. Father Wood built a rectory, a hall under the church, a playground, and paved the parking lot. He formed the parish Chi Rho youth club, with outings to the Long Beach swimming plunge. After World War II, with Father Wood's blessing, the fiestas moved to the paved parking lot. The church became the center of the community's social and religious life. Today some of the settlers' descendants continue to worship there; Caroline Salinas Villa has attended Mass there for 70 years. In 2007, the church and its new pastor, Fr. Raymond Mallett, OFM, Conv., will celebrate the 50th anniversary of the Franciscan fathers' presence in the parish.

The old Redondo Barn was another center of community life. This dance hall attracted hundreds of Mexican Americans from surrounding communities for *tardeadas* (Sunday afternoon dances), where many listened to Tony Alvarez's band, describing him as the "Mexican Glenn Miller." Albert Castillon remembers the Redondo Barn opened one last time to celebrate his marriage to Emma Hernandez. Their wedding party of 44 attendants included many of the area's prominent Mexican American families. Sadly, the barn closed in the 1950s.

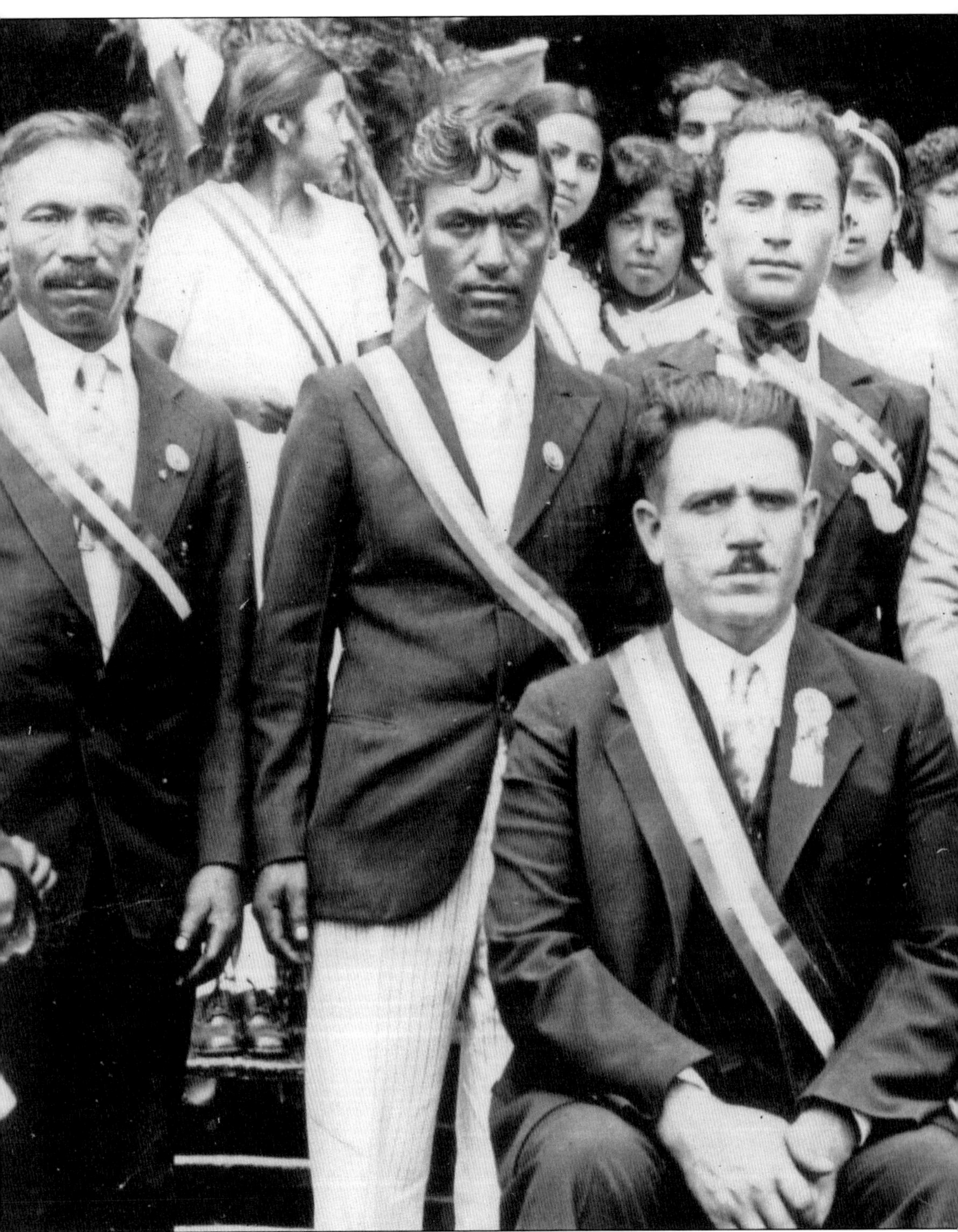

Around 1924, Mexican American community leaders formed the *club morelos* at Our Lady of Guadalupe Church in Hermosa Beach. This photograph, taken around 1933, shows members commemorating Mexico's independence from Spain at Clark Stadium in Hermosa. Pictured

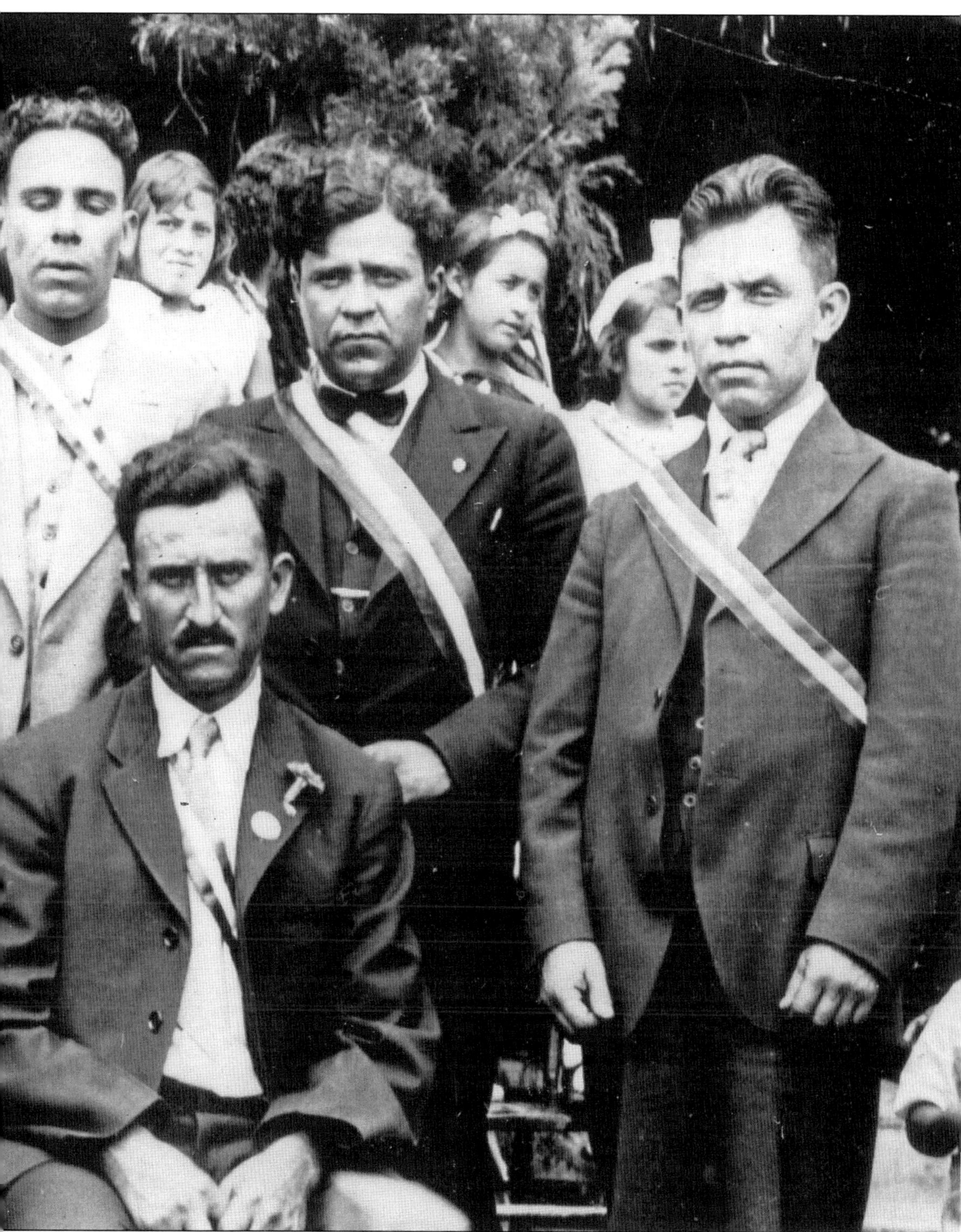

here are, from left to right, (first row) Alfredo Flores and Domingo Moreno, president; (second row) Mauricio Colin, Victoriano Gomez, Jesus Camarena, unidentified, Alphonso Limon, and Romaldo Saldana. (Courtesy John Luna Moreno.)

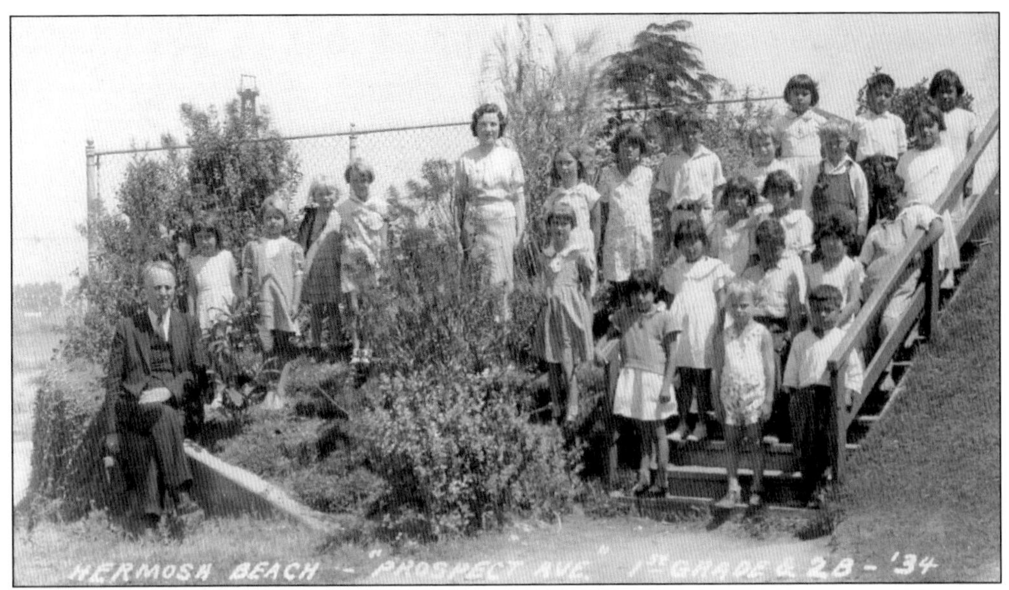

Prospect Avenue School in Hermosa Beach provided a playground with an ocean view for these children in 1934. The school, located at Sixth Street and Prospect Avenue, was where first graders Porfiria Moreno, Bonifacio Moreno, and Clara Murillo attended school. They are the three children at the top of the stairs. (Courtesy Porfiria Banda.)

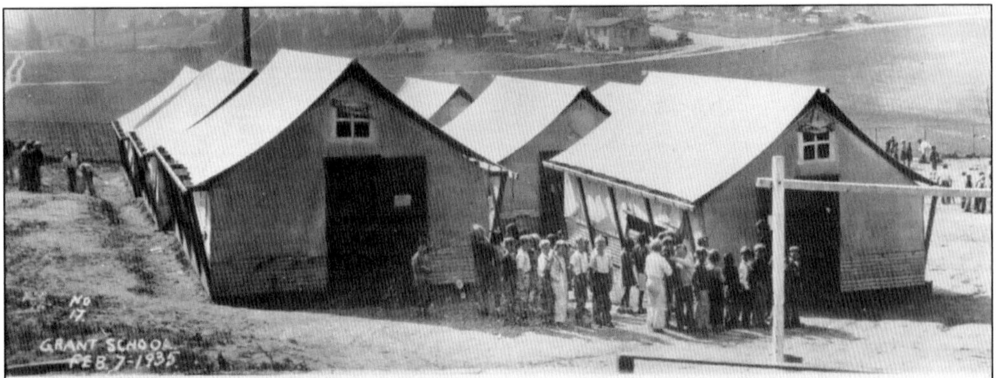

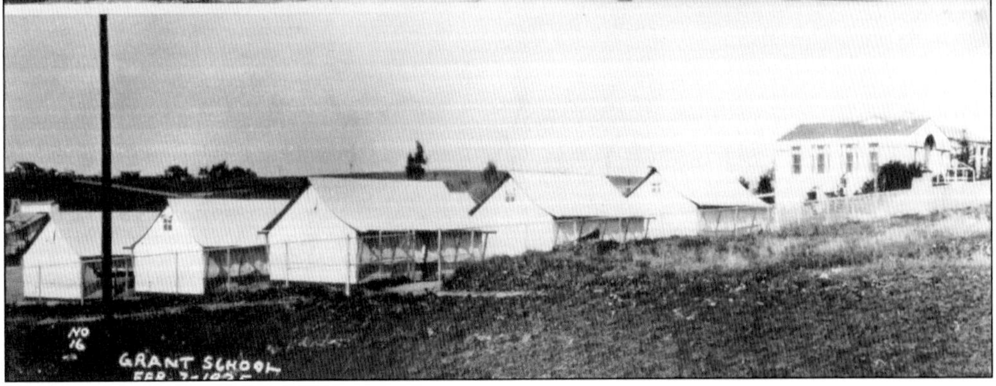

Children in northern Redondo attended Grant School, located at Artesia Boulevard and Aviation Boulevard. The top image shows the temporary tent classrooms, and the bottom one shows the tent classrooms and the first permanent school. (Courtesy Roberta Moreno.)

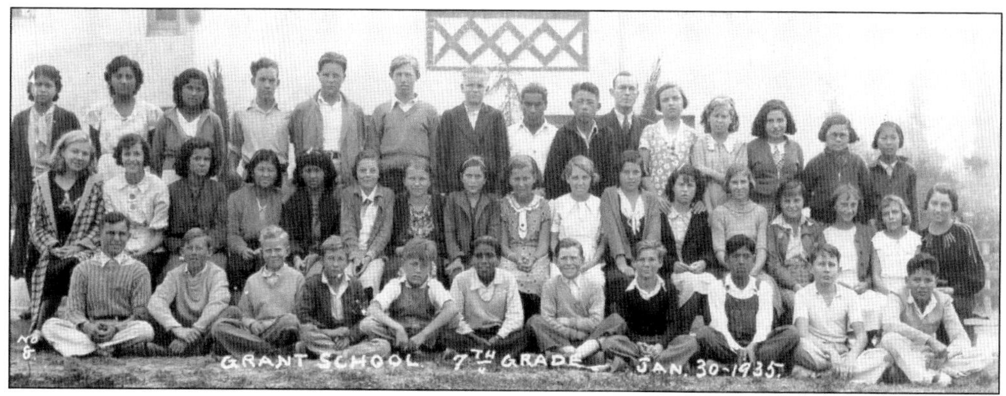

These seventh graders called themselves the "Tent House Gang." They occupied the first temporary classrooms at Grant School in northern Redondo. Pictured here are Rose Camereno (second row, fifth from left), Rafaela Colin (third row, second from left), and Dora Moreno (third row, third from left). (Courtesy Roberta Moreno.)

Jack Renke grew up speaking Spanish as a second language, learning Spanish from his next-door neighbors, the Torres and Solis families. It could be said that he was Mexican American by diet and association since he was a frequent guest at these families' homes. Renke, Amador Espinosa, and other police department retirees still gather for breakfast meetings. (Courtesy Jack Renke.)

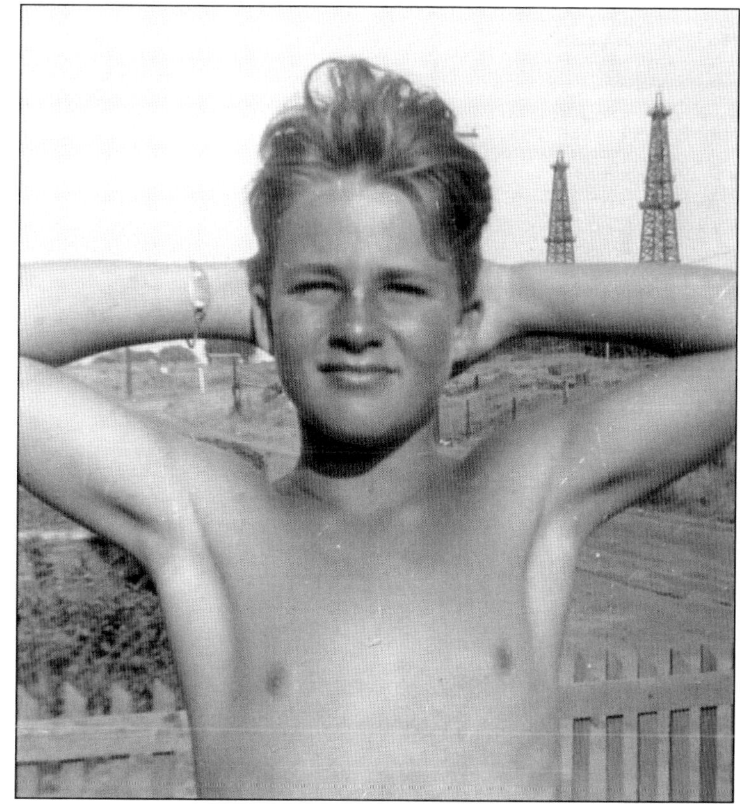

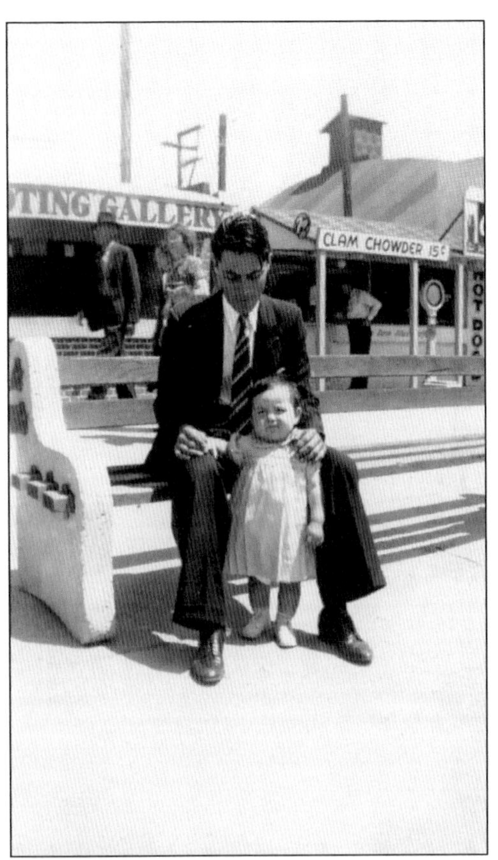

In this photograph, Jesse Gonzalez is on a Sunday outing with his daughter Rose Marie at the Redondo Beach Pier, always a popular family attraction. This 1938 photograph shows that the clam chowder advertised on the sign for 15¢ was a bargain. (Courtesy Darlene Swarz.)

Although this Pullman car appears derailed, it is actually separated from its wheels in a salvage yard in Wilmington, California. Here Jesse Gonzalez pretends to upright the car. The train wheels to the right were part of the original car. (Courtesy Darlene Swarz.)

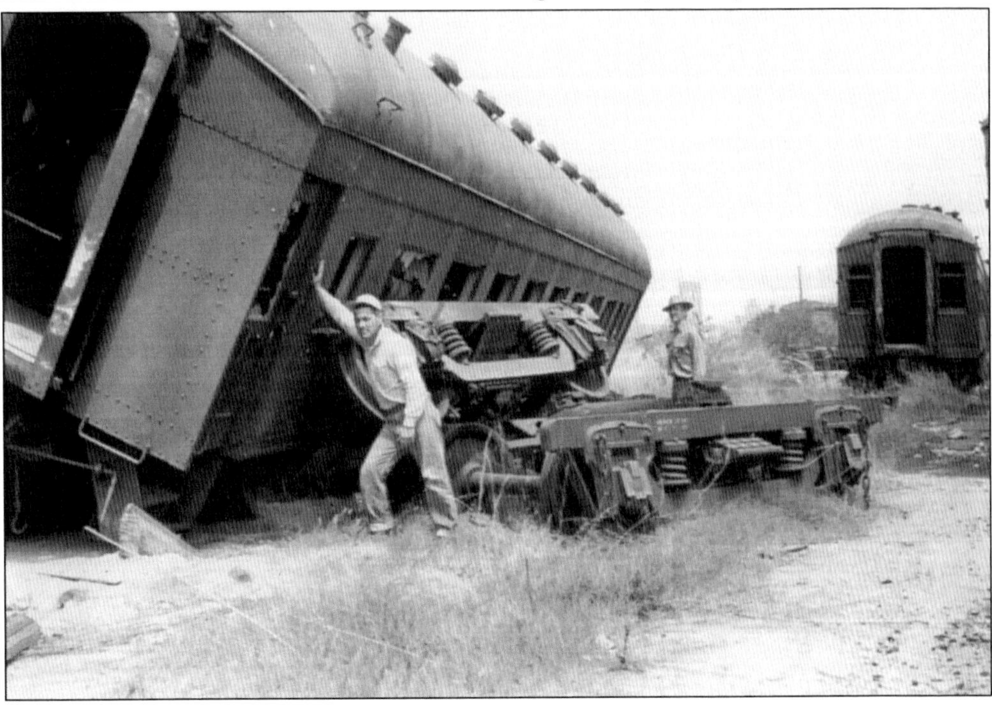

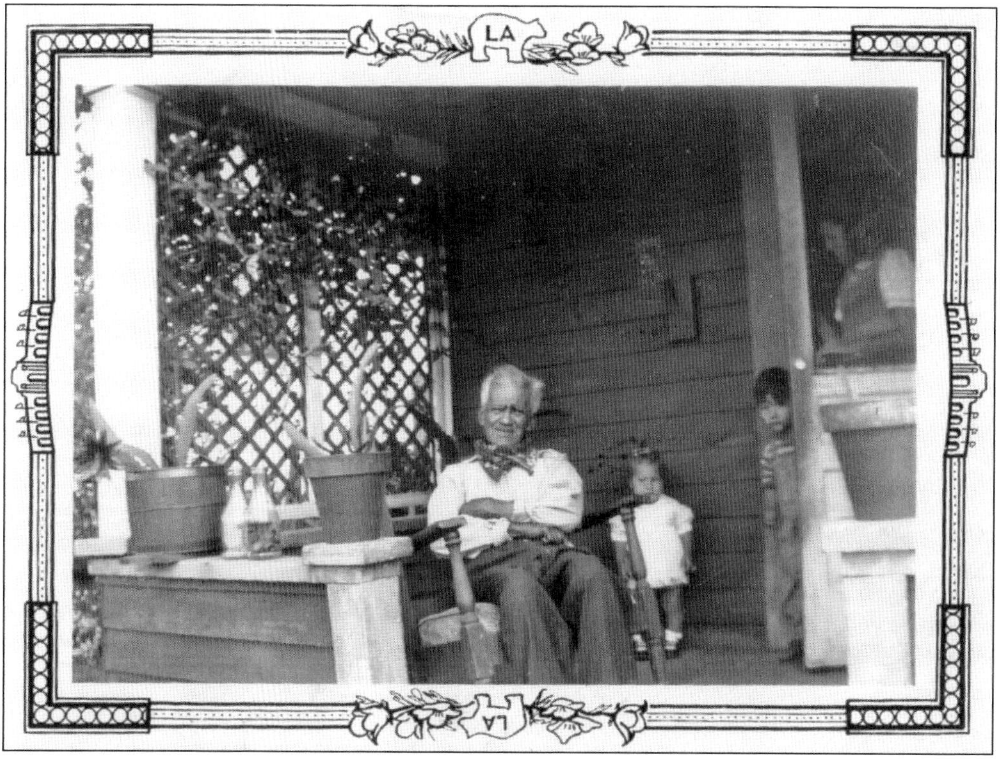

Abelardo "Polin" Rodriguez lived to the age of 107. This photograph, taken in Hermosa Beach, California, in 1940, shows him sunning on the porch with Armida and Evaristo Gonzalez Jr. At that time, he was reported to be the oldest Mexican American resident of Hermosa Beach. (Courtesy Nieves Gonzalez.)

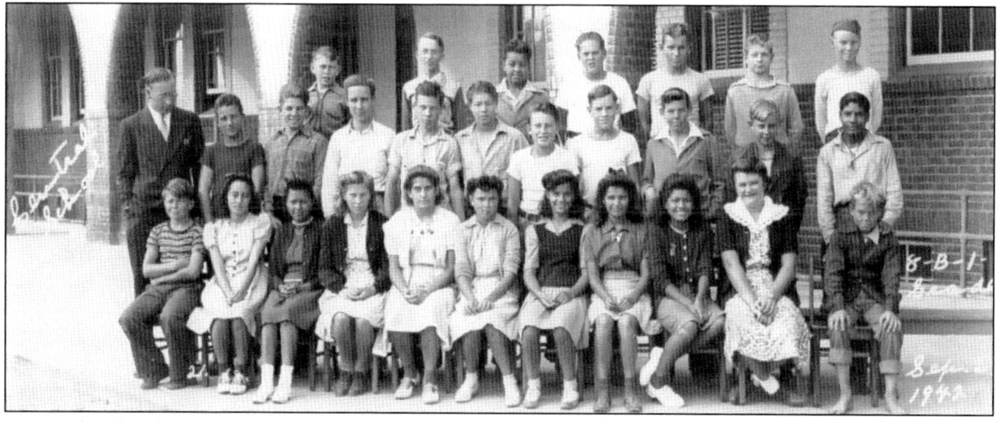

Central School was the next stop after Grant and Beryl Schools. In this 1942 school photograph are (first row) Emma Hernandez (second from left), Rosie Garcia (third from left), and Emilia Rodriguez (ninth from left); (second row) Dr. Brown (far left), Jack Renke (second from left), and Salvador Ambriz (eleventh from left); (third row) Frank Garcia (third from left). (Courtesy Jack Renke.)

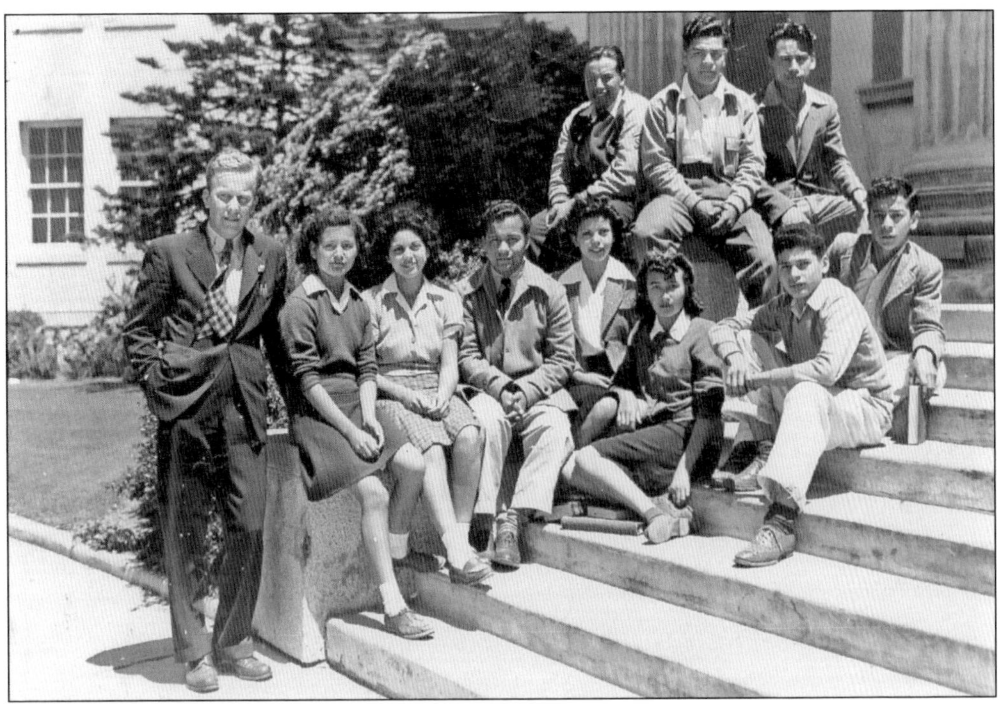

Spanish class scholars at Redondo Union High School appear in this 1941 snapshot, taken in front of the old auditorium. From left to right are the unidentified instructor, Lorenza Enriquez, Kathy Tarango, Paul Saldana, Norma Tarango "Ordie" Hernandez, "Pipin" Reyes, Julian Mendoza, Rudy Anaya, Joaquin "Jack" Mendoza, and Marcus Torres. (Courtesy "Socko" Torres.)

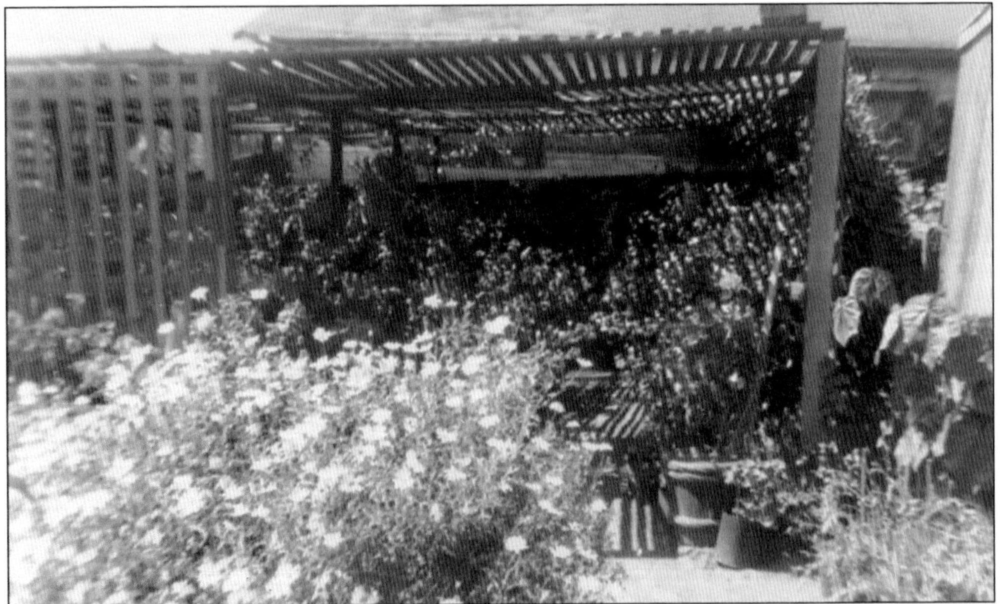

Sadie's Hat Nursery, located on First Street in Hermosa Beach, appears in this 1944 photograph. Senaida "Sadie" Lopez, who also had a flower shop, owned the nursery. Sadie was well known in the community as a resource person who helped citizens deal with the Redondo Beach City Hall bureaucracy. (Courtesy Alice Buffington.)

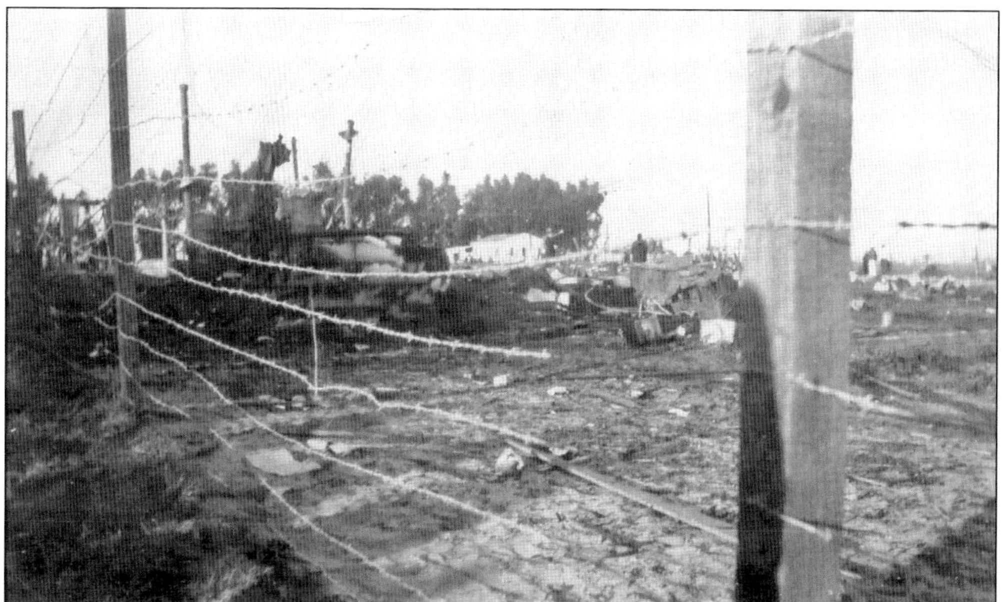

This site was located on Inglewood Avenue near Ralston Street in northern Redondo and produced fireworks before World War II. During the war, it produced signal flares. In 1944, an explosion leveled most of the buildings but fortunately, no employees were at work when it happened. (Courtesy Caroline Villa.)

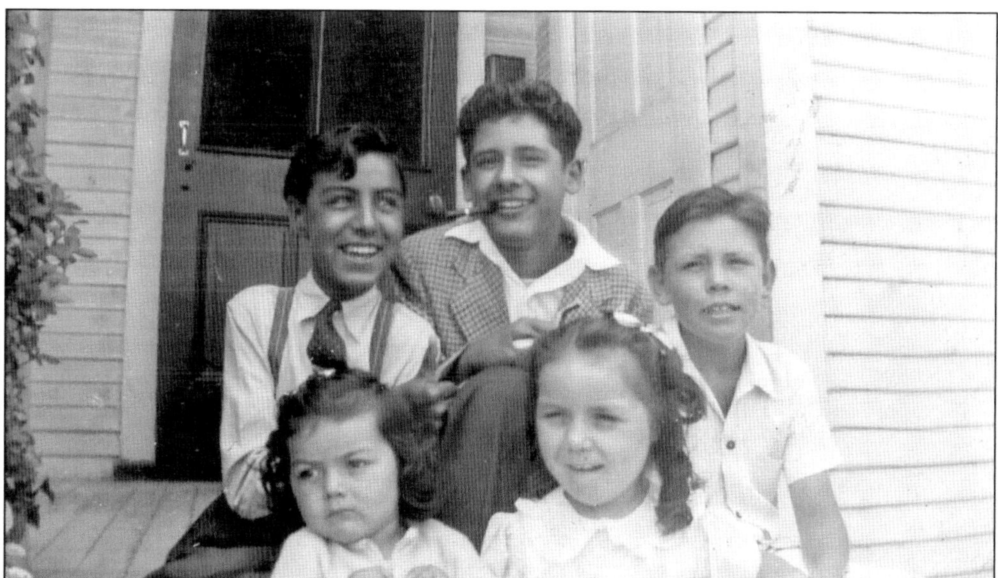

The Castillon and Gonzalez children visit at the Gonzalez home in Redondo around 1945. Pictured here are, from left to right, (first row) Darlene and Rosemarie Gonzalez; (second row) Mauro Gonzalez and Albert and Richard Castillon. The Gonzalez and Castillon children were cousins as well as the grandchildren of Mauro Gonzalez, the first Mexican American resident of Redondo Beach. (Courtesy Darlene Swarz.)

42

Marriage

No.	CONTRACTING PARTIES	RESIDENCE	DATE AND PLACE OF BAPTISM	PARENTS
1	CLEMENTE COLIN	1710 MORGAN LANE R.B.	16 JUNE 1918 PLAZA CHURCH LOS ANGELES	MAURICIO COLIN / CATALINA BRAVO
	REFUGIO GONZALES	WILMINGTON	ST ANNE'S NEEDLES, CALIF JULY 4 1917	DAVID GONZALES / GUADALUPE SAENZ
2	ERNEST R VALENZUELA	U.S.N.	ST JAMES REDONDO 5 JUNE 1921	RAMON VALENZUE / MARY BRAMBILA
	ELOISA F ESPINOZA	R.B. 619 GUADALUPE	LOMPOC, LA PURISIMA (Born Oct 4, 1921)	ENRIQUE ESPINOZA / WILFREDA CONTRE
3	MANUEL A. GARCIA	2741 E 5th L.A.	SOLOMONVILLE, ARIZ. Oct 3 1918	SIXTO GARCIA / MANUELA AMADO
	ADELINA SALDAÑO	316 N. Gertruda	PUEBLO, COLO. O. Lady of Mt Carmel 24 May 1921	ROMUALDA SALDAÑ / PASCUALA CONTRE
4	BONIFACIO MORENO	1314 Carmelita R.B.	St. JAMES, REDONDO AUG 8th 1926	DOMINGO MORENO / MARIA BRAVO
	JOSEPHA CARRANZA	1727 Carlson Lane R.B.	SAN LUIS REY, 27 Dec. 1925	JESUS CARRANZA / LEOVIJILDA PERE
			PUREFBRO, MICH	BAUTISTA AMA

Pictured here is a *c.* 1945 marriage register from Our Lady of Guadalupe Church in Hermosa Beach, completed by Fr. Cyril Wood. It lists families from Lompoc, California, and other locations that intermarried. Prior to the arrival of Father Wood, all sacramental records were kept at St. James Church in Redondo. (Courtesy Alex Moreno Areyan.)

63 [Dec. 25 1943 – See Opposite Page]

First Communion Register

Date June 4 (1944) Administered by Rev. C. J. Wood

No.	BAPTISMAL AND FAMILY NAME	Age	RESIDENCE
1	Clara Contreras (at Hermosa)	8	1245 1st St. R.B.
2	Cora Solis	10	1723 Carlson Lane R.B.
3	Julia Areyan	9	1718 Morgan Lane R.B
4	Gloria Salinas	10	2204 Marshallfield R.B.
5	Caroline Salinas	9	2204 Marshallfield R.B.
6	Mary Muniz	11	1822 Clark Lane R.B.
7	Flavio (Floyd) Garcia	12	1822 Clark Lane R.B.
8	Andrew Garcia	14	1822 Clark Lane R.B.
9	Leduvina Duarte	13	546 N. Gertruda R.B.
10	Lilian Valdez	9	816 1st St H.B.
11	Marta Enriquez	9	571 2nd St H.B.

Date Dec.

No.	BAPTISMAL
1	Jose Torres
2	Florencio
3	Clemente
4	Juana To
5	Ernesto H
6	Jesus He
7	Salvador
8	Robert Vill
9	Elvira Vill
10	
11	SUNDAY

This photograph is a first communion register from 1944, also completed by Father Wood, and provides names and addresses of those receiving this sacrament. Only a partial listing of their sponsors can be seen. (Courtesy Alex Moreno Areyan.)

In 1948, couples dance on Pacific Avenue in downtown Redondo Beach in front of the old D&D drugstore. Delfina Gonzalez Reynaga, center right, and a military friend are part of the crowd enjoying the parade. The occasion was Fiesta Days, celebrated from about 1938 to 1950, when the entire Mexican American community participated in celebrating the city's early Spanish and Mexican heritage. (Courtesy Alice Buffington.)

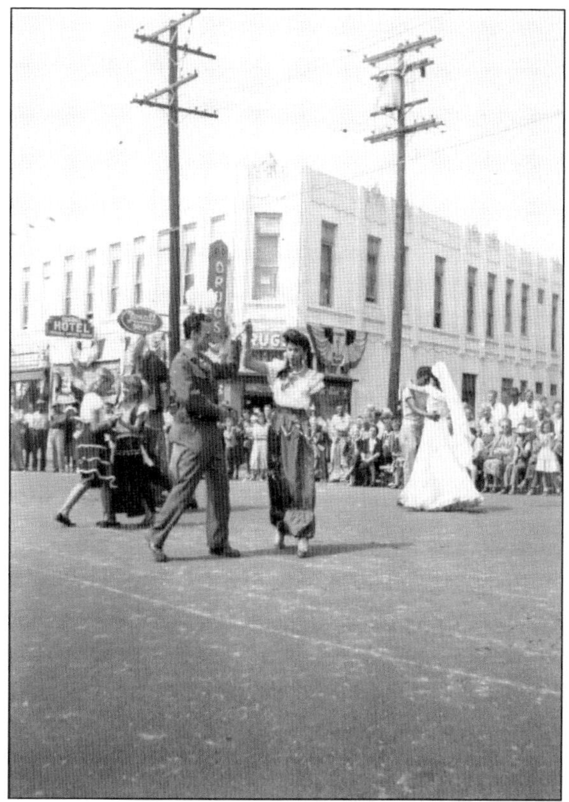

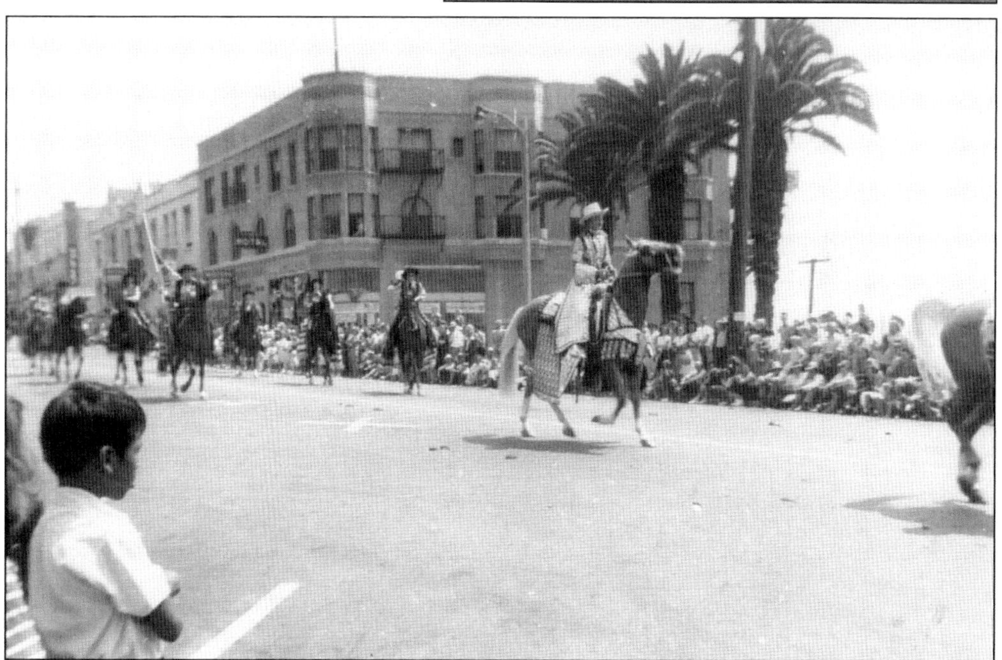

In 1951, Frontier Days replaced Fiesta Days and continued until 1956. Frontier Days paid tribute to the city's Western heritage. According to "Chuey" Hernandez, Albert Castillon was the winner of Frontier Days' grand prize of a 1956 Chevrolet station wagon. (Courtesy Alice Buffington.)

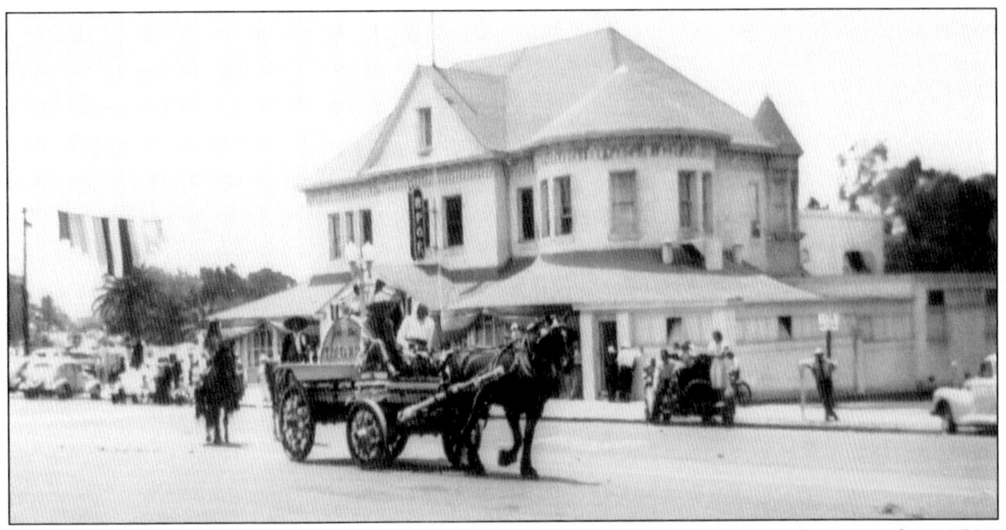

Fourteen-year-old Candy Millan rides behind a hay wagon during Fiesta Days in the 1950s. The old Redondo Beach Elks Lodge on Catalina Avenue is visible in the background. Prior to occupancy by the Elks, it served as the central station for the old Pacific Electric Railway. (Courtesy Candy Millan.)

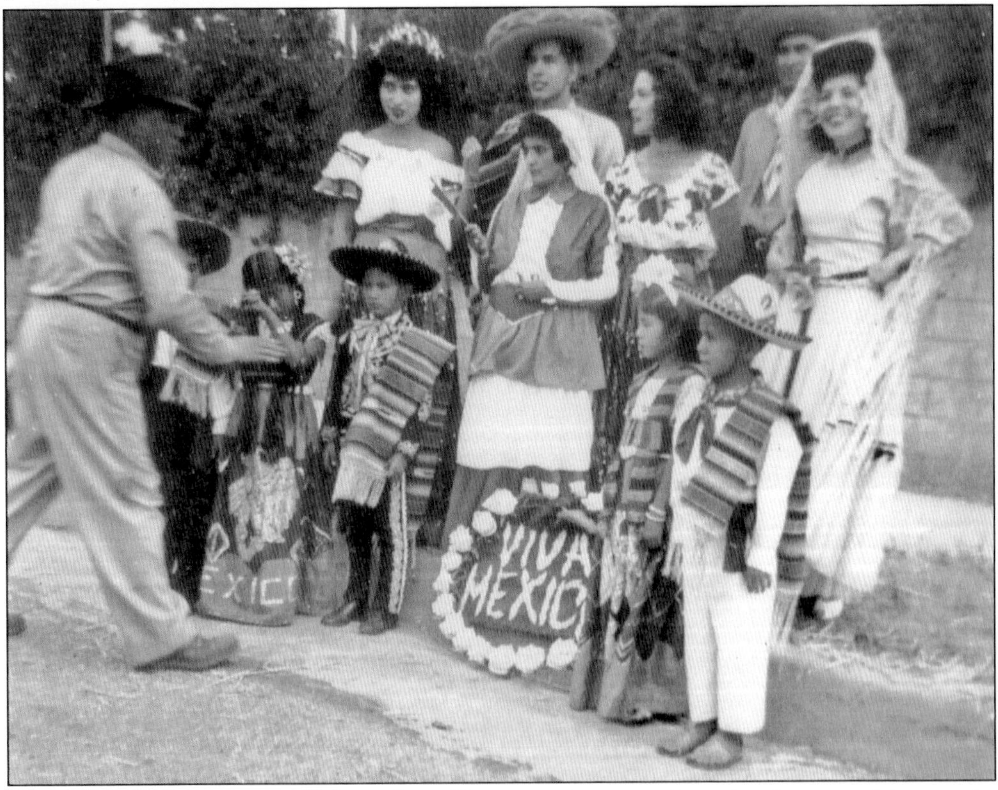

This photograph taken in 1947 shows Fiesta Days participants anticipating the start of the parade. The man at left and the children in front are unidentified. Emilia Hurtado is in the second row, center. In the third row, pictured from left to right, are Alice Lopez, Jack Warner, and unidentified. (Courtesy Alice Buffington.)

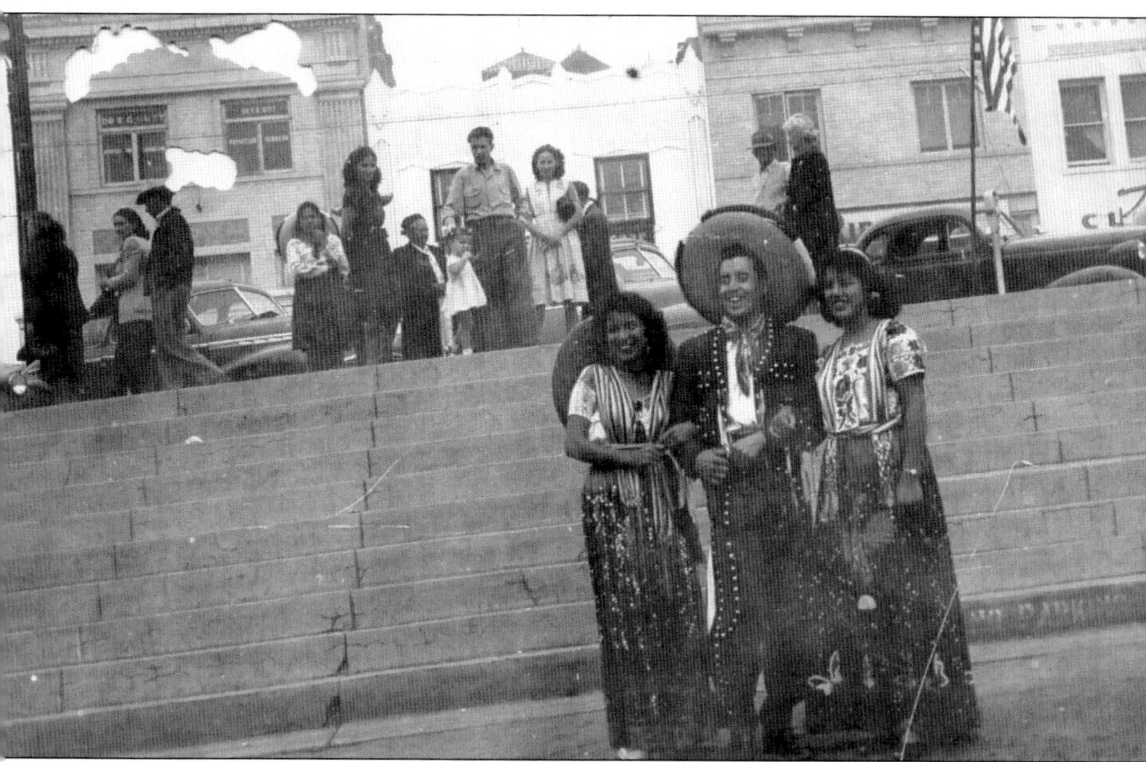

Dressed in Mexican *china poblana*, outfits of white, colorfully embroidered blouses and red, white, and green skirts, and a Mexican cowboy *charro* suit in 1947 are three eager Fiesta Days participants. Pictured from left to right are unidentified, Senaido Vargas, and Carmen Hernandez. Senaido, a talented tenor, later sang and acted in more than a dozen musicals as an El Camino College student. (Courtesy Alice Buffington.)

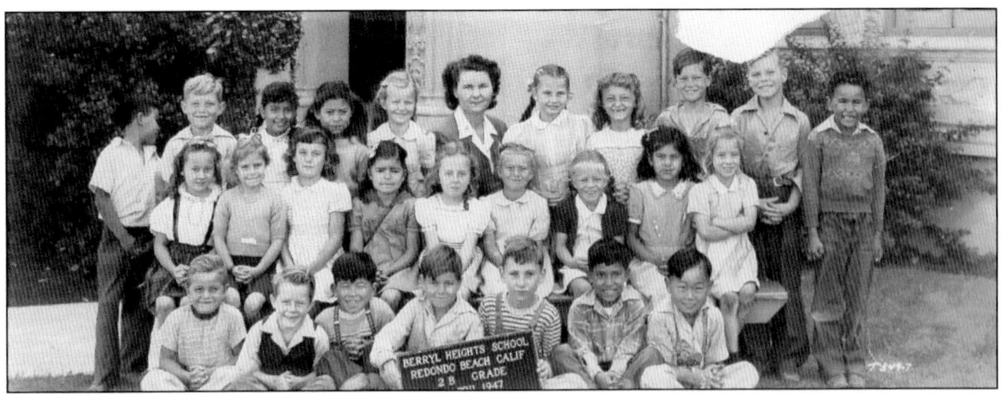

Pictured here in 1947 at the entrance to Beryl Elementary School in Redondo Beach are Richard Moreno (first row, sixth from left), Gilbert Savedra (third row, far left), and Jenny Gonzalez (third row, third from left). The rest of the children and the teacher are unidentified. The school boasted an ocean view and an underground cafeteria. (Courtesy John Luna Moreno.)

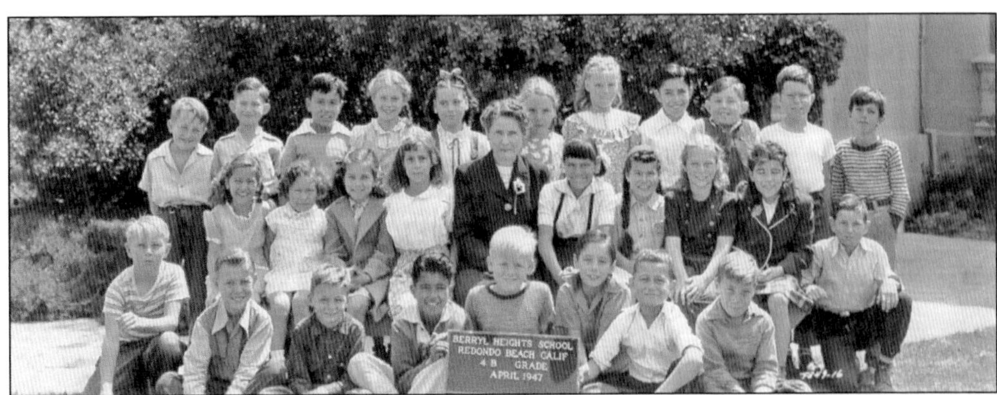

Pictured in this 1947 photograph of the fourth grade at Beryl Elementary School are Manuel Savedra (first row, fourth from left), Armida Gonzalez (second row, second from left), and Piedad Leon (second row, sixth from left), who is next to the teacher. The rest of the students are unidentified. Armida and her brother Evaristo performed traditional Mexican dances in full costume at Beryl Elementary School assemblies. (Courtesy Ordie Fernandez.)

This 1946 Buick Roadmaster serves as a backrest for Rudy M. Areyan in this 1947 image. The photograph was taken in the driveway of the Colin residence, his next-door neighbors. In later years, Rudy operated a concrete construction business and teamed with the Trevino brothers on South Bay construction projects. (Courtesy Mary Lou Ordaz.)

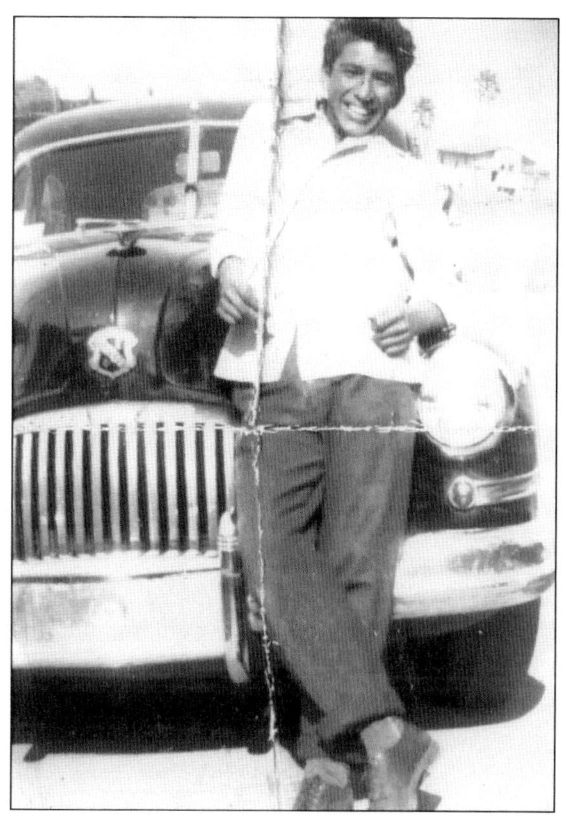

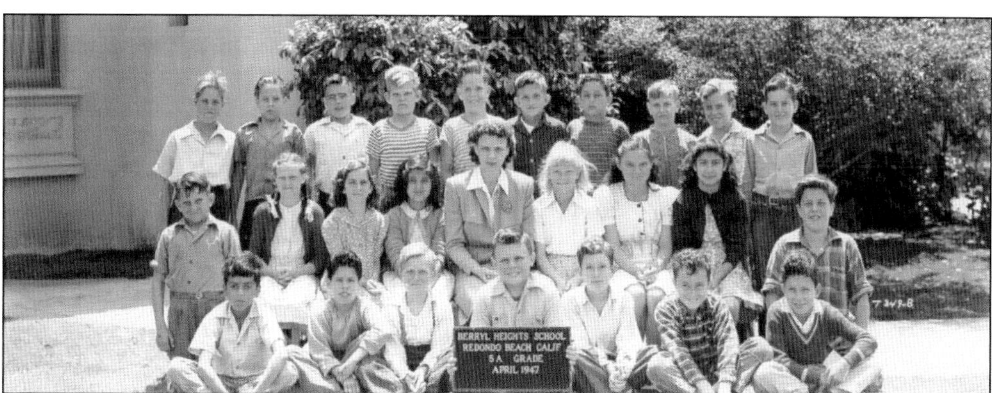

Pictured in this 1947 photograph of the fifth grade at Beryl School are Alfredo Escobar (first row, second from left) and Caroline Salinas (second row, second from the right, in the black sweater), who in high school was selected as the Girls Athletic Association's fiesta queen. The rest of the students and the teacher are unidentified. (Courtesy Ordie Fernandez.)

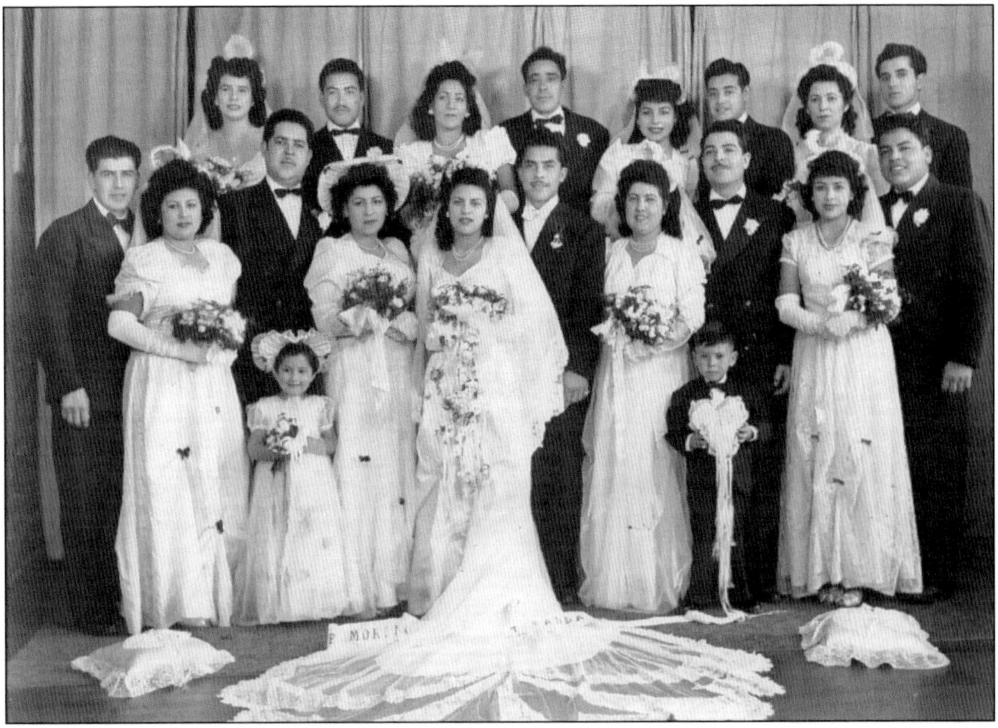

Trino Banda and Porfiria Moreno's wedding is featured in this 1947 photograph. Trino was a resident of the pueblo colony called La Rana (Spanish for frog) in Torrance. Many Mexican American families from surrounding communities intermarried during the 1940s and 1950s. The flower girl is Roberta Moreno, and the ring bearer is the author. (Courtesy Rosie Salazar.)

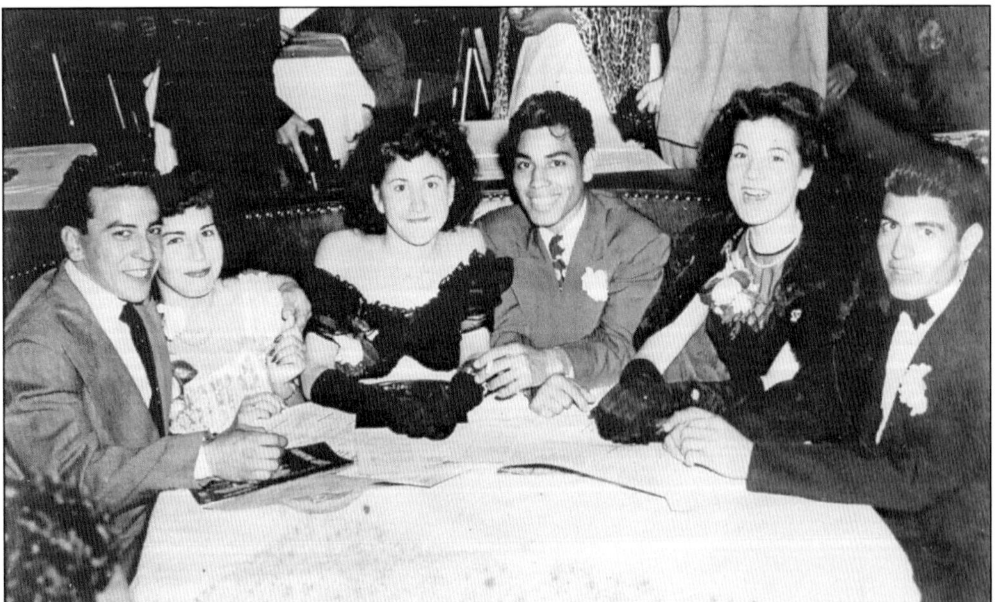

The Florentine Gardens in Hollywood was the premier place for after-prom celebrations in 1947. Pictured from left to right are Julian Mendoza, Jenny Valencia, Adela Enriquez, Mike Sierra, Nieves Santana, and Joe Valencia. (Courtesy Nieves Gonzalez.)

Tommy Pacheco resembles well-known 1940s Mexican singer Jorge Negrete in this photograph taken in 1948. He frequently entertained family and friends by playing old Mexican ballads at gatherings. His father operated a tree felling business in northern Redondo in the early 1930s. (Courtesy "Fellie" Pacheco.)

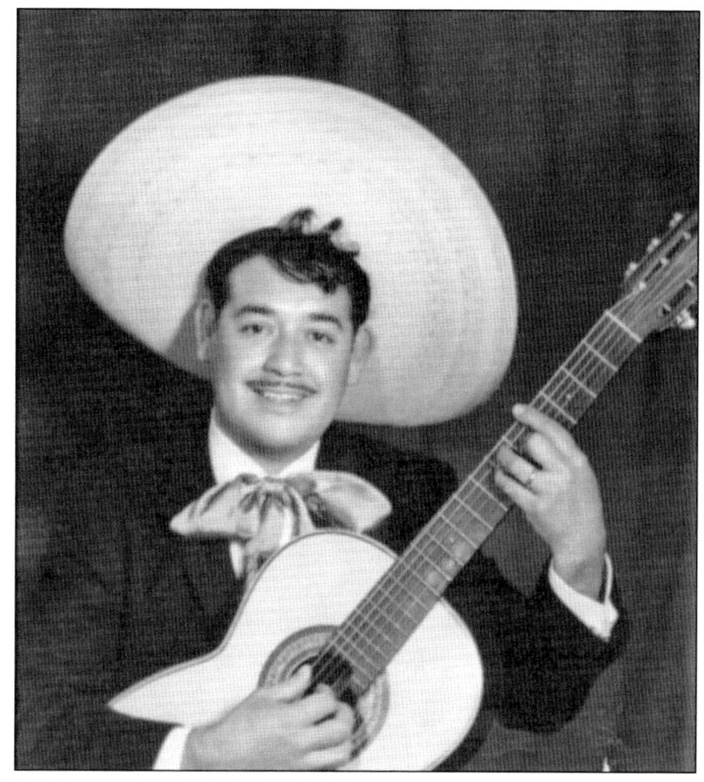

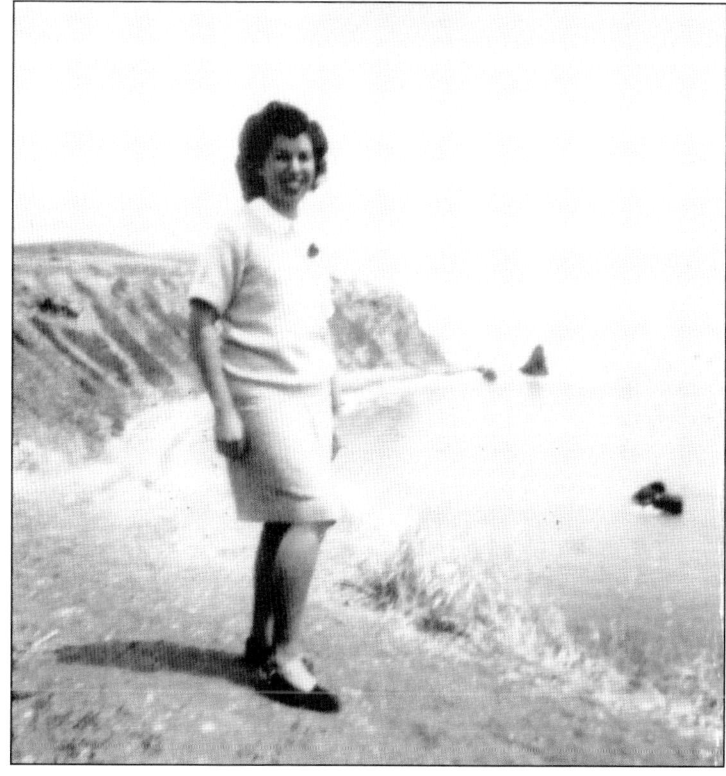

The Palos Verdes Peninsula was a favorite spot to visit on Sunday afternoon drives. This photograph shows Ophelia "Fellie" Saucedo enjoying the ocean view in 1948, near what became Marineland of the Pacific's aquatic park. Fellie later married Tommy Pacheco, seen in the prior photograph. (Courtesy Tommy Pacheco.)

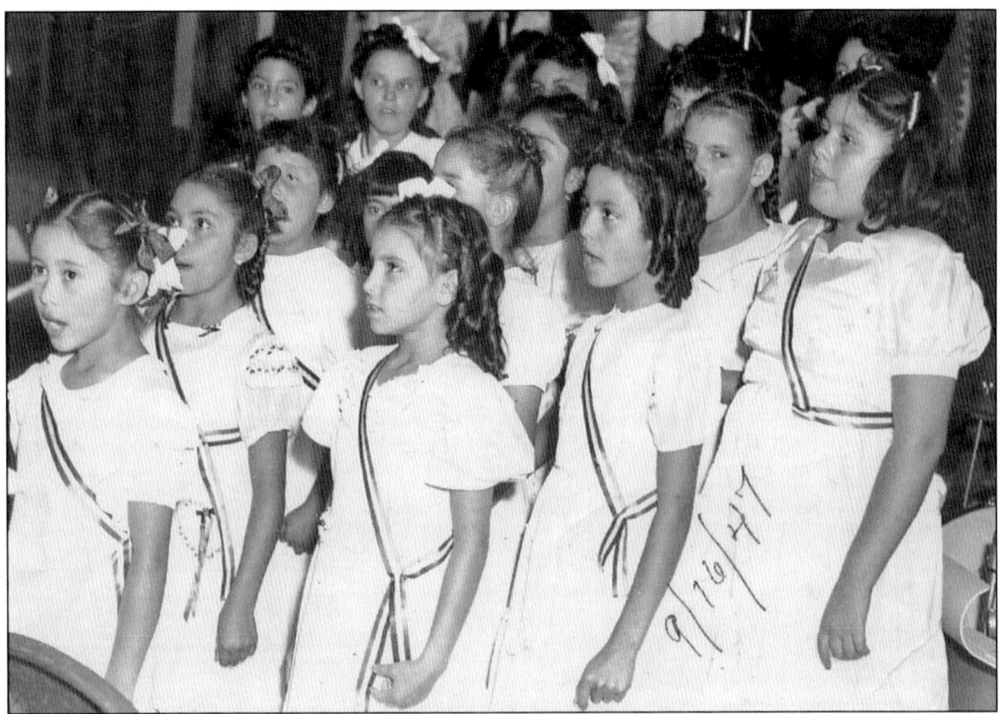

These young parishioners at Our Lady of Guadalupe Church sing at a church fiesta on September 16, 1947, celebrating Mexico's independence from Spain. Identified in this photograph are Esther Solis (in front), Ordie Fernandez (second row, far right), Rachel Garcia (third row, far right), Joan Garcia (fourth row, far left), and Piedad Leon (fourth row, far right). (Courtesy Ordie Fernandez.)

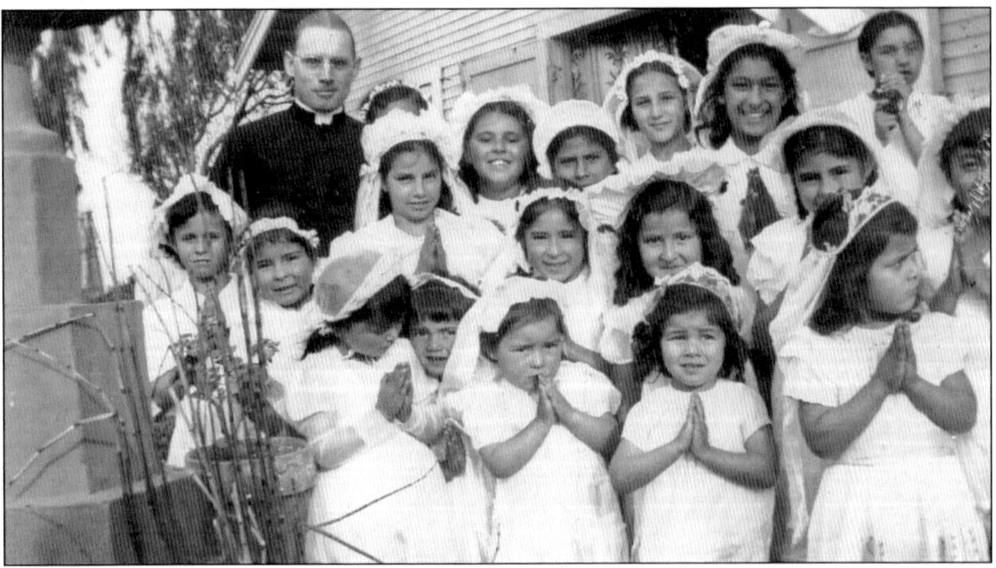

In this rare photograph, Fr. Cyril Wood is pictured with a group of young ladies bringing flowers to Our Lady of Guadalupe during the traditional May offering. Represented in this photograph are the Cortez, Estrada, Leon, Moreno Areyan, Ortiz, Ruiz, and Savedra families. Father Wood, beloved by his parishioners, formed several youth groups during his tenure at the church. (Courtesy Herminda Banda.)

The ornate altar of Our Lady of Guadalupe Church in Hermosa shows the charm of the early church. Alice Lopez, the daughter of the late Sadie and Joe Lopez, who moved to Redondo Beach in the early 1930s from Culver City, California, is seen in this 1949 wedding photograph. (Courtesy Alice Buffington.)

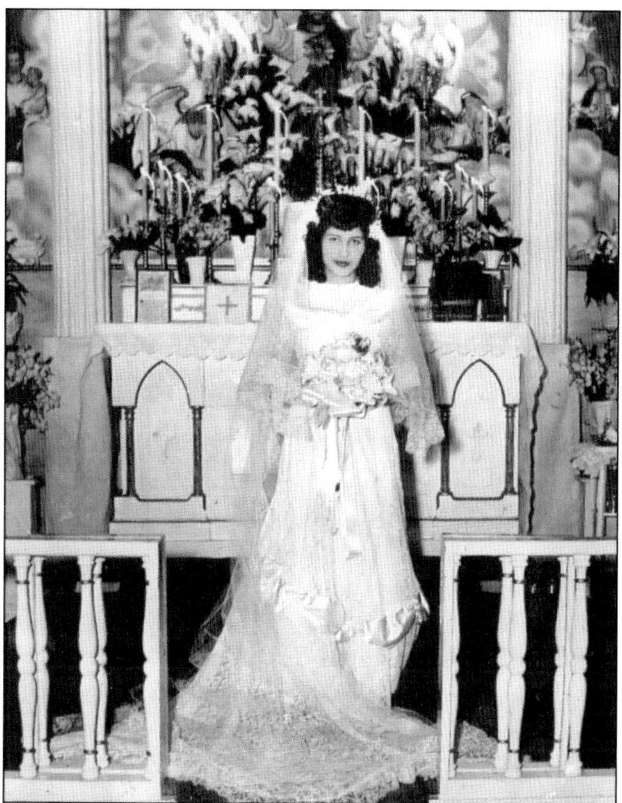

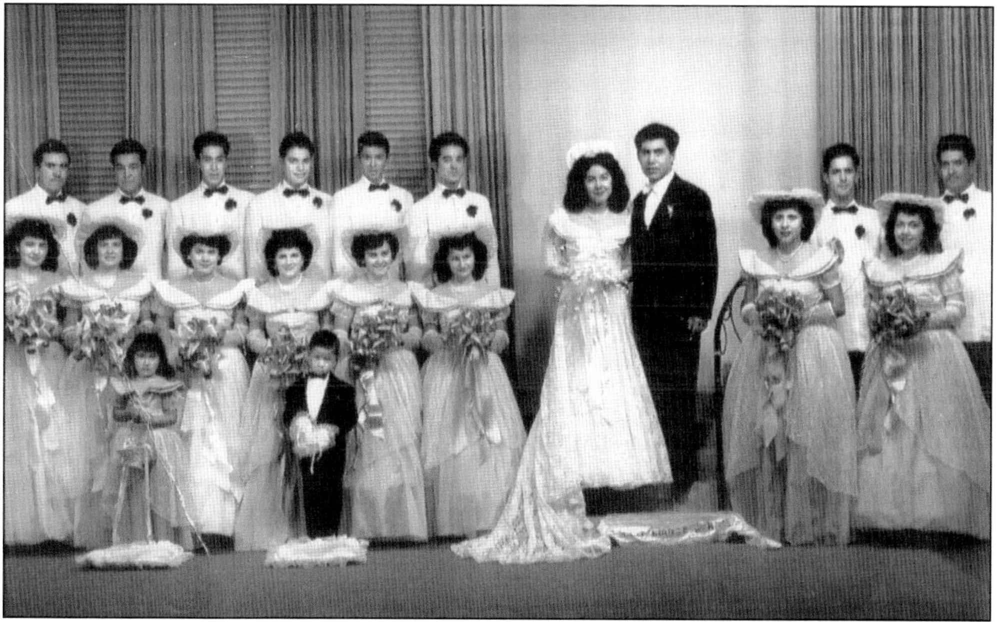

This wedding photograph of Mary Louise Hernandez and Ramiro Ordaz was taken in 1950. Their wedding dance was at the Old Redondo Barn, where they danced to the music of the Tony Alvarez band. They met on a blind date approved by her father, Ignacio, who worked at Columbia Steel in Torrance with Ramiro's father. (Courtesy Mary Lou and Ramiro Ordaz.)

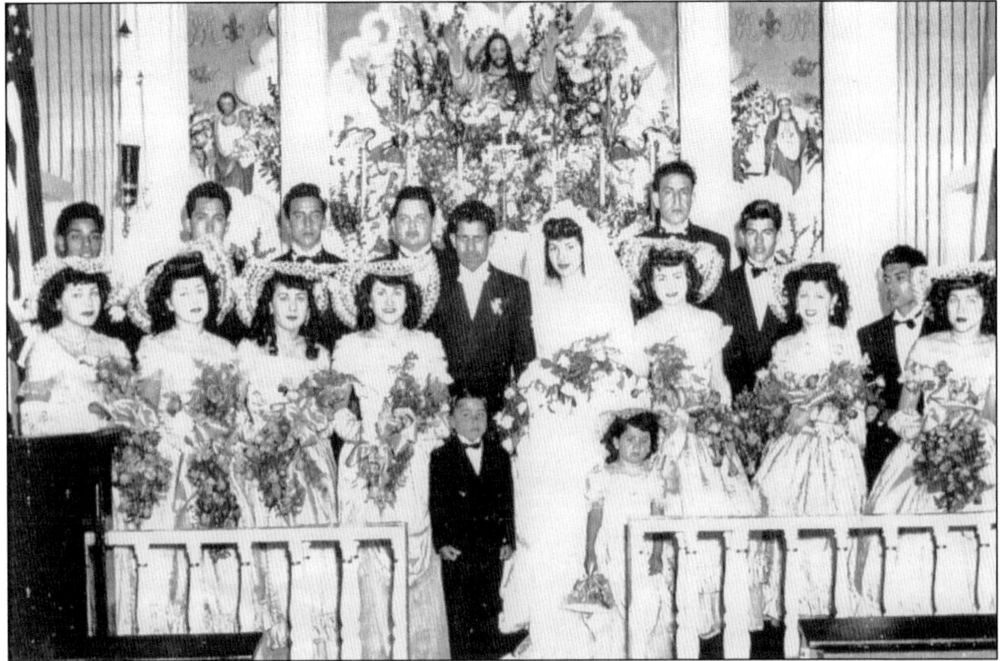

Calistro "Cal" Gonzalez and Nieves "Neva" Santana were married on March 28, 1948, at Our Lady of Guadalupe Church. The wedding party represented the Santana, Hernandez, Anaya, Enriquez, Sierra, Cortez, Mendoza, Garcia, Luna, and Valencia families. The flower girl is Tommie Navarro and the ring bearer is Armando Moreno. (Courtesy Nieves and Calistro Gonzalez.)

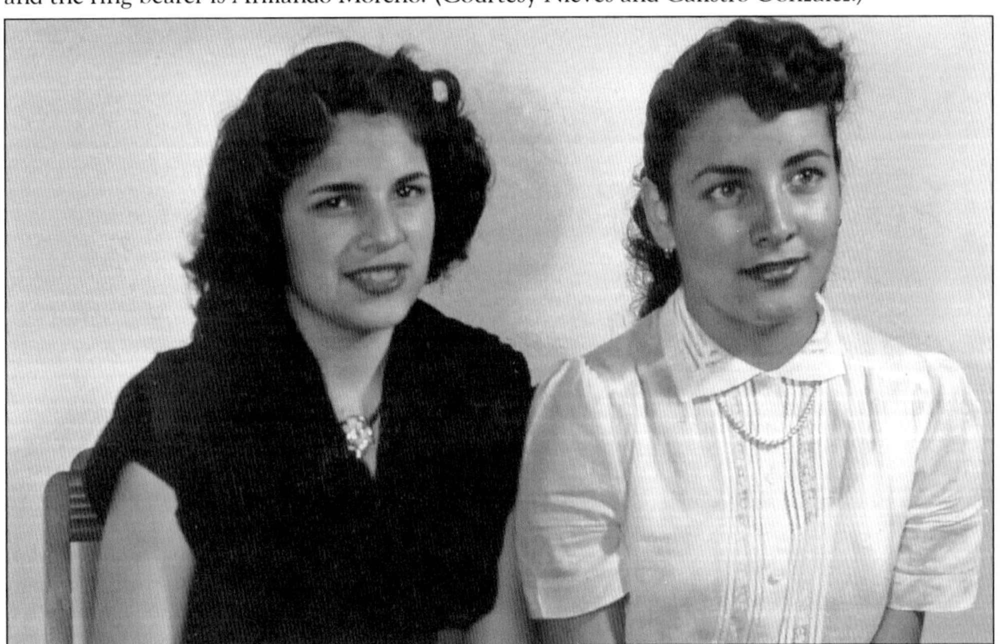

Candy Millan (left), age 15, and Gloria Saucedo, around age 17, posed for this photograph in 1950 as fiesta queen candidates at Our Lady of Guadalupe Church. The queen competition was not a beauty contest, but a fund-raiser based on the total number of raffle tickets sold. The fiestas began in the early 1930s and continued until around 1957. (Courtesy Candy Millan.)

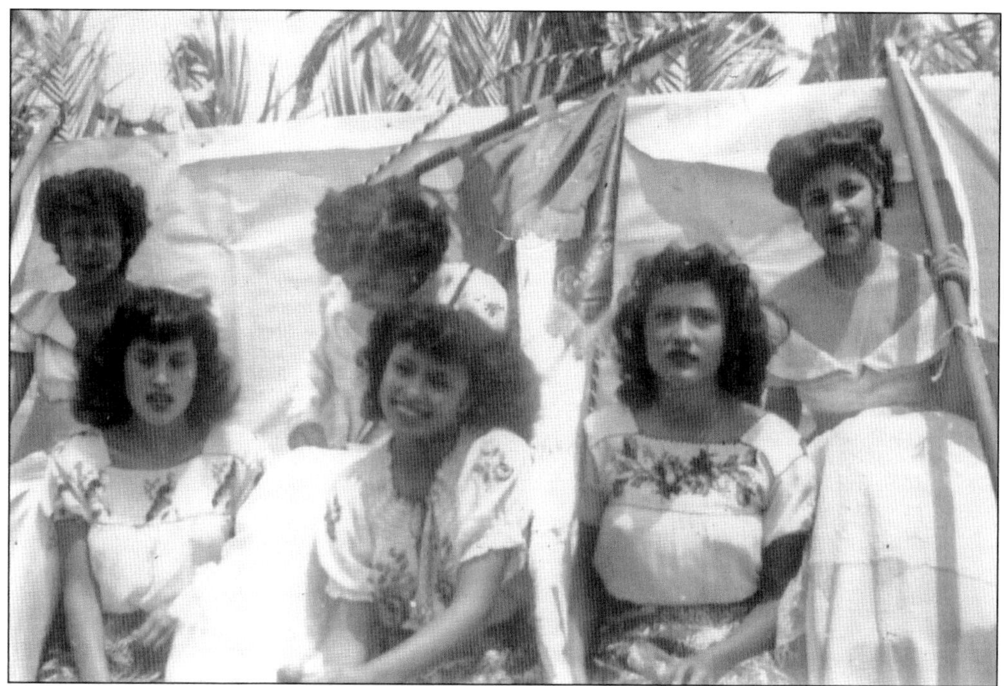

The Redondo Beach Fiesta Days were not complete without a float and the parade queen and her court. On this 1950s float are, from left to right, (first row) unidentified, Rachel Garcia, and Joan Garcia; (second row) unidentified, Mary Louise Gomez, and Candy Millan. (Courtesy Candy Millan.)

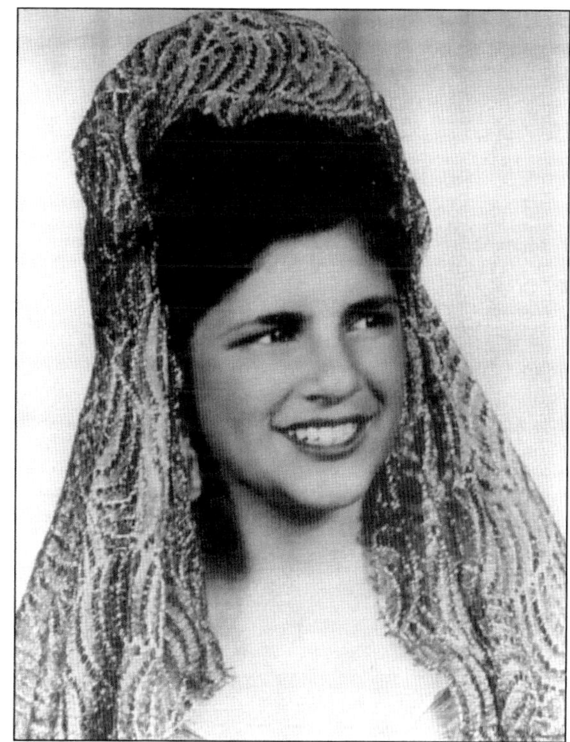

This is a 1950 *Daily Breeze* newspaper publicity photograph announcing the selection of Candy Millan, age 15, as queen of the Our Lady of Guadalupe Church fiesta. She is dressed in the traditional *peineta* (comb) and *mantilla* (head scarf) of old Spain and Mexico. (Courtesy Diana Millan.)

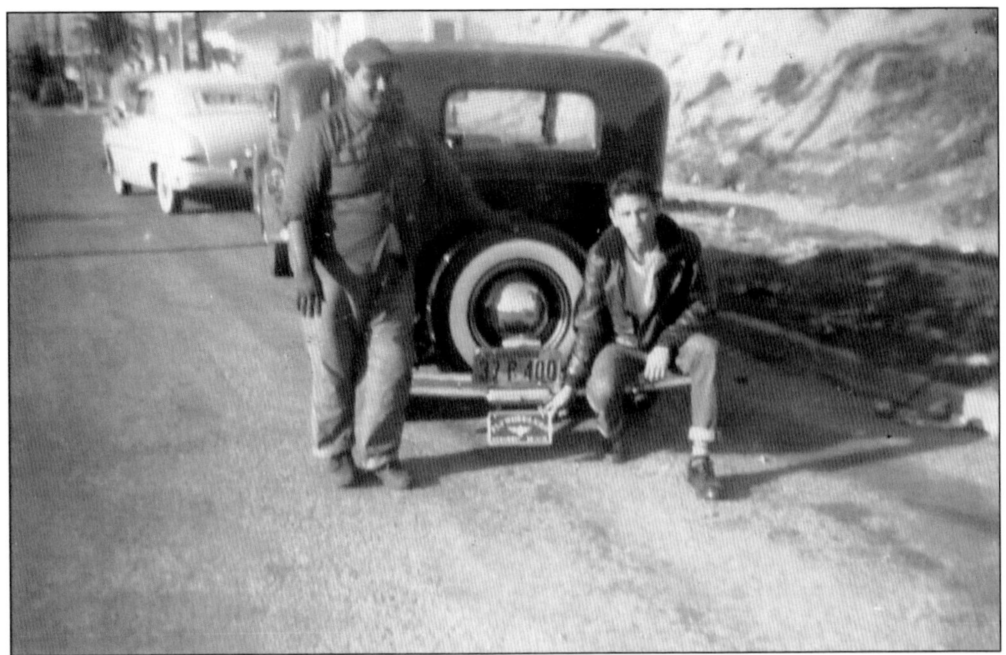

The Flywheelers car club was one of several in Redondo Beach in the 1950s. This photograph taken on Elena Street shows Clemente Torres (left) and Richard Castillon proudly displaying their Flywheelers club plaque on Clemente's early 1930s Ford Victoria, complete with a rear-mounted spare tire continental kit. (Courtesy Richard Castillon.)

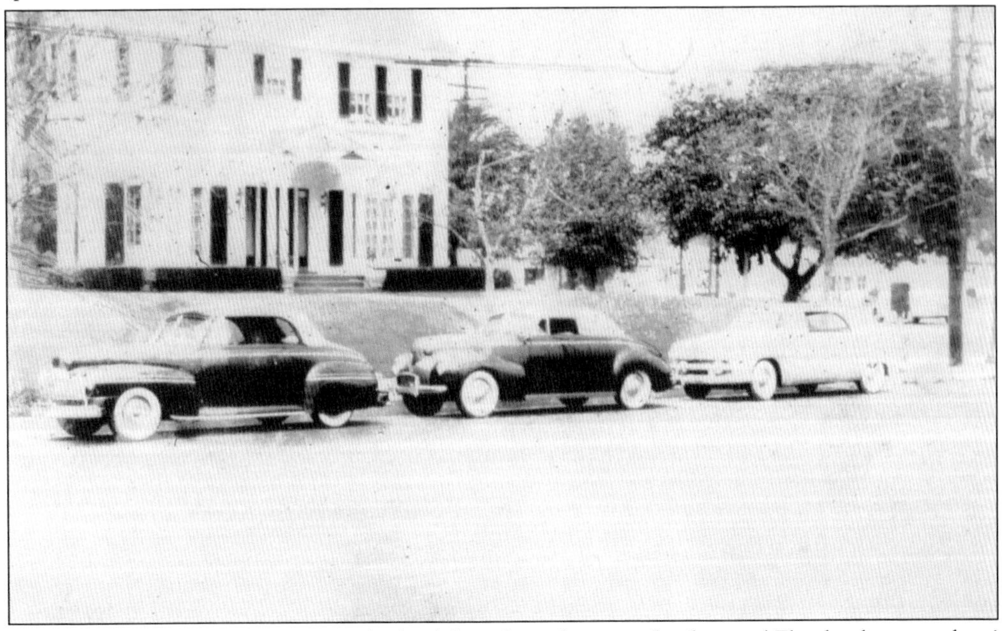

The front of the Sweetser Estate is the backdrop for a photograph of several Flywheelers members' cars. Pictured are, from left to right, Richard Castillon's 1949 Mercury convertible, Frankie Fernandez's "Chopped" 1940 Mercury, and Ronnie Saldana's 1950 Ford hardtop. Clemente Torres, a Flywheelers member, was the groundskeeper at Sweetser's for many years. Other car clubs were the Drifters and the Magoos. (Courtesy Richard Castillon.)

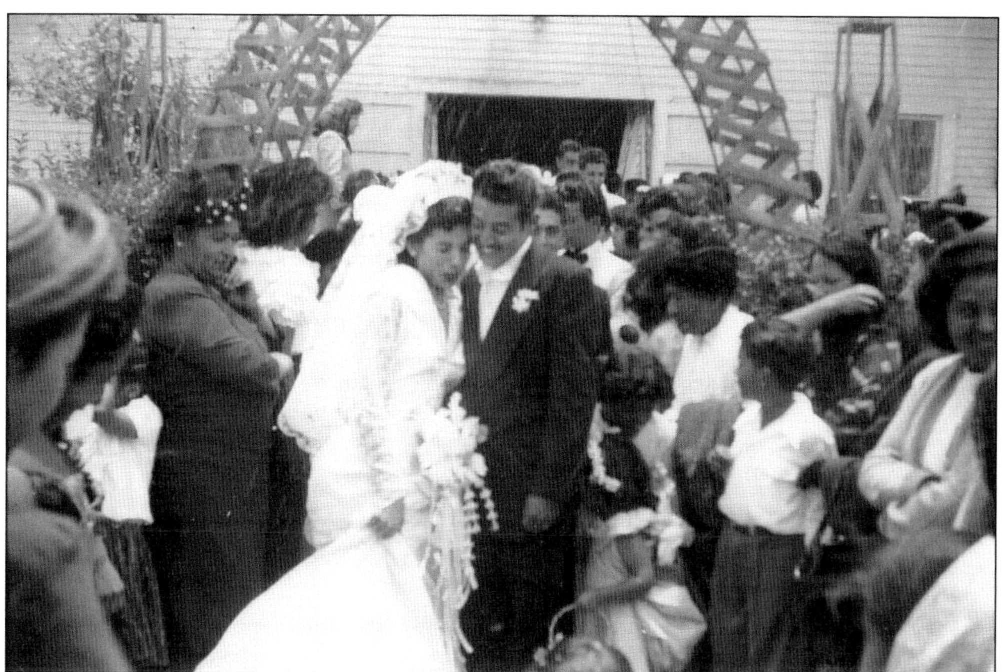

Tommy Pacheco's marriage to Ophelia Saucedo at Our Lady of Guadalupe Church is captured in this 1950 photograph. The church was the religious, cultural, and social nexus for the communities of Redondo, Hermosa, and other Mexican American neighborhoods in the area. Eight years after this wedding, the old church was demolished to make way for the new one. (Courtesy "Fellie" Pacheco.)

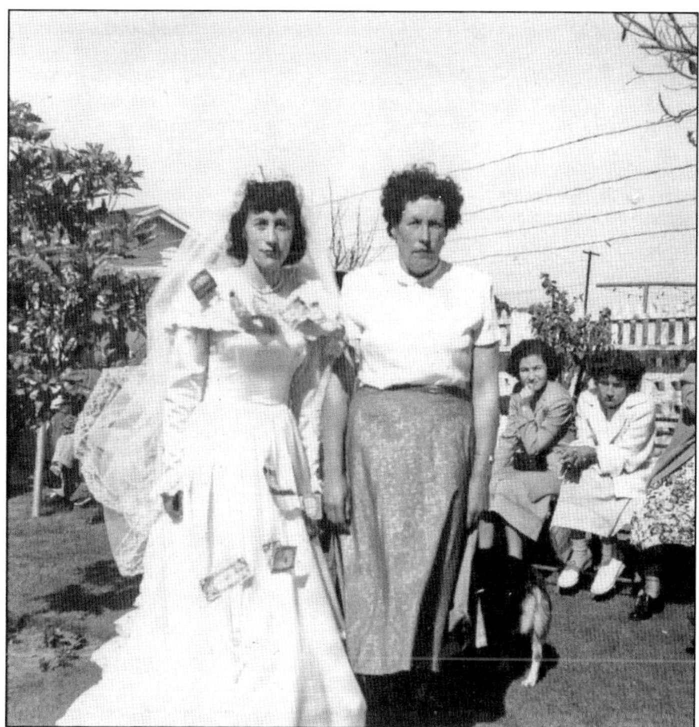

"Chavela" Leon and her mother, "Cuca," are pictured in their backyard on Morgan Lane in northern Redondo, where they celebrated her marriage to Luis Cordova in 1951. The dress is adorned with money given to her by guests dancing with the bride at the reception. Money is the traditional Mexican American manner of wishing a couple prosperity. (Courtesy Luis Cordova.)

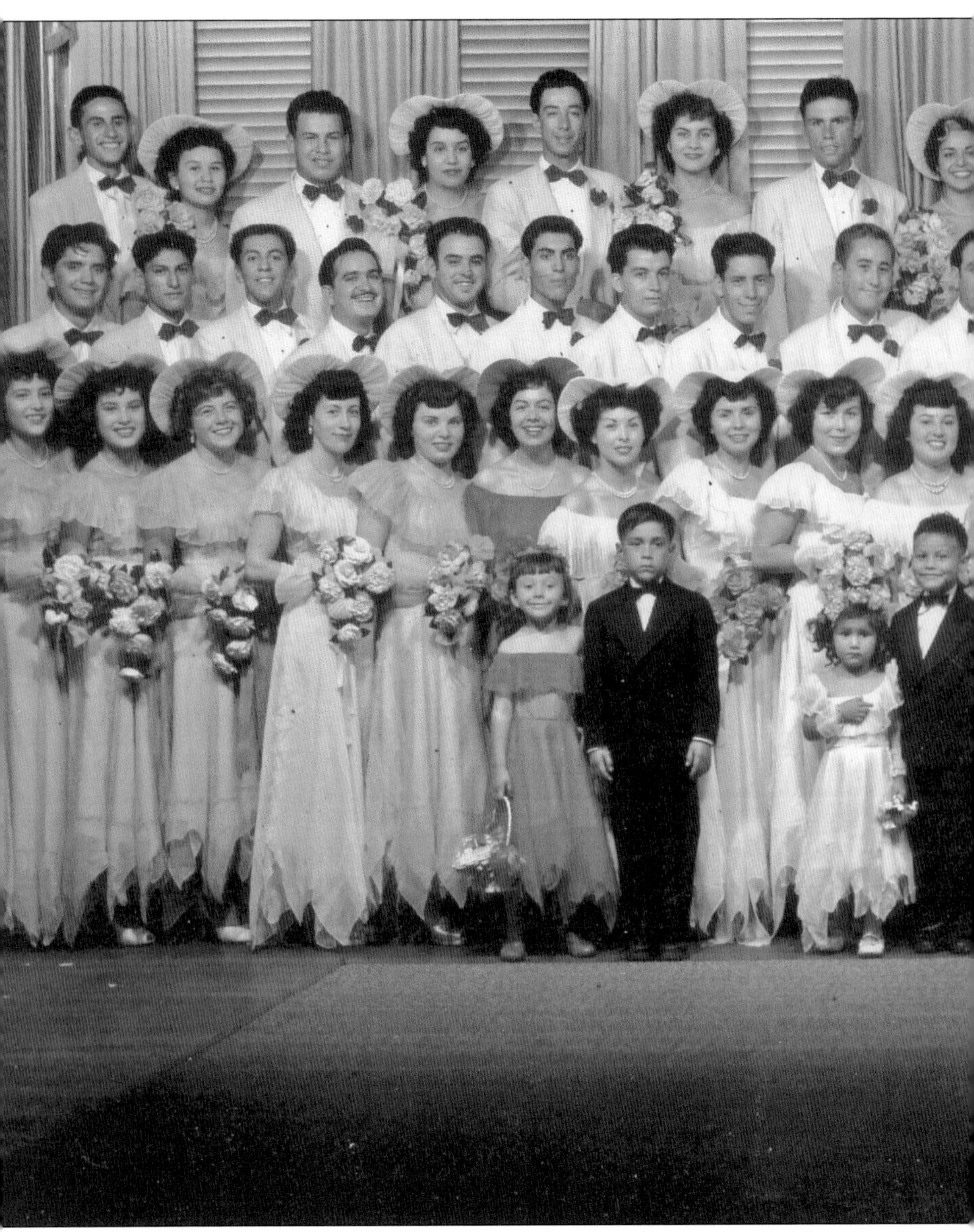

Forty-four attendants, which included two flower girls and ring bearers, were in Albert Castillon and Emma Hernandez's wedding party in 1950. The wedding brought together more than 20 of the most prominent Mexican American families from the South Bay communities. The wedding dance was held at the Old Redondo Barn, with music provided by the orchestra of Tony Alvarez.

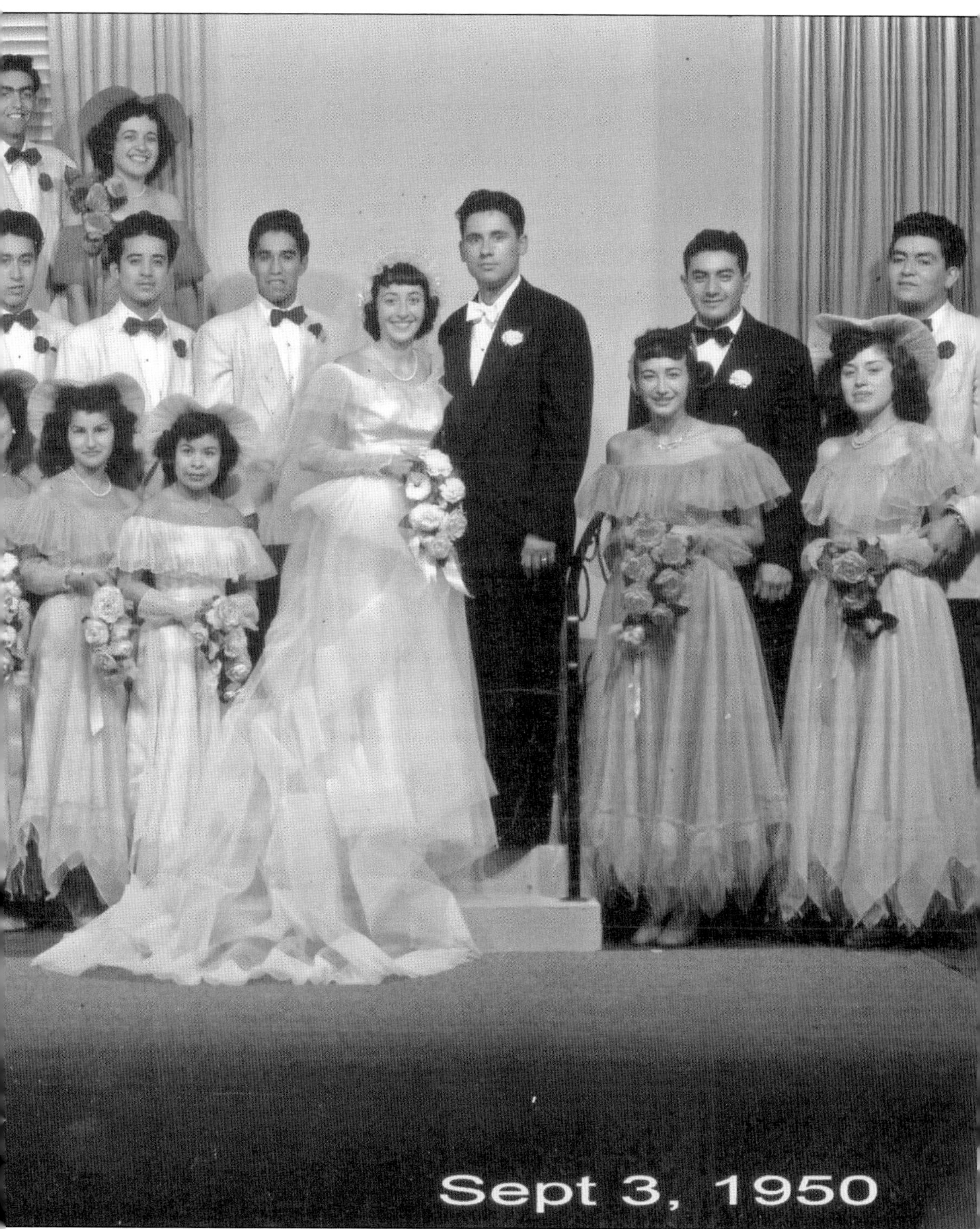

Albert proudly recalls that the barn was opened one last time for their reception. The Castillons remain residents of Redondo Beach, where Albert engages in his passion of sailing. This photograph was taken at a studio in downtown Los Angeles, since no local studios were equipped to take pictures of this size. (Courtesy Emma Castillon.)

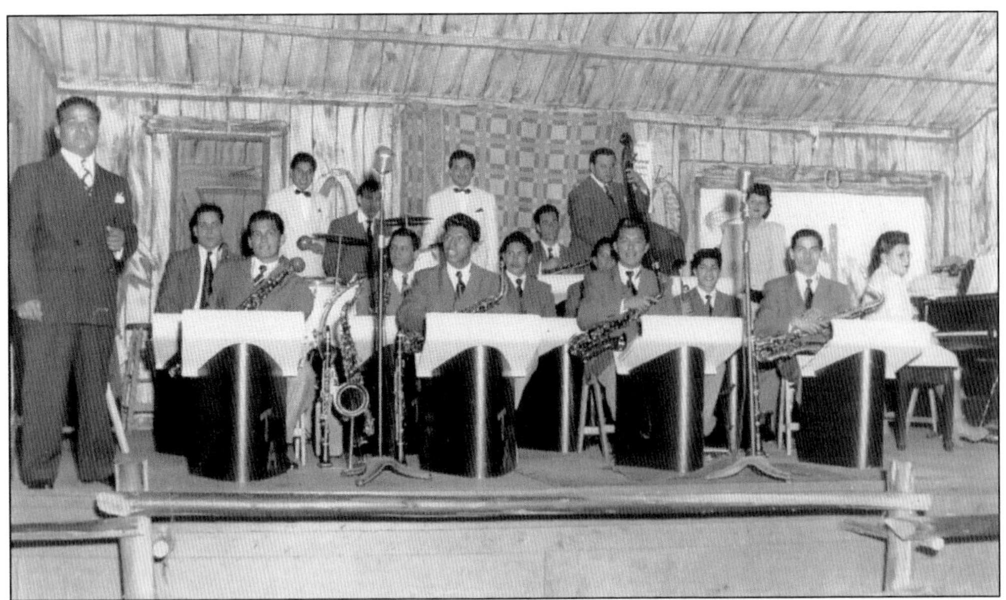

Tony Alvarez, pictured in this *c.* 1948 photograph at far left, and his orchestra were legendary in the Mexican American communities. He played to sell-out crowds at the Long Beach Auditorium, where he was booked almost continuously. Note the artificially painted wood on the ceiling and the imitation corral in front. Spade Cooley's western band also played here. (Courtesy Richard Alvarez.)

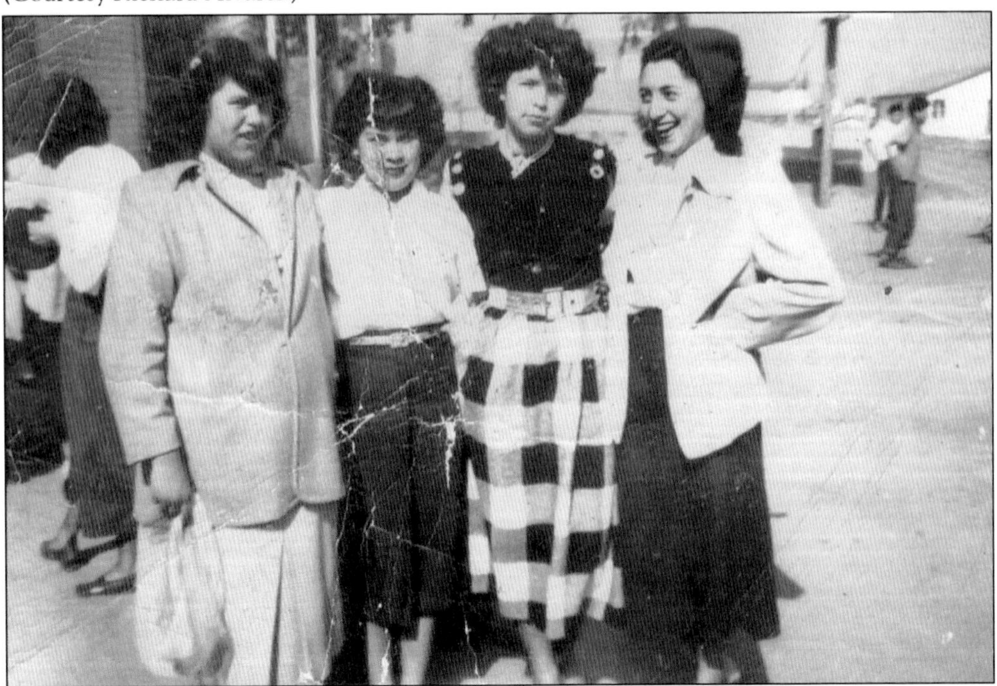

Jenny Torres, Natalie Hernandez, Lupe Areyan, and Toni Torres pose from left to right in the parking lot of Our Lady of Guadalupe Church, after a Chi Rho club event. The club was one of several founded by Fr. Cyril Wood, who, sadly, was transferred to a parish in Santa Monica in 1953. (Courtesy Natalie Herrera.)

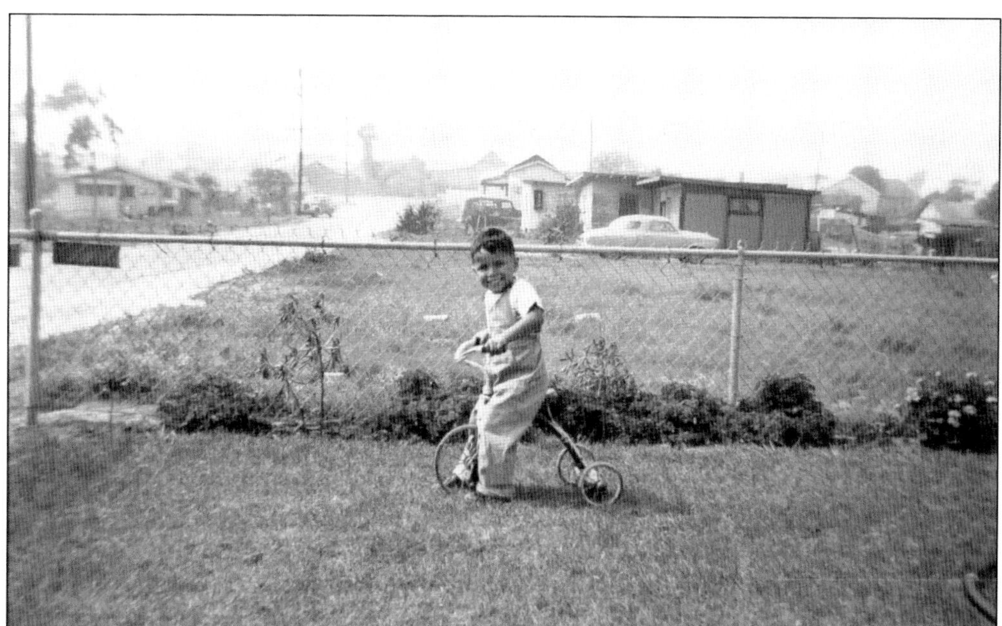

Rudy Adame, the son of Constantino and Andrea Adame, rides his tricycle in the family's front yard on Carlson Lane, a half block from Our Lady of Guadalupe Church, in this *c.* 1953 photograph. The empty field behind Rudy was the site of the old church's *jamaicas* (fiestas), which started in the late 1920s. The church was at the end of the street on the left. (Courtesy Andrea Adame.)

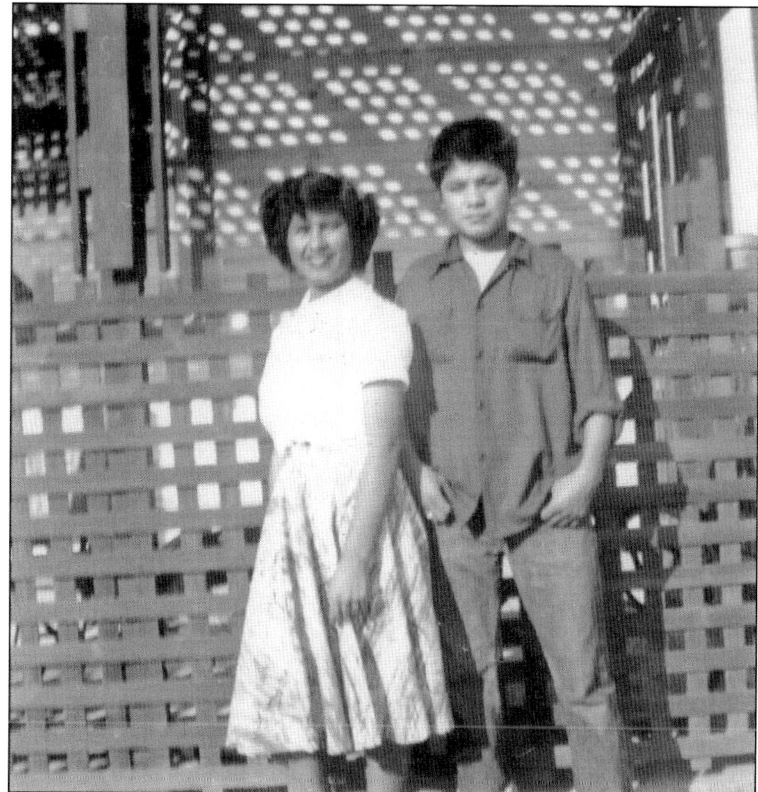

Mary Areyan and Ernest "Little Ernie" Hernandez enjoy the summer sun on Mary's patio in 1953. "Little Ernie" earned his reputation as a fiercely competitive wrestler at Redondo High School in the 1950s. His maternal grandfather, Blas Mendoza, was an early settler of northern Redondo Beach. (Courtesy Mary Martinez.)

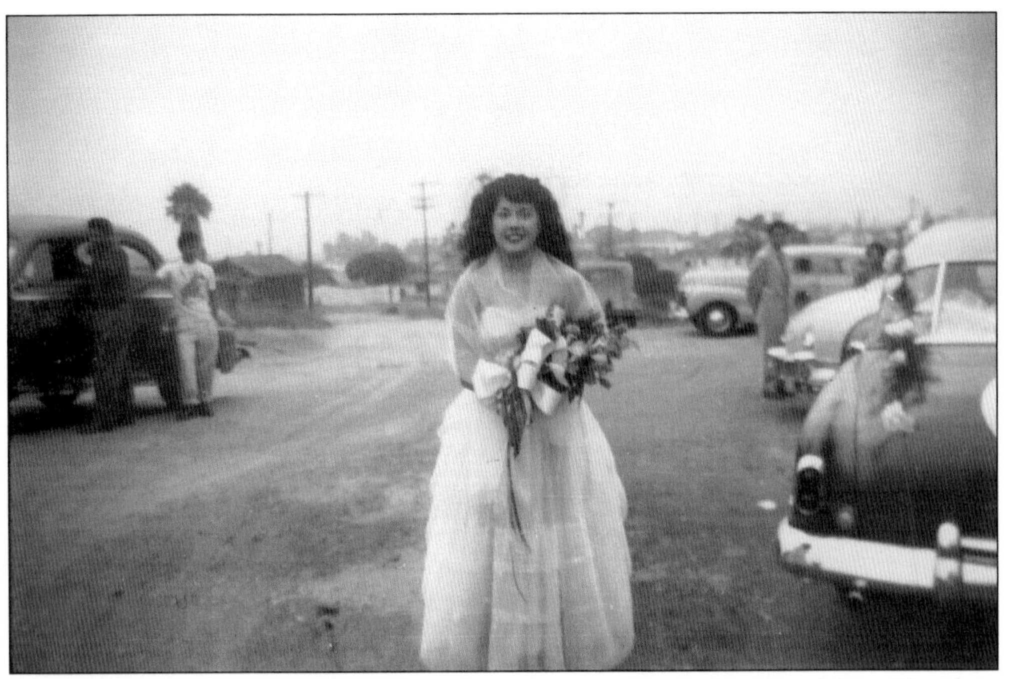

This photograph, looking northeast from the entrance to Our Lady of Guadalupe Church in 1952, shows Mary Lou Hernandez as a wedding attendant. The road behind her leads to Carlson Lane, the main street to the church from northern Redondo. Only the area where the cars are parked was paved. (Courtesy Mary Lou Hernandez.)

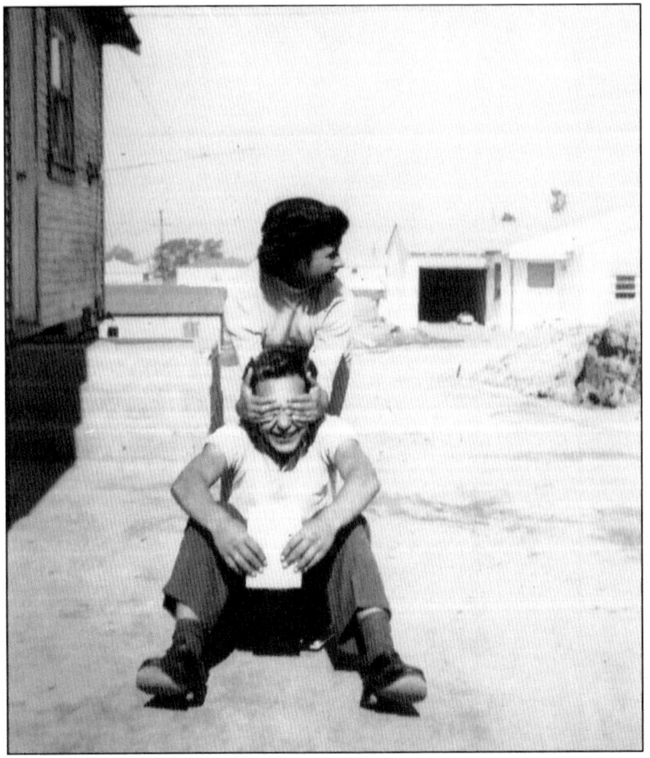

John Luna Moreno (seated) is pretending not to see his U.S. Navy report date letter, and Mary Areyan, his cousin, is helping him not to see the letter. Over Mary's right shoulder is a building behind which a P-38 trainer airplane crashed in 1943. Mary witnessed the crash, which was heard at Rosa's Restaurant in Hermosa, over a mile away. (Courtesy Mary Martinez.)

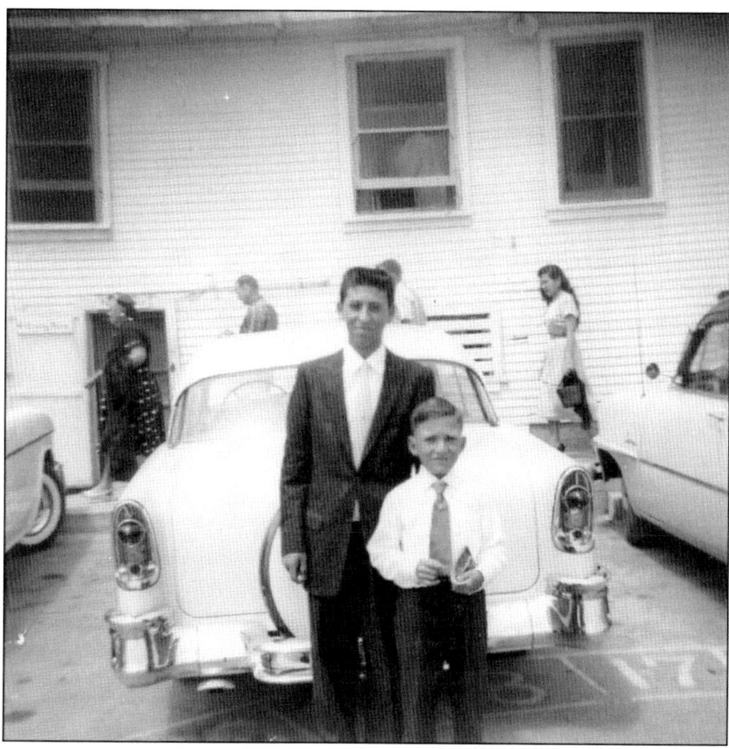

Mexican American families often bonded through religious events such as first communions. This 1957 photograph shows Hendry Felix standing with his godfather, the author. The door to the rear left was the entrance to the small kitchen in the church hall, which doubled as a boxing ring set up by Father Wood. (Courtesy Alice Buffington.)

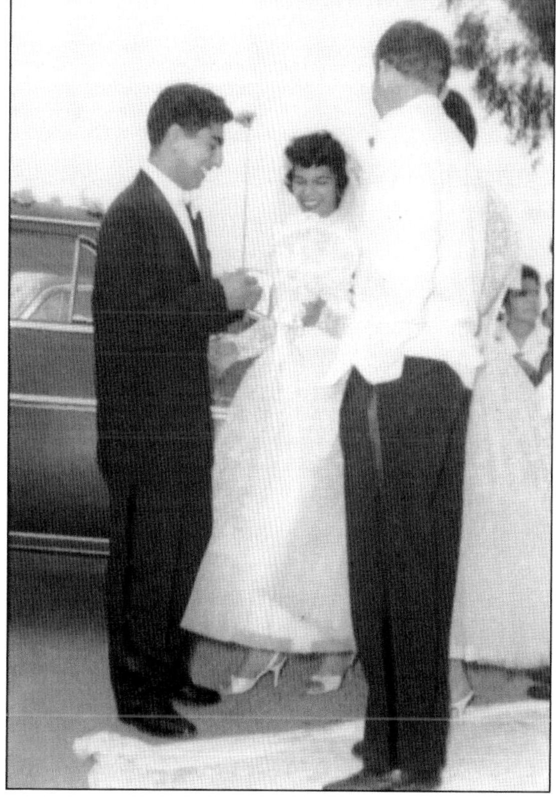

Occasionally local girls married men outside of their Mexican American community. In this photograph, Julia Areyan, raised two blocks from Our Lady of Guadalupe Church, marries Charles Donald Martinez from Eaton, Colorado. They met while he was serving in the U.S. Navy and married in 1956. (Courtesy Porfiria Banda.)

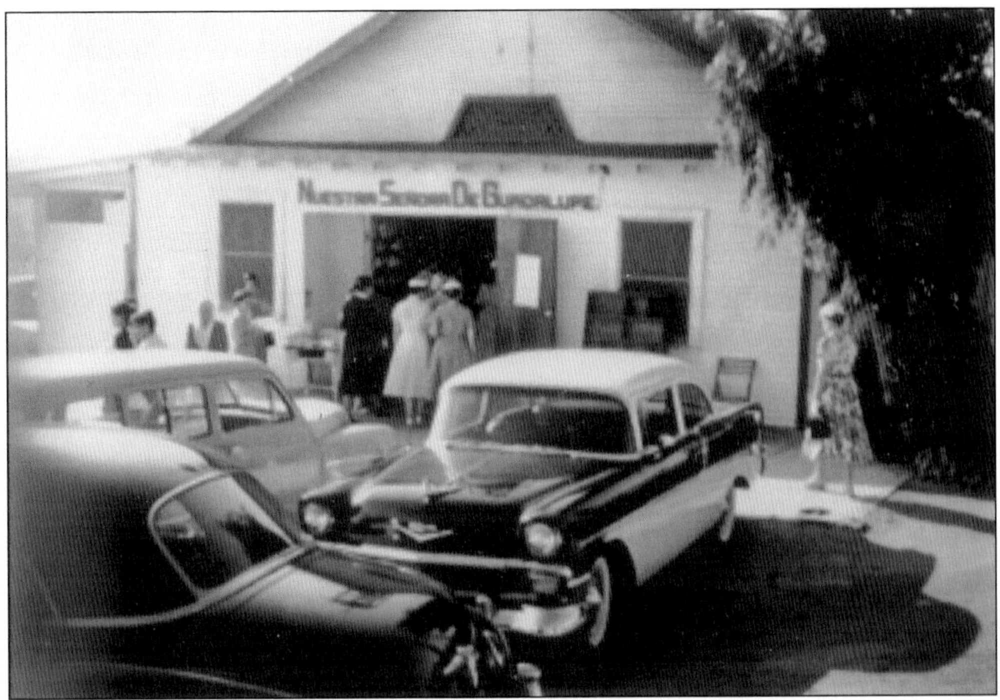

For 35 years, this small church was a familiar place for the hundreds of families who attended Nuestra Senora De Guadalupe. In 1958, the rebuilt church was officially renamed Our Lady of Guadalupe by the Los Angeles archdiocese. Because of the new demographics of the present parish, the church's historical roots and history are not well known. (Courtesy David Serrano.)

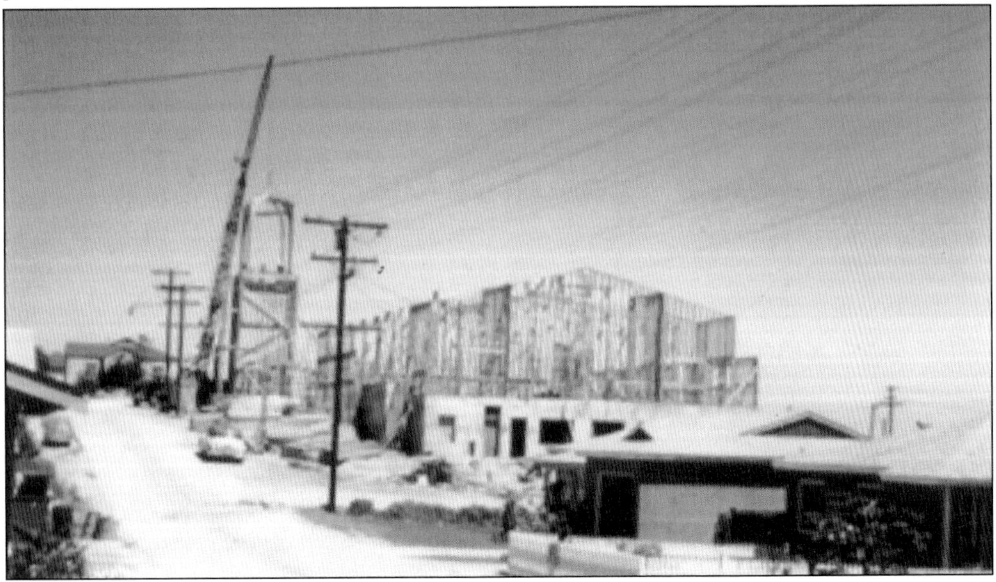

For Our Lady of Guadalupe, 1958 and 1959 were years of transformation. Despite the plans of the archdiocese to change its name and image, a committee of pioneer families personally visited the archdiocesan offices to protest any change and succeeded in retaining the original name. This 1958 photograph shows the foundation and framework stage of the new church. (Courtesy David Serrano.)

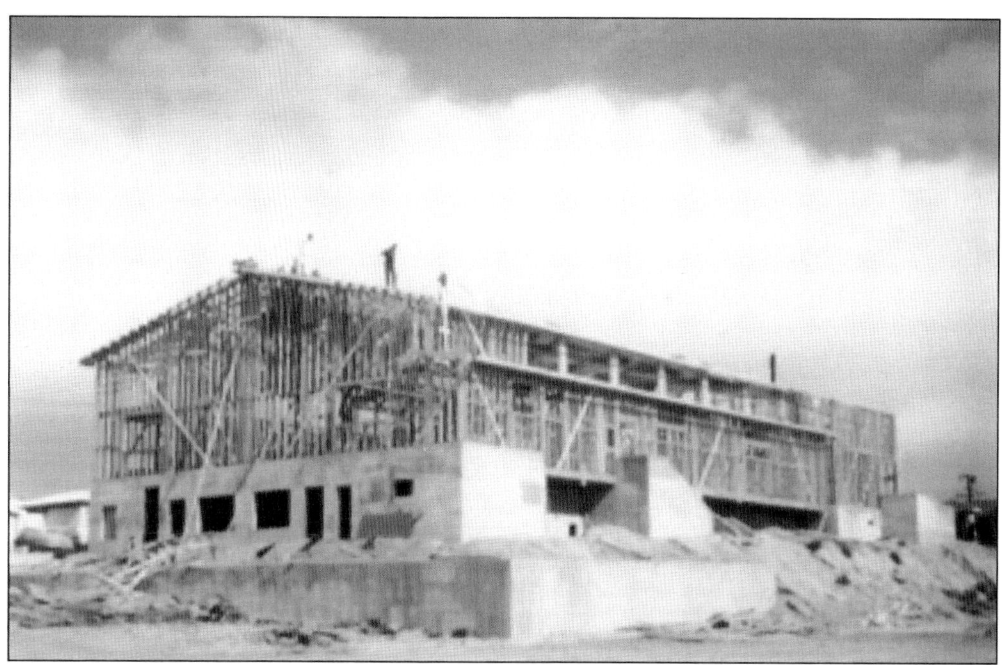

This 1958 view of Our Lady of Guadalupe, looking northwest, reveals the outline of the new church. The new design faithfully followed the church's original layout and orientation. (Courtesy David Serrano.)

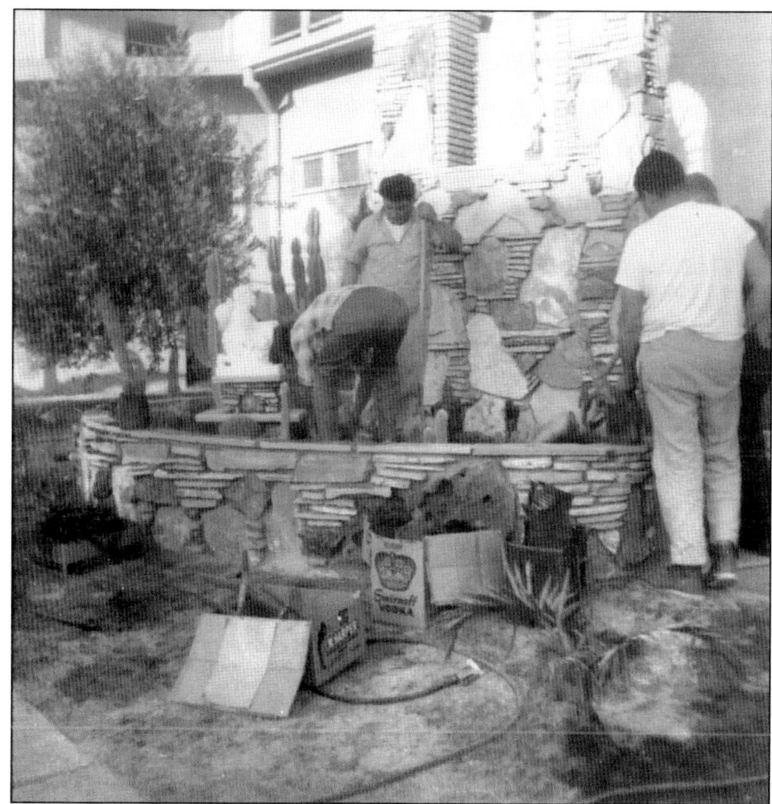

In 1961, Ignacio "Nacho" Estrada and Isaias "Chayo" Moreno undertook construction of a grotto, which paid tribute to Our Lady of Guadalupe. Both were longtime parishioners who built the grotto from native Palos Verdes flagstone in memory of both families. The grotto is on the west side of the church. (Courtesy Irene Cota.)

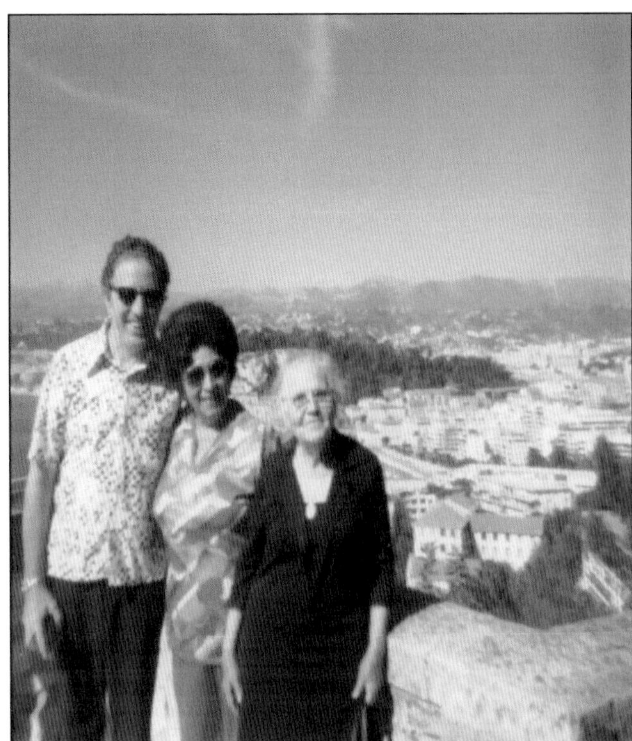

This rare photograph of Francisca "Panchita" Vail (right) was taken on a church pilgrimage to Lourdes, France, in 1961. Panchita, beloved by many parishioners at Our Lady of Guadalupe, prayed eloquent rosaries for deceased parish members. Her magnificent litanies were described as almost religious poetry. She is accompanied here by a fellow parishioner Inez Areyan and an unidentified friend. (Courtesy Inez Areyan.)

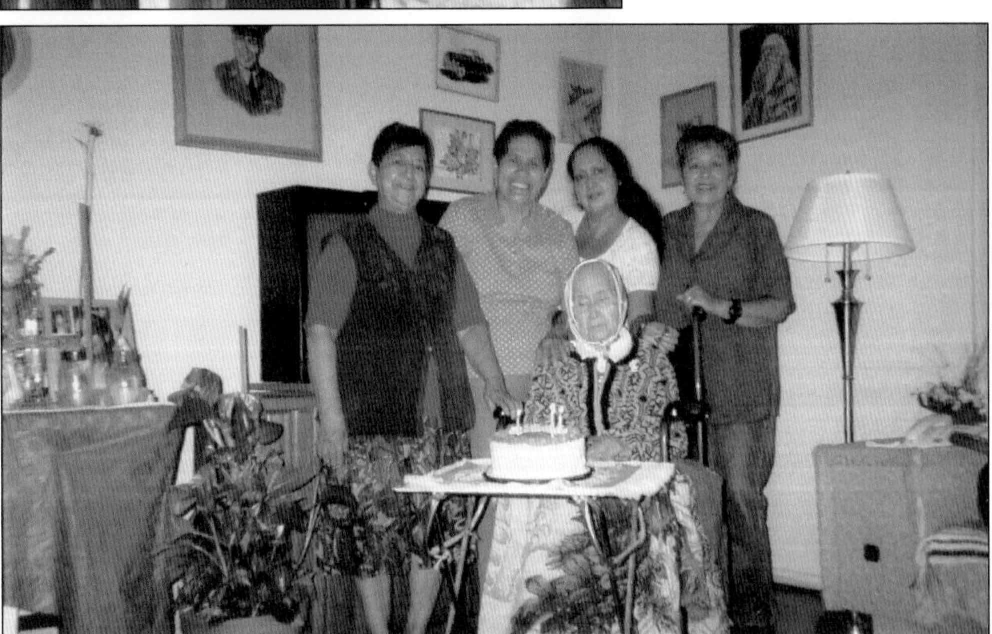

Bertha Gomez, born in Coahuila, Mexico, celebrated her 103rd birthday on August 7, 2006, in Hermosa Beach. Sharing the cake are, from left to right, Irma Palacios, Alba Sierra, and granddaughters Robin Marquez and Margaret Carillo. Bertha was the subject of John Bogert's column in the July 23, 2006, edition of the *Daily Breeze* newspaper and is reportedly the city's oldest resident. During World War II, she helped Japanese Americans neighbors by keeping their household goods while they were interned. (Courtesy Robin Marquez.)

Four

Work Life

The early Mexican American families in Redondo Beach and Hermosa Beach were attracted by work on nearby farms and to affordable land, when lots could be purchased for $50. They provided much of the needed labor for dozens of Japanese American truck farms dotting the Torrance and Gardena area, producing vegetables for the Los Angeles produce market. Mexican and Japanese Americans survived the Depression by consuming the food grown on these farms. After the Depression, the Japanese Americans also grew flowers on the Palos Verdes Peninsula, creating even more jobs.

In 1941, when Japanese Americans were interned, a number of Mexican Americans, such as Ignacio Hernandez, who grew gladiolus and marigolds, started their own businesses. Amador Fernandez was another successful flower grower. He also worked for the City of Pasadena's Rose Parade, traveling to many parts of the world purchasing exotic flowers. Greek American farmers, such as the Karavas and Priamos families, also filled the void left by the Japanese internments, providing employment for many of the Mexican American women. With Greek American growers, flower fields expanded to Torrance, Hermosa, and Manhattan Beach. During these years, the Mexican Americans' strong work ethic stimulated the area's economy and contributed to the expansion of the Los Angeles flower market.

During the 1930s, the Dicalite Mine in Walteria and the Columbia Steel foundry in Torrance provided work to support the growing Mexican American community. Their industriousness made them a valuable resource for these companies. Others worked in construction or started gardening businesses. Domingo Moreno, a stonemason by trade, worked on the construction of the old Hermosa Beach theater and installed the massive slabs of Palos Verdes flagstone at the Palos Verdes Library. Later he and his son Gonzalo worked on the estate of the 1940s actor Charles Laughton.

World War II saw Mexican American women join the female workforce that replaced the men who went to war. Porfiria and Dora Moreno and others became "Rosie the Riveters," building airplanes at Douglas Aircraft for wages of $1 per hour. In the early 1950s, General Telephone, Redondo Tile, Chic Lingerie, and Metlox Potteries employed many more women.

Know all Men by these Presents, That R. Saldana (R. Saldana) of the Serene County of Weld, in the State of Colorado, party of the first part, for and in consideration of the sum of Five hundred and Twenty-eight and no/100 ($528.00) Dollars, to him in hand paid by Todd & Wyatt of the city and County of Denver, in the State of Colorado, parties of the second part, the receipt whereof is hereby acknowledged, does hereby grant, bargain and sell unto the said parties of the second part their heirs, executors, administrators and assigns, the following goods and chattels, viz.:

One Star Automobile
Model F 1924 touring
Serial No. L248262 Engine No. 212 287
Together with all parts and equipment now used in connection therewith or which may hereafter be added thereto.

TODD & WYATT
OCT 15 1925

In 1925, Romaldo Saldana purchased a 1924 Star touring sedan to bring his family to Redondo Beach. This is a copy of the sales contract for the car. His prior work experience at the Columbine Mine in Colorado made him an ideal worker for the Dicalite Mine in Walteria, California, where he worked for a number of years. (Courtesy Carmen Daugherty.)

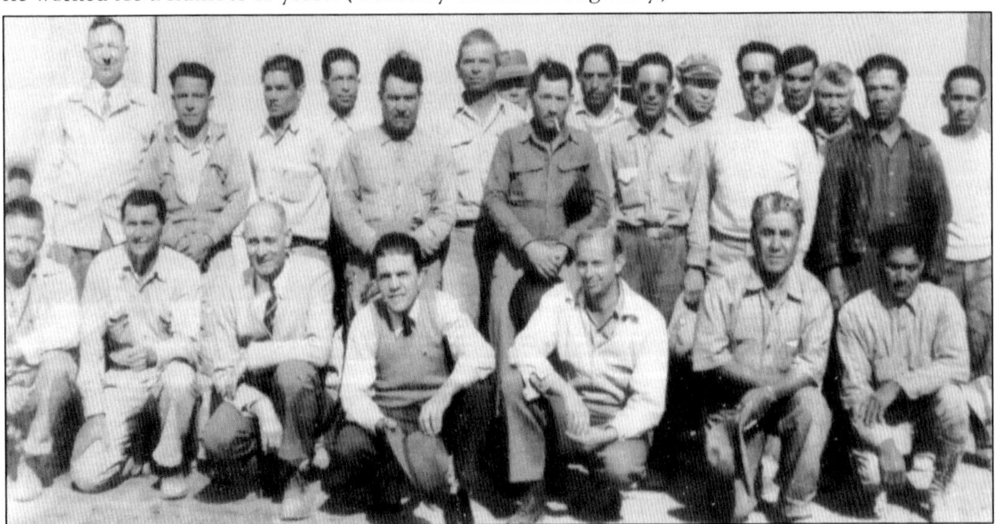

Mine workers at the Dicalite Mine pose for a 1932 photograph in Walteria, California. Included in this photograph are (first row) Narciso Herrera (sixth from left) and Calistro Gomez (seventh from left); (second row) unidentified, Senaido Flores, Jose Guardarrama, Martin Martinez, Julio Manriquez (with cigarette), Silvano Monge, Gaspar Tarango and unidentified; (third row) Manuel Gonzalez, unidentified, Isabel Madrid, unidentified, Galdino Granados, Ponciano Santana, and unidentified. (Courtesy public archives.)

SCO—SST

NOTICE OF TERMINATION OF EMPLOYMENT

(Duplicate for Employee)

AME OF EMPLOYEE (rint last name first)	POSITION OR NATURE OF WORK	DATE OF TERMINA
Moreno, Gonzalo	laboratory helper.	3/15/36.
		DATE OF EMPLO If after Jan. 1, 193

REASON FOR TERMINATION

- [x] LEFT VOLUNTARILY
- [ ] DISCHARGED
- [ ] LAID OFF—WHY?
- [ ] OTHER REASONS—EXPLAIN

rage Weekly Wage	Number of Hours for Normal Work Week	Average Number of Weekly Hours Worked During Past 52 Weeks	Total Number of Weeks Duri Previous 104 Weeks for W Contributions Were Ma
15.02	48	48	10

NOTE—If under $30.00 show actual amount, if over $30.00 state: "In excess of $30.00 per week."

EREBY ACKNOWLEDGE THAT MY EMPLOY-NT TERMINATED FOR THE ABOVE REASON	NAME OF EMPLOYER STREET & NUMBER POST OFFICE

This 1936 termination notice from Dicalite Mine laboratory worker Gonzalo Moreno reveals that he earned $15.02 for a 48-hour week, or about 30¢ an hour. This pay was probably typical for the period at the end of the Depression. (Courtesy John Luna Moreno.)

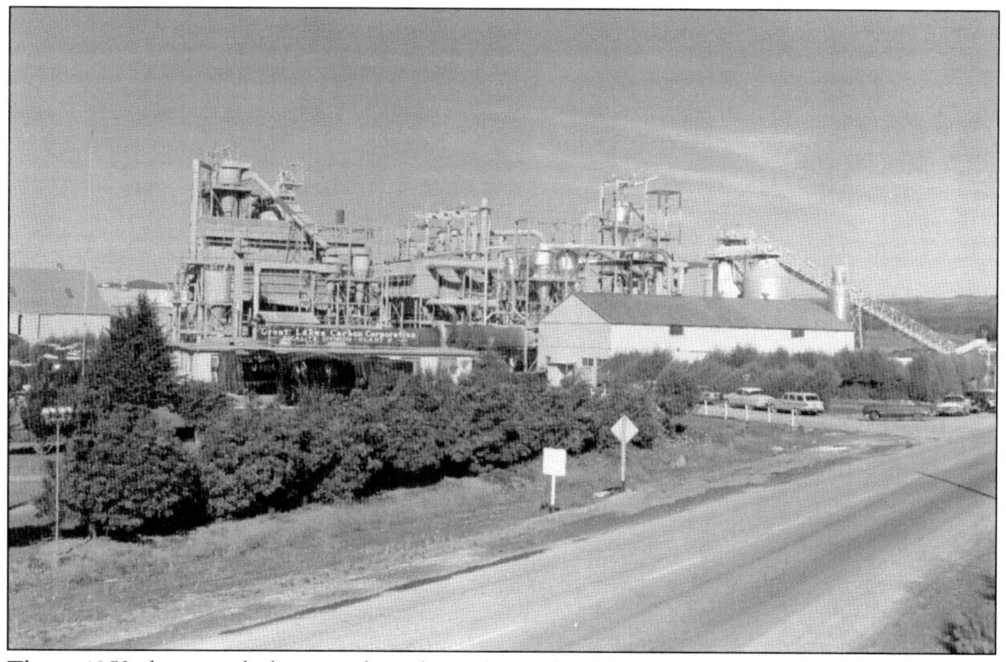

This c. 1953 photograph shows a relatively modern celite (dicalite) processing facility in Lompoc, California. The material was mined from quarries nearby and transported to the facility for grinding and processing. Many Mexican American men worked at the Celite mine before coming to work at the new mine in Walteria, California, around 1930. (Courtesy public archives.)

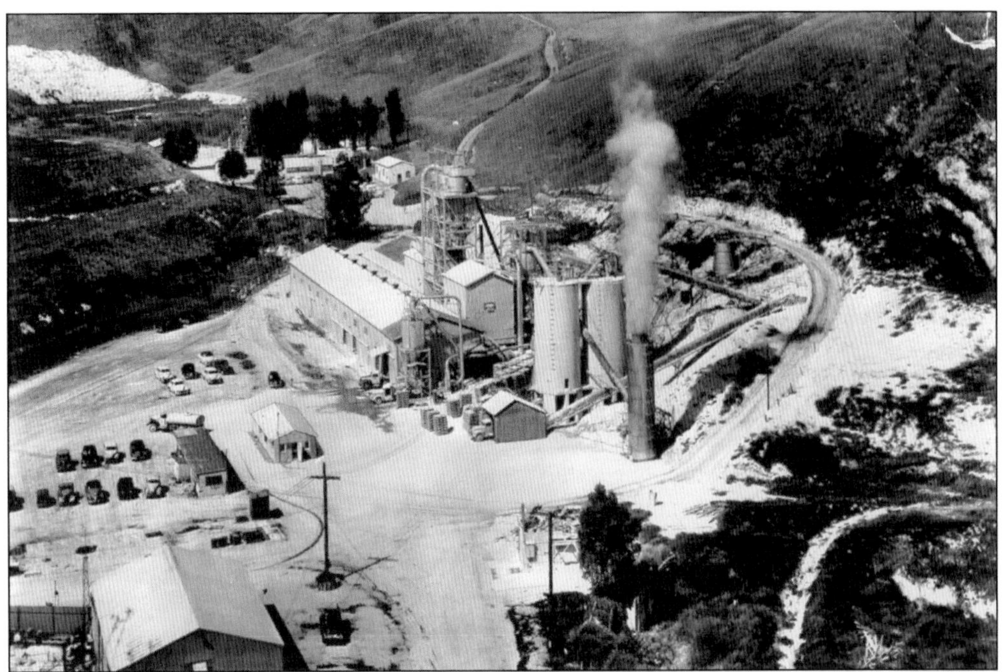

This 1940s photograph is of the Dicalite Mine, located in a canyon in Walteria. Beginning in 1930, many Mexican American men from the cities of Redondo and Hermosa Beaches, Torrance, Gardena, Harbor City, Wilmington, San Pedro, and other outlying areas worked here. In the hills to the extreme right is the Palos Verdes Peninsula. (Courtesy public archives.)

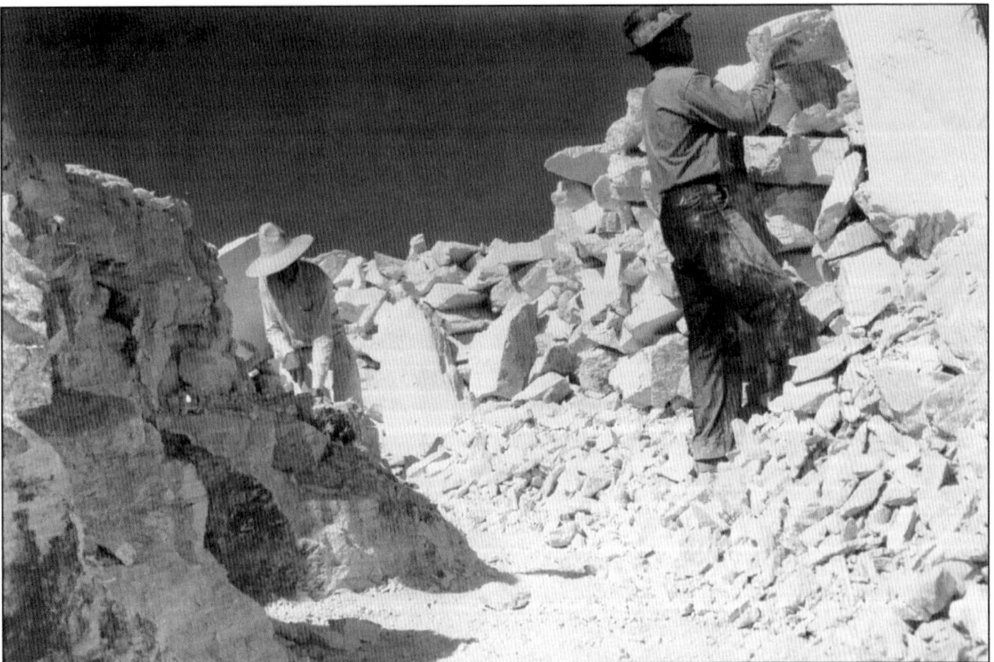

Hand quarrying of diatomaceous earth assured the selection of the highest grade of material for the mill. In this photograph, workers carefully select and mine the blocks of dicalite product. (Courtesy public archives.)

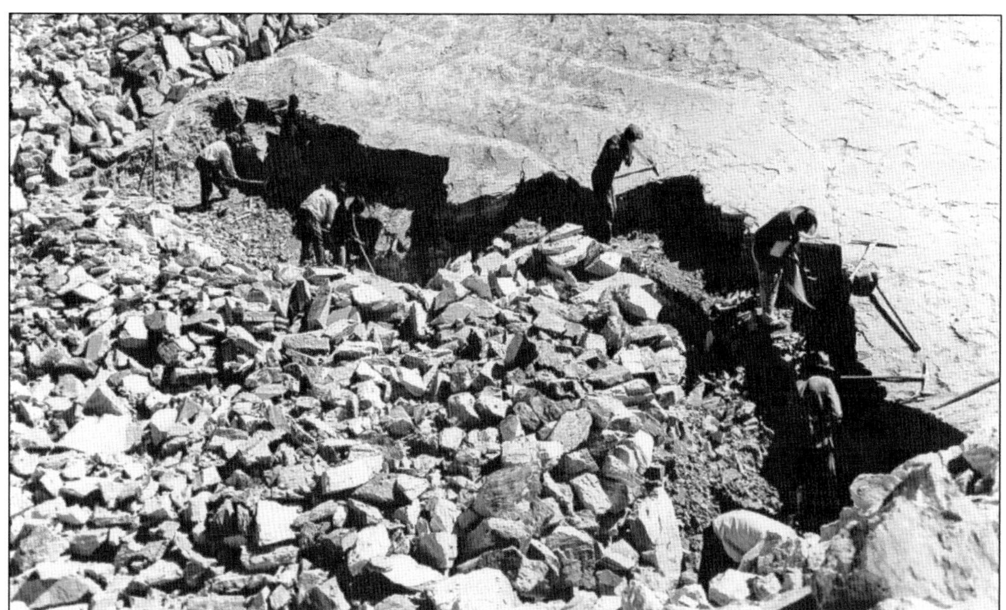

These seven workers use picks and shovels to slice and remove the dicalite material from the quarry beds. Material was pried up with leverage bars, lifted, and stacked on wagons for transportation to the mill. This photograph was taken about 1930 at the Walteria mine. (Courtesy public archives.)

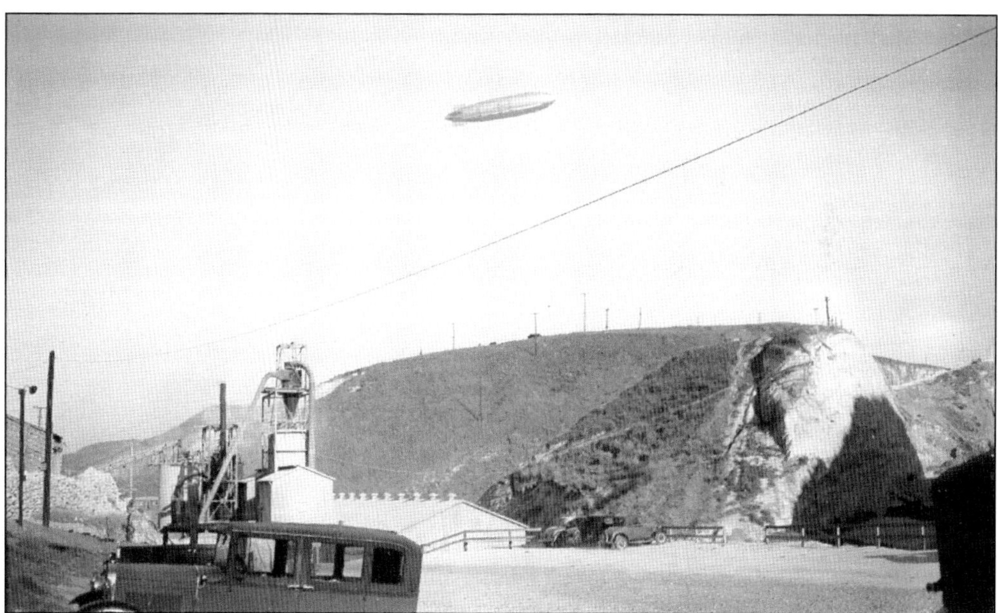

A historical moment occurred over the Dicalite Mine in Walteria on August 26, 1929, when the world's largest airship flew over the mine on a leg of its world tour. William Randolph Hearst sponsored the trip in order to secure newspaper rights to the story. From Los Angeles, the airship went to Lakehurst, New Jersey, then returned to Germany. (Courtesy public archives.)

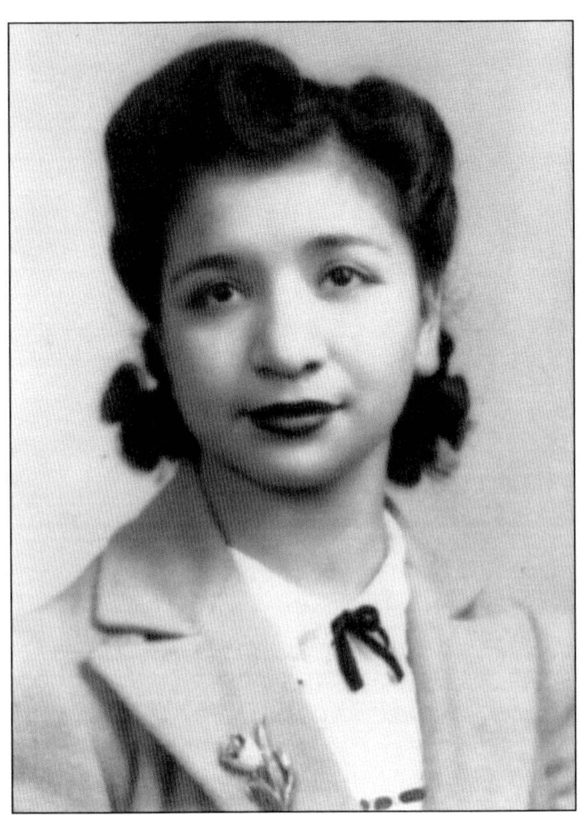

Carmen Saldana operated Louise's House of Beauty in Manhattan Beach for more than 50 years. She was active in civic affairs and was instrumental in developing the sister city program with Culiacan, Mexico. She remains a resident of Hermosa Beach. (Courtesy Carmen Daugherty.)

Form 1099
SURY DEPARTMENT
RNAL REVENUE SERVICE
NITED STATES
MATION RETURN FOR
LENDAR YEAR 1947
RUCTIONS TO PAYORS
one of these forms for each ccordance with the instruc- return Form 1096. This not required with re- wage payments report- orm W-2a.
d with return Form 1096 reach the Commissioner of evenue, in care of Processing C. C. Station, Kansas City ri, on or before February 15.
f this form as filed with the nt should be furnished to yee whose income is reported olumn to assist him in pre- income tax return.

To Whom Paid: Gonzalo Moreno, 1633 Havermeyer Street, Rdeondo Beach, Calif.
(Print full name and home address) (Show employee's social security number, if any. If employee is a married woma[n] name of husband should also be furnished)

1947

KIND AND AMOUNT OF INCOME PAID

Salaries or Other Compensation. Do not include amount reported on Form W-2a	Interest on Notes, Mortgages, Etc.	Rents and Royalties	Other Fixed or Determinable Income	Foreign Items ($500 or more)	Dividends ($100 or more) (Total paid, including amounts claimed nontaxable)
	($500 or more aggregate amount of above items)				
$	$	$	$ 1,280.00	$	$

16—52717-1

By Whom Paid (Name and address): Charles Laughton, 14954 Corona Del Mar, Pacific Palisades, Calif.

[OVER]

This 1947 tax withholding form shows the diversity of jobs held by Mexican American families. Gonzalo Moreno worked as a groundskeeper on the Rolling Hills estate of the late Shakespearian actor Charles Laughton. Gonzalo's father, Domingo, was given two peacocks by Laughton, which he kept at his home on Carmelita Avenue for many years. (Courtesy John Luna Moreno.)

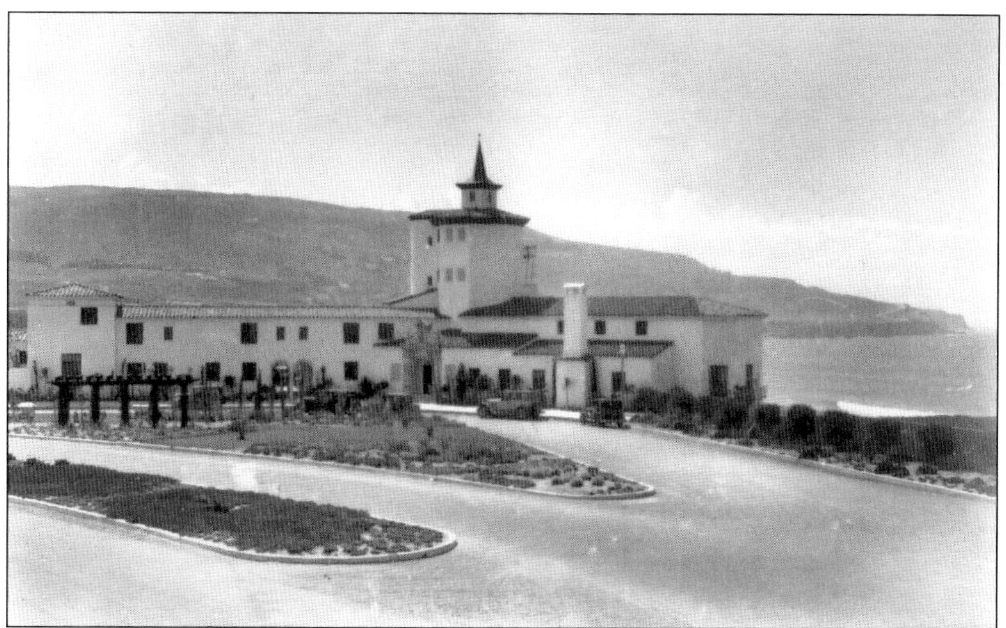

By using their bulldozers, Evaristo and Calistro "Cal" Gonzalez saved the old Riviera Beach club from collapsing into the Pacific Ocean during severe winter storms in the 1950s. Evaristo owned a grading and topsoil business that also graded the land for the many condominiums on the Esplanade in Redondo Beach. (Courtesy Caroline Villa.)

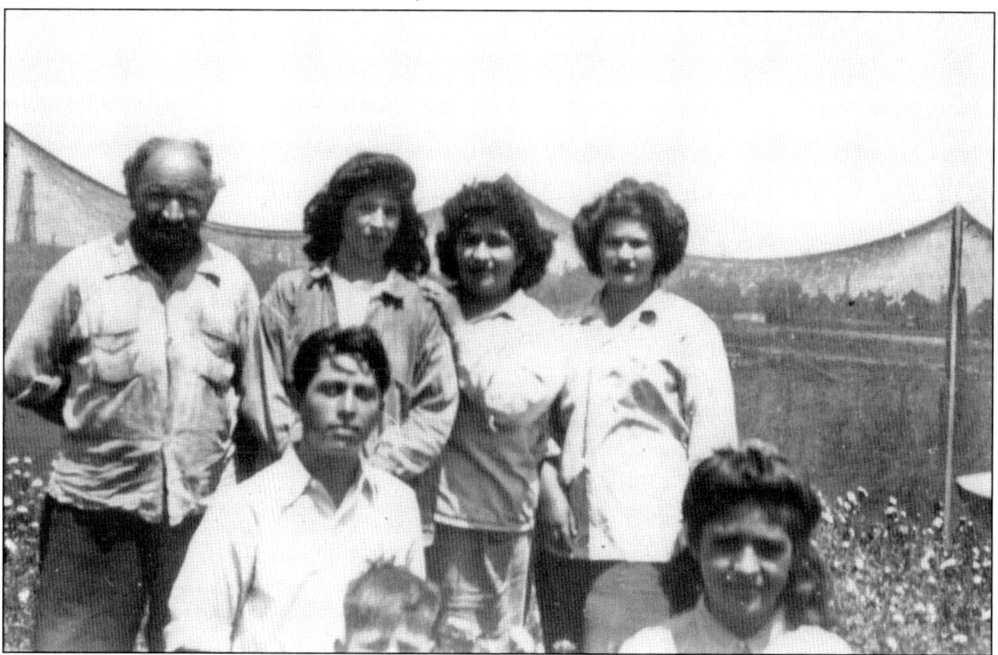

Flower "de-budding" was an important source of work for women in the community. This field at the corner of Hawthorne and Torrance Boulevards in Torrance was operated by Greek American growers. Pictured are, from left to right, (first row) Michael Areyan (partially visible) and Carmen Areyan; (second row) Pedro Jimenez; (third row) Tony "Push 'Em Up," Rose Camereno, Inez Areyan, and Alma Camereno. (Courtesy Inez Areyan.)

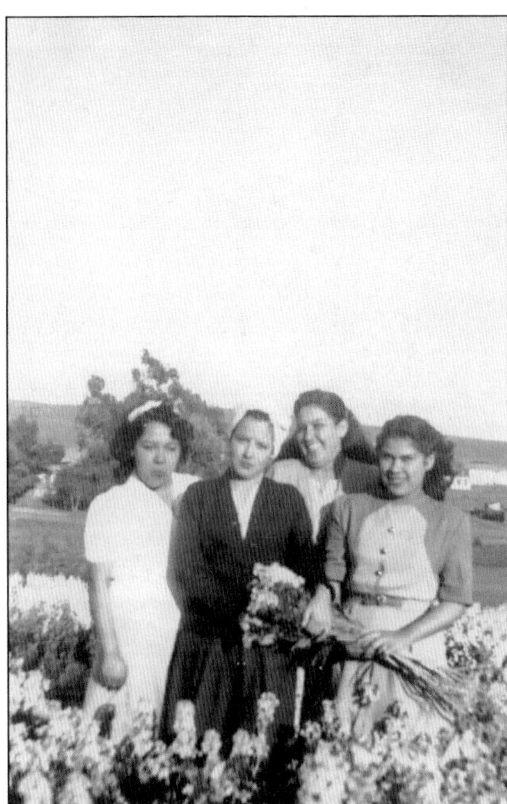

In 1947, Ignacio Hernandez owned this flower field at the corner of Knob Hill and Prospect Avenues in Redondo; it is seen here with snapdragons. Pictured are, from left to right, Grace Hernandez, Jenny and Beatriz Leon, and Natalie Hernandez. Natalie complained that working for her father interfered with her social life. (Courtesy Ordie Fernandez.)

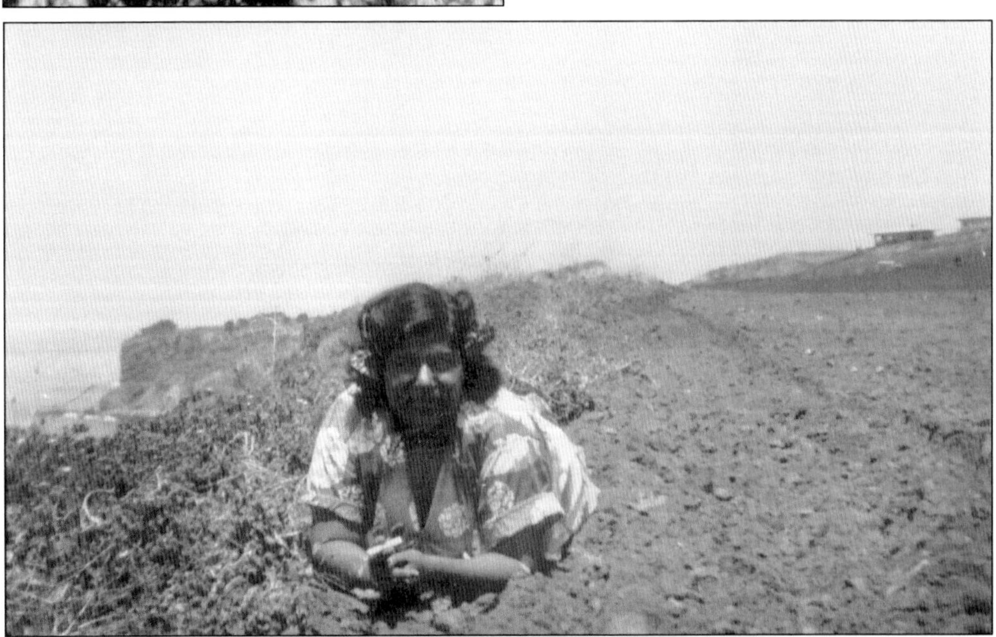

This c. 1951 photograph shows the flower fields operated by Greek American growers on the Palos Verdes Peninsula. Pictured here is Henrietta Torres, taking a break near the cliffs. Before World War II, Japanese American and Mexican American growers operated these same fields. (Courtesy Roberta Moreno.)

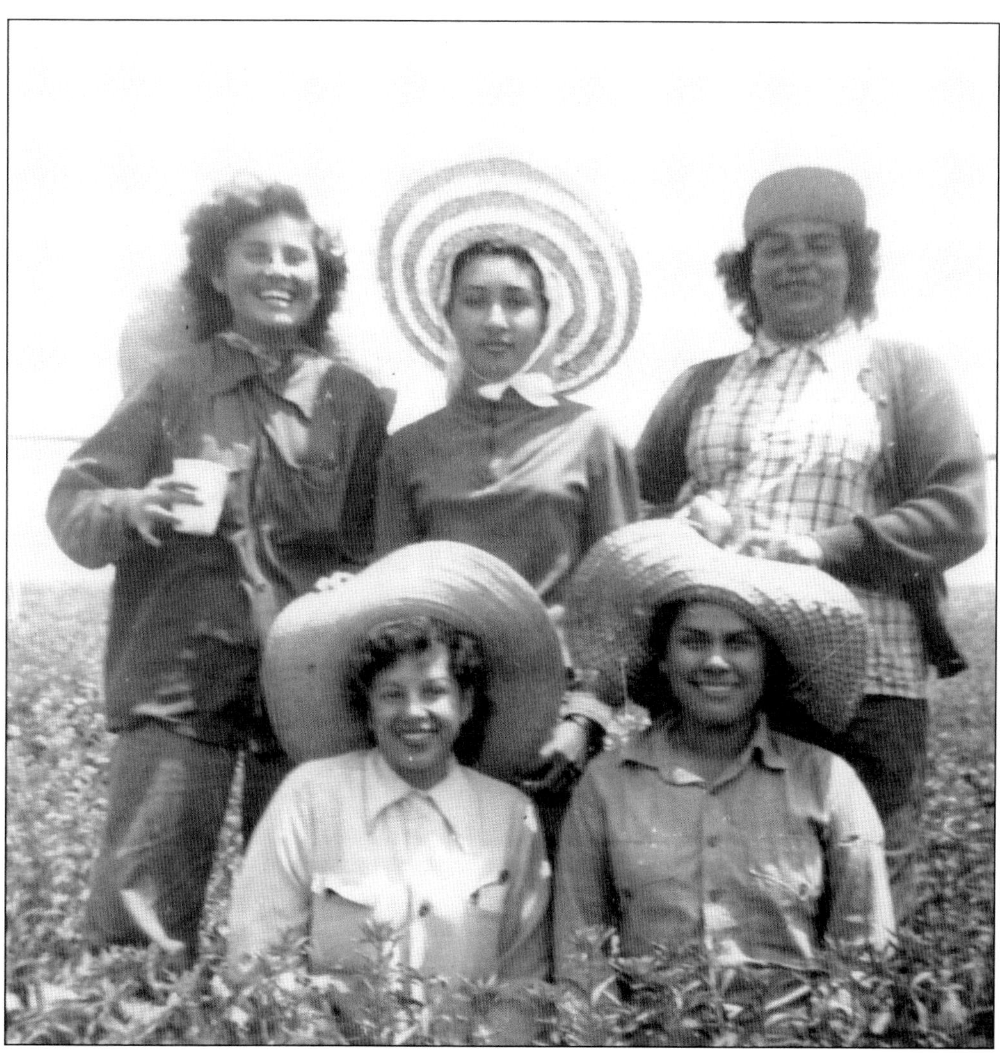

Around 1952, this flower "de-budding" crew, in whimsical hats, is pictured in Amador Fernandez's flower field in Torrance, near Del Amo Boulevard. From left to right are (first row) Velia Alvarez and Natalie Hernandez; (second row) Teddy Fernandez, Victoria Rodriguez, and Jenny Torres. (Courtesy Natalie Hernandez.)

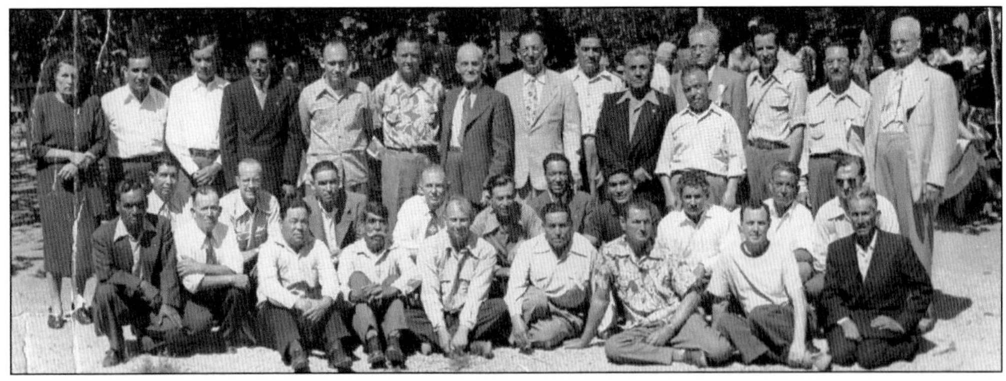

A 1954 Dicalite picnic at Walteria Park attracted both workers and managers. Pictured are, from left to right, (first row) Victoriano Gomez, unidentified, Lorenzo Salinas, Jose Gomez, unidentified, Enrique Espinoza, and three unidentified; (second row) two unidentified, Julian Lujan, two unidentified, Silvano Monge, Ismael Mendoza, Jose Guardarrama, Senaido Flores, and unidentified; (third row) "Cuca" Leon, Joe Ybarra, Ponciano Santana, Isabel Madrid, next five unidentified, Narciso Herrera, Romaldo Saldana, three unidentified, and Gaspar Tarango. (Courtesy Mendoza brothers.)

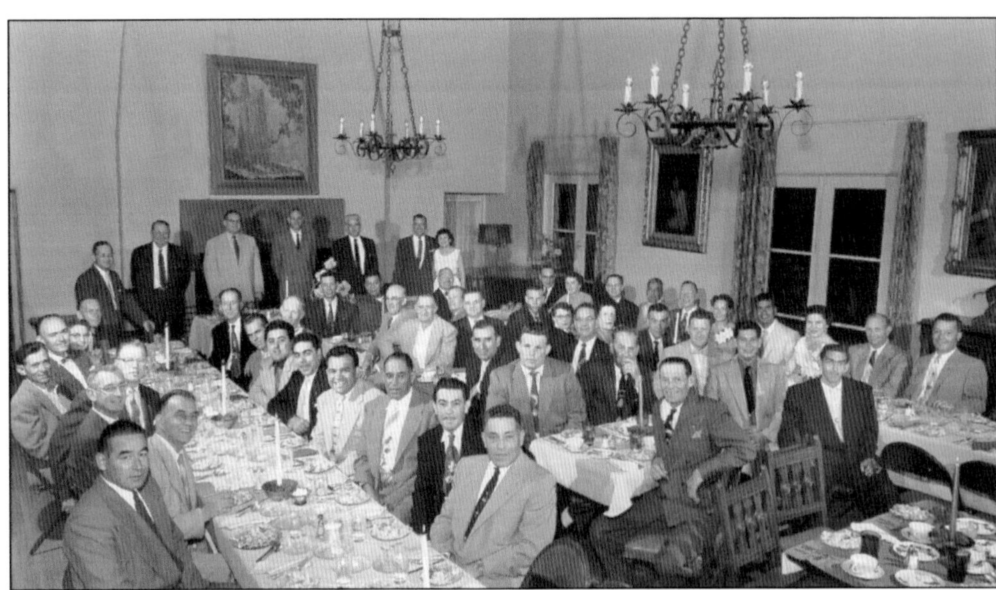

La Venta Inn in Palos Verdes, pictured here, was the site of the Dicalite Corporation's employee recognition dinner in 1955. The mine closed in 1958, according to Louis Saldana, who worked with the author's father, Alejo, at the company's warehouse. They loaded boxcars at the present site of Sears Del Amo, in the early 1930s. (Courtesy Danny Espinoza.)

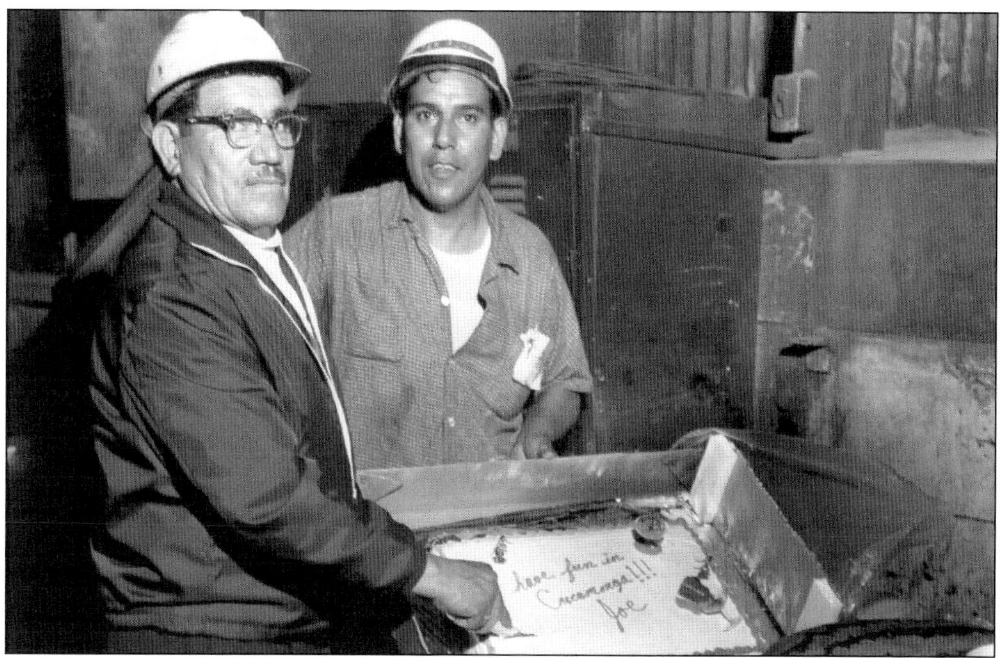

Columbia Steel was another important employer of the community's men, from the 1930s to the 1960s. Pictured here at his retirement celebration is Jose Olloque with Orlando Rodriguez. The humorous inscription on the cake reads, "Have fun in Cucamonga!!! Joe." (Courtesy Pearl Vidal.)

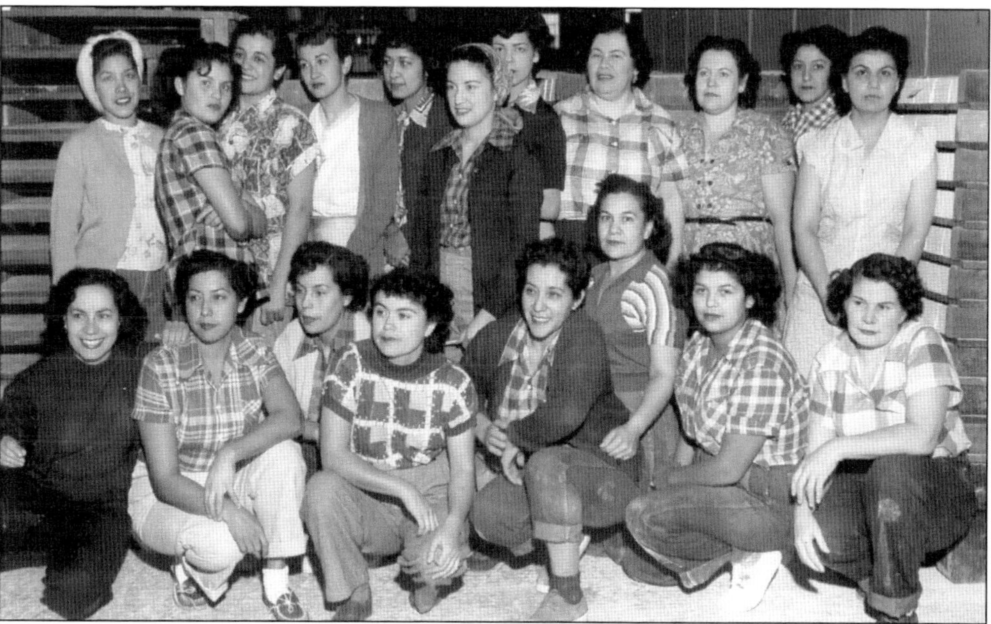

Redondo Tile's workforce was comprised mainly of women from the Mexican American community from the late 1940s to the late 1950s. Pictured are, from left to right, (first row) unidentified, Virginia Ortiz, Eleanor Fernandez, Lupe Torres, Connie Valenzuela, and three unidentified; (second row) Mary Lou Hernandez, Teddie Fernandez, Celia "Sally" Hernandez, "Ordie" Hernandez, unidentified, Nonie Anaya (with bandana), unidentified, Lina Castillon, Socorro Leon, Jenny Zamudio, and Ruby Moore. (Courtesy Mary Lou Ordaz.)

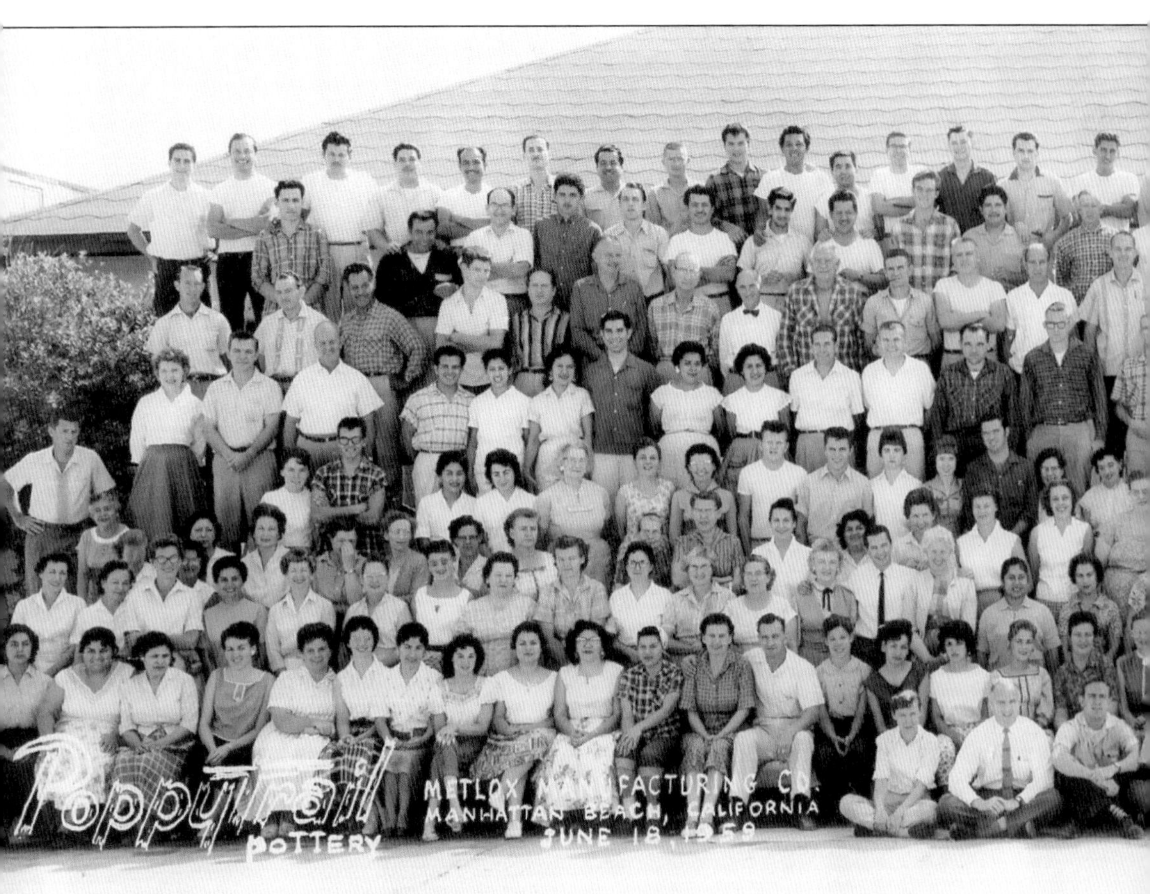

Pictured in this 1959 photograph is the workforce of Metlox Potteries. The plant was located one block from the Manhattan Pier and employed several hundred people, many from the Mexican American communities of the South Bay. The Contreras, Enriquez, and Maldonado families

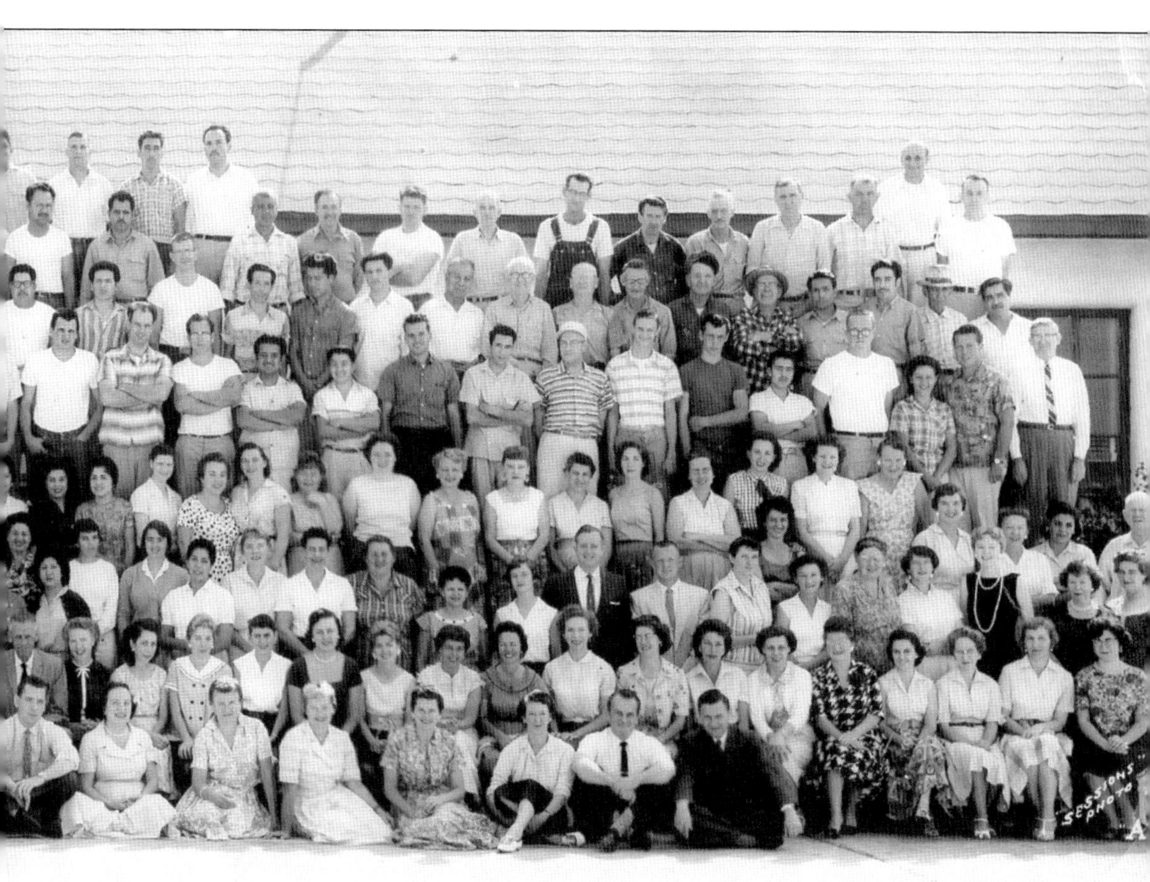

figured prominently among the diverse workforce. In 2006, the former site became an upscale boutique shopping mall. (Courtesy Lupe De Anda.)

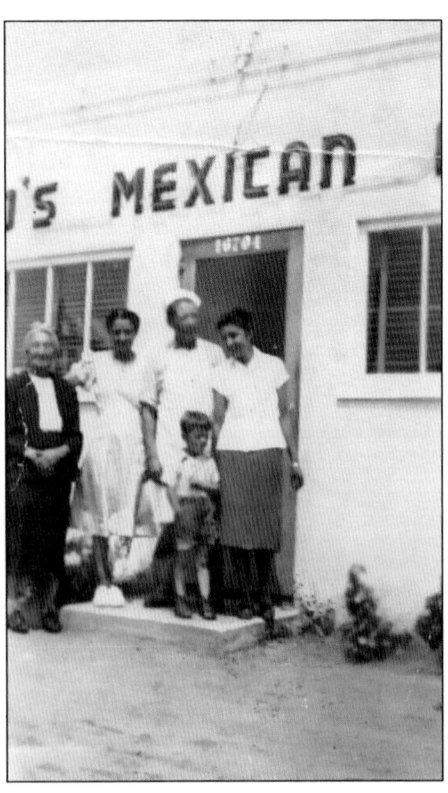

Leo's Mexican Foods opened in 1948 on Inglewood Avenue, later moving to 160th Street and Inglewood Avenue, and has been in continuous operation for nearly 60 years. Pictured here from left to right are Teresa Preciado, Josefina Preciade, Leonel Preciado (owner), and daughter Maria Real Preciado. At front center is young Leonel Preciado Jr., who currently operates this landmark restaurant. (Courtesy Ricardo Real.)

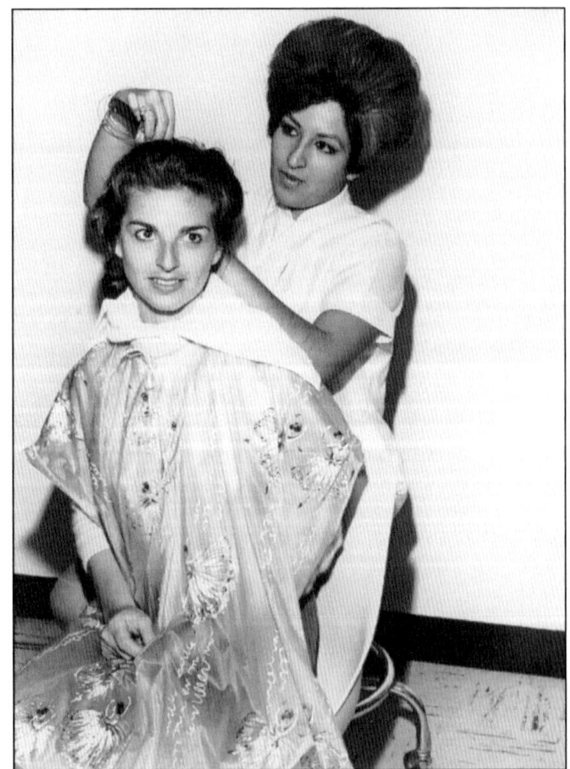

Here Roberta Moreno styles the hair of Miss Gardena, California. Roberta, a registered cosmetologist, managed the Crowning Glory Beauty Salon in the early 1960s. (Courtesy Roberta Robles.)

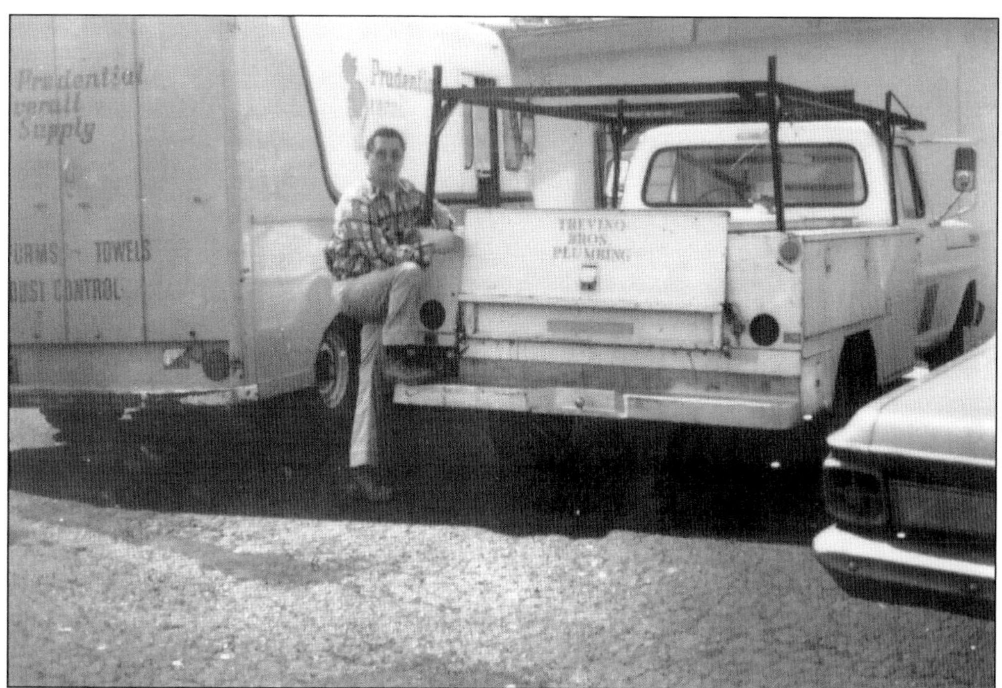

Robert Trevino is pictured at Trevino Brothers Plumbing Company in this 1960s photograph. (Courtesy Lupe Trevino.)

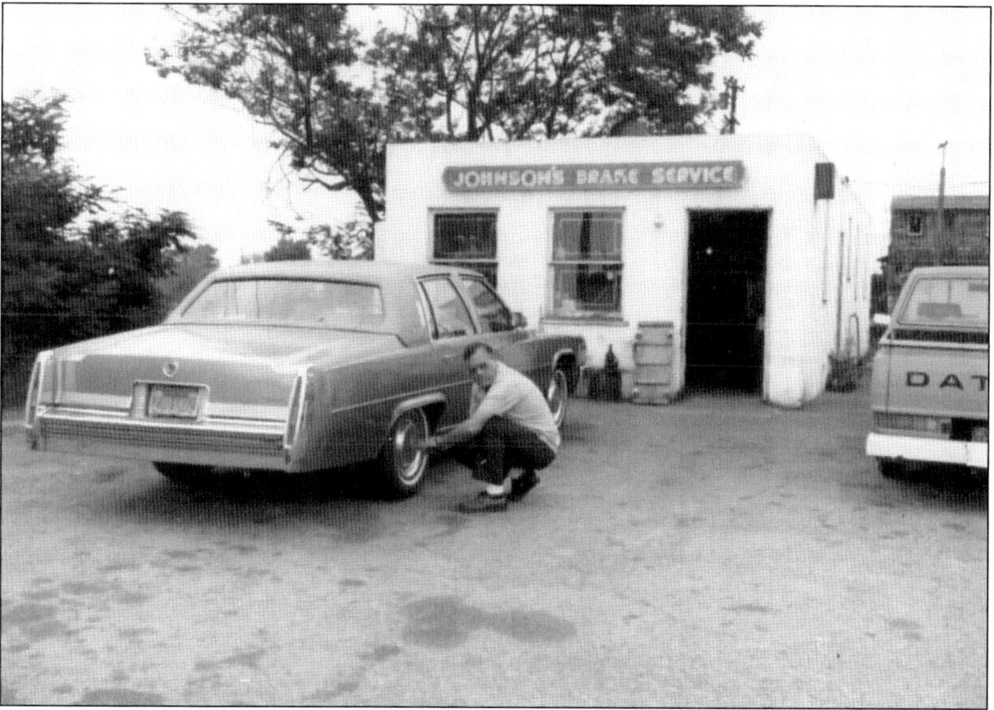

Albert Castillon owned and operated Johnson's Brake Service in Manhattan and Hermosa Beaches for over 20 years. His expertise was used when movie studios required restoration of brake mechanisms for antique foreign autos. (Courtesy Albert Castillon.)

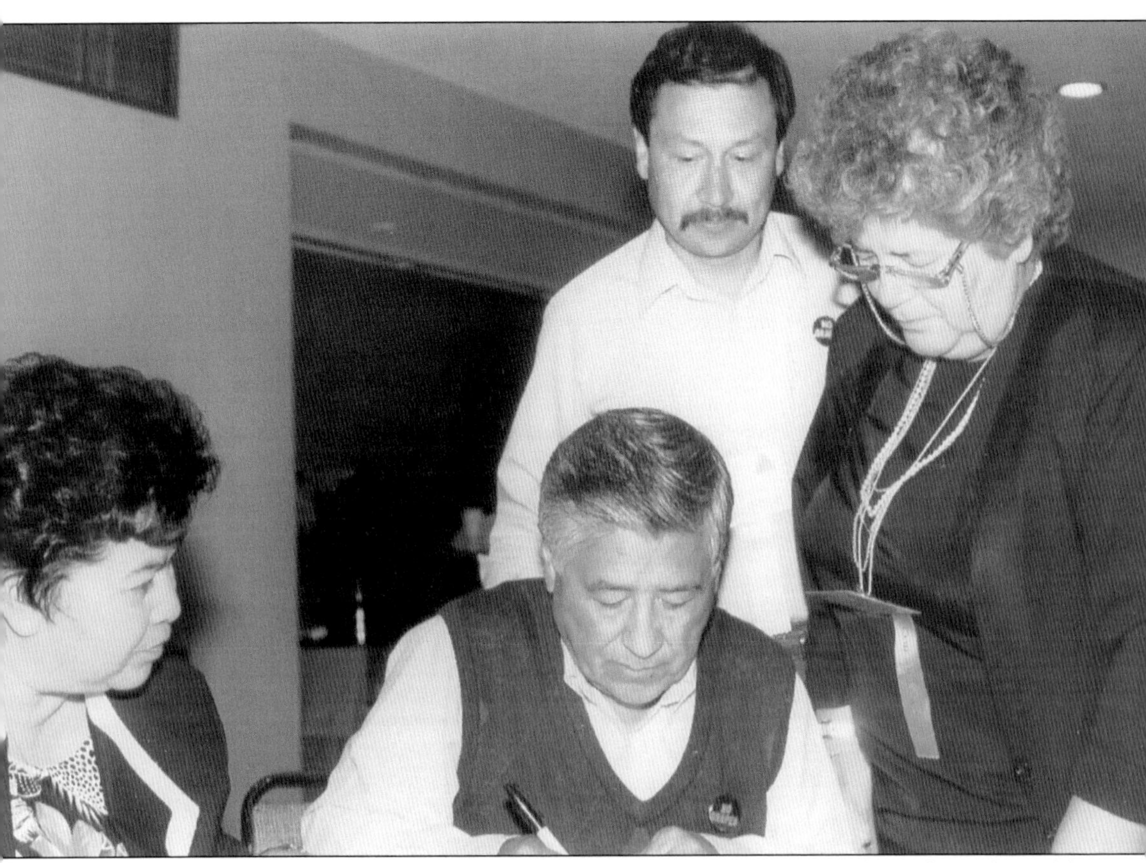

Seated in the middle is Mexican American labor leader Cesar Chavez, founder and president of the United Farm Workers Union. Behind him is Robert Rodriguez, and on the right is labor activist Carmen Hernandez of Redondo Beach. Hernandez, a union vice president, was a founder of the Nationwide Conference of Trade Union Women in Chicago in the 1970s, and despite retirement, she continues to advocate for union workers. (Courtesy Carmen Hernandez.)

Five

Sports and Recreation

The first priority of the family was its financial well-being, so Mexican American involvement in sports in the early years was largely dependent on family economics and parental permission. Because families were traditionally large, participation was decided by how much revenue would be lost by the family if someone played sports. Despite this, by the late 1930s, adult men were playing baseball on Mexican American teams and competing in the Los Angeles Negro League. In 1938, Vincent Lopez managed the Hermosa Beach White Sox baseball team at Clark Stadium.

In the late 1930s, Amador Espinoza ran track at Redondo High School and played first violin in the school band. Between 1939 and 1948, the Torres brothers—Marcus, Emo, and "Socko"—succeeded in breaking the traditional limitations and competed in football, baseball, basketball, and track, becoming Redondo High sports legends. Marcus was a star pitcher, who struck out Ted Williams, one of the greatest hitters in American baseball, in a game between Redondo High School and San Diego's Hoover High School. He later signed a baseball contract with the Hollywood Stars of the Pacific Coast League. Emo was an accomplished football player, who played football for Cal Poly University. In 1948, after competing in four sports, "Socko" earned 15 sports letters at Redondo High School. He played football at El Camino College and was inducted into the El Camino College Sports Hall of Fame. Between 1944 and 1949, Marty Acosta, "Lencho" Gomez, Orlando Gutierrez, Joe Saldana, Albert Castillon, and Nick Vargas left impressive marks on the Redondo High football and baseball programs. By 1950, "Chuey" Hernandez, Ricardo Real, Richard Castillon, Phillip Gonzales, and others continued the tradition of sports achievements in basketball, track, football, and wrestling. Between 1950 and 1960, Peter Serrato, John and Frank Lujan, Alex Madrid, Angel Contreras, Mike Salsido, Joe "Chuy" Rodriguez, and Ronnie Serrato added their contributions to the football, baseball, basketball, and wrestling programs at Redondo High.

Today some sports pioneers belong to the Senile Seahawks, an informal organization that meets at Las Brisas Restaurant, where a photograph of Orlando Gutierrez, a former teammate who became a U.S. Navy pilot, hangs behind the cash register.

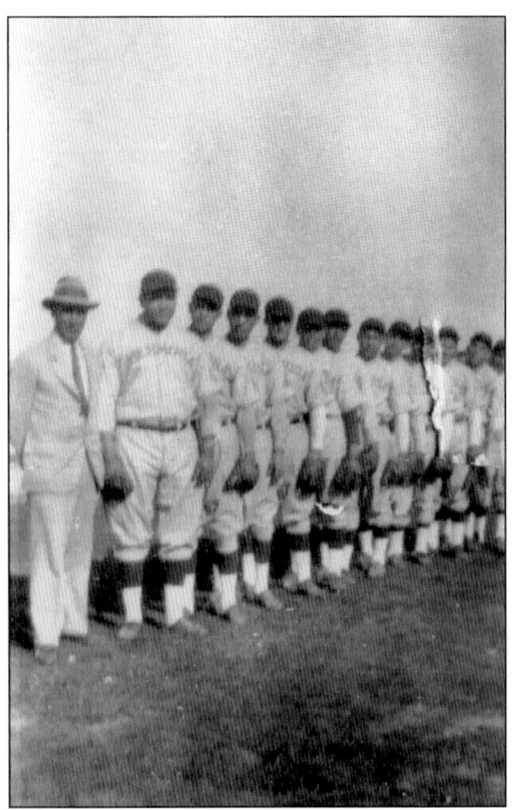

Vincent Lopez managed the Hermosa Beach White Sox in 1937. The players were all Mexican Americans and competed in the Los Angeles Negro League. Professional baseball was not open to persons of color until 1947, when Jackie Robinson, a UCLA graduate, broke the color line to play for the Brooklyn Dodgers. (Courtesy Alice Buffington.)

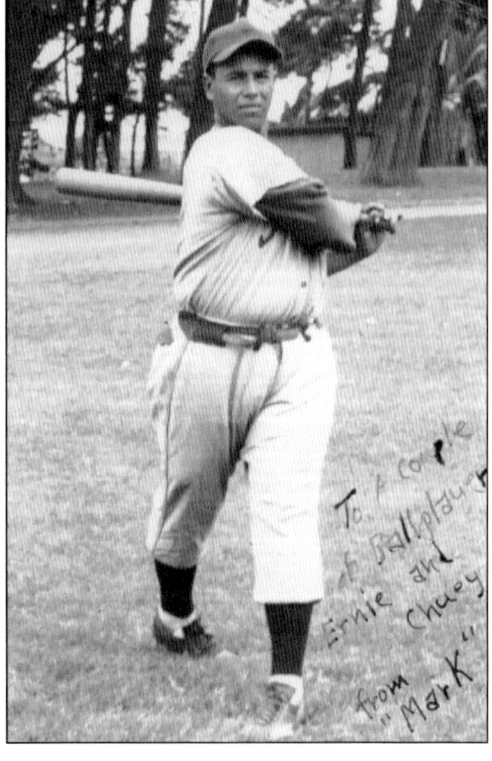

Marcus Torres was a standout baseball player at Redondo Union High School from 1940 to 1944. This 1946 photograph was taken while he played minor league professional baseball in Reno, Nevada. (Courtesy "Chuey" Hernandez.)

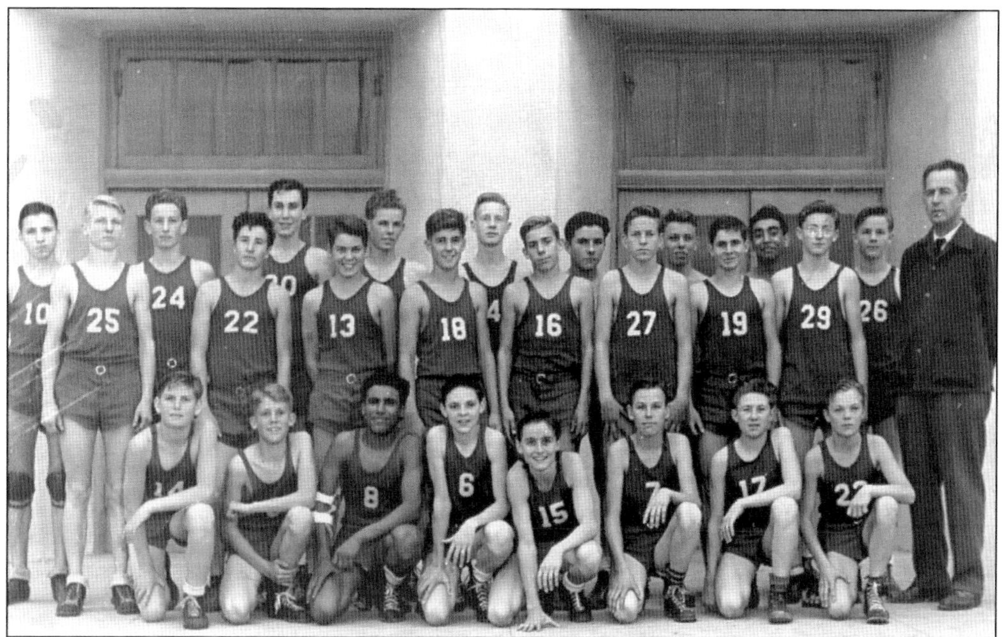

In 1946, the varsity, B, and D basketball teams posed for this unusual combination photograph at Redondo High. Included in this photograph are "Socko" Torres (first row, third from left) and Danny Espinoza (third row, eighth from left). (Courtesy "Socko" Torres.)

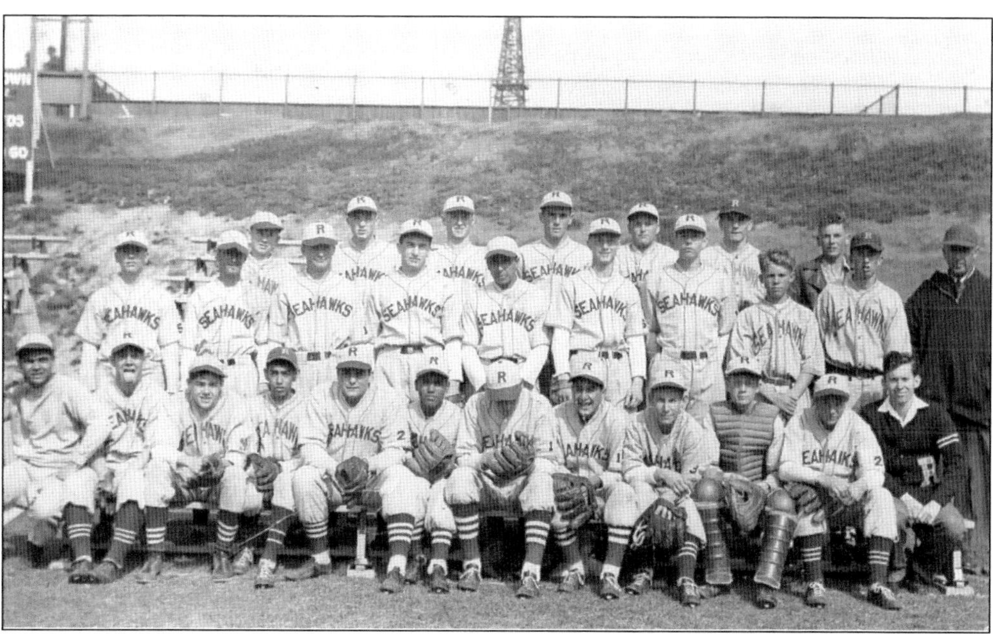

Redondo High's 1945 varsity baseball team had lost 12 games before a friendly talk from Coach Harold Grant helped them tie Beverly Hills High for the Bay League title. Pictured are, from left to right, (first row) Danny Reyes, two unidentified, Artie Espinoza, unidentified, "Socko" Torres, unidentified, "Lencho" Gomez, four unidentified; (second row) Phillip Gonzalez (fifth from the left). (Courtesy "Socko" Torres.)

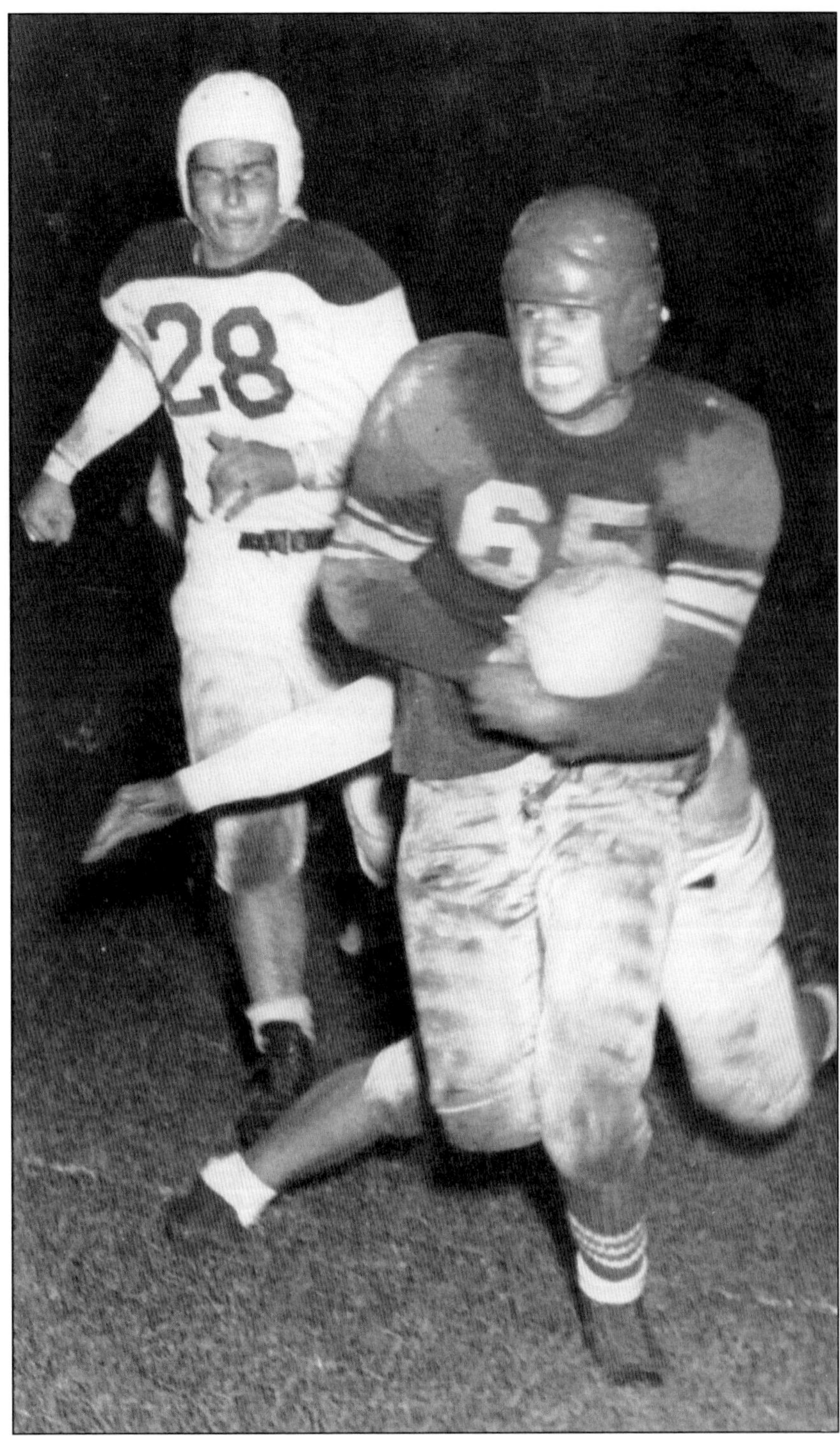

In this photograph, football standout Nick Vargas eludes two opponents in a 1946 game at Redondo High School against Mount Carmel, a tough opponent. Vargas excelled as a varsity athlete in four sports at Redondo High. He later played football at El Camino College and became a successful radio DJ, restaurateur, and engineering construction business owner. (Courtesy Nick Vargas.)

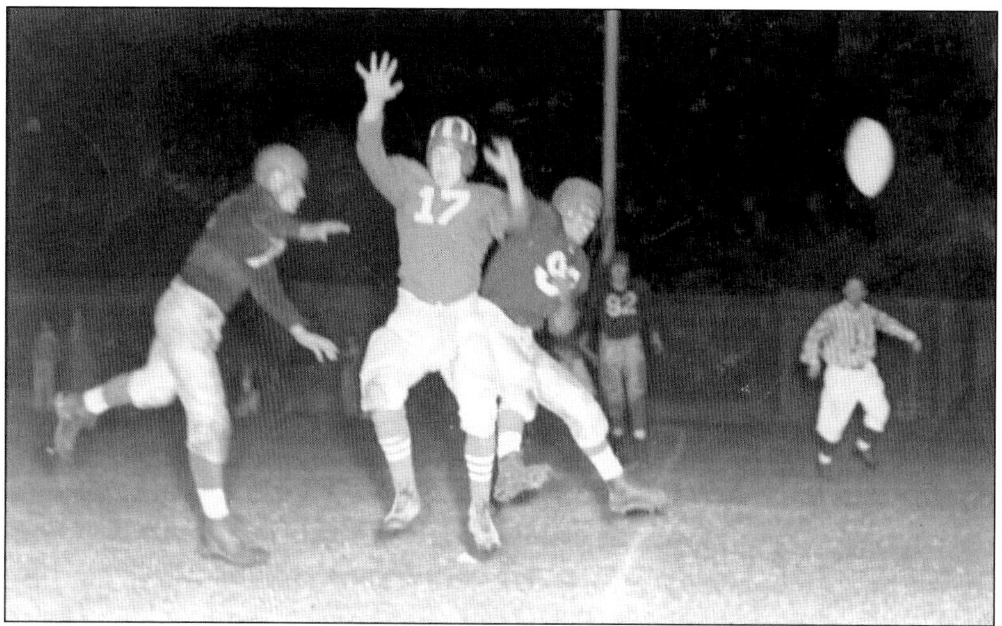

In this 1946 snapshot, "Socko" Torres, No. 93, and Bob Bacon, No. 17, scramble for the ball at Seahawk Stadium at Redondo High in a game against Inglewood High School. At 120 pounds, Torres was a sophomore varsity running back.

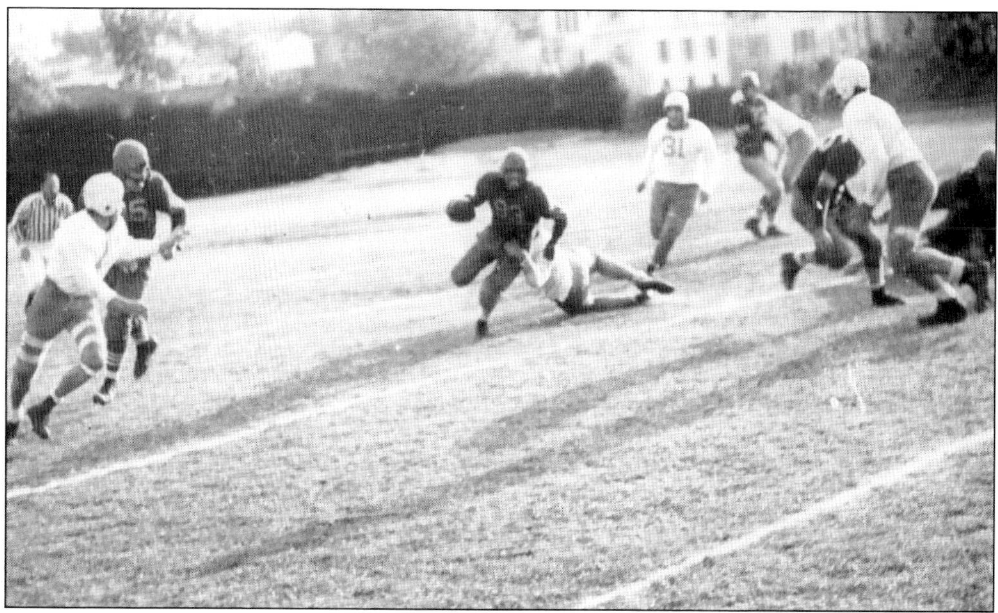

During a daytime football game against Beverly Hills High, "Socko" Torres evades a tackler on his way to a touchdown. The final score was tied at 20-20. Torres was the only athlete in the history of Redondo High School to earn 15 sports letters in four years. (Courtesy "Socko" Torres.)

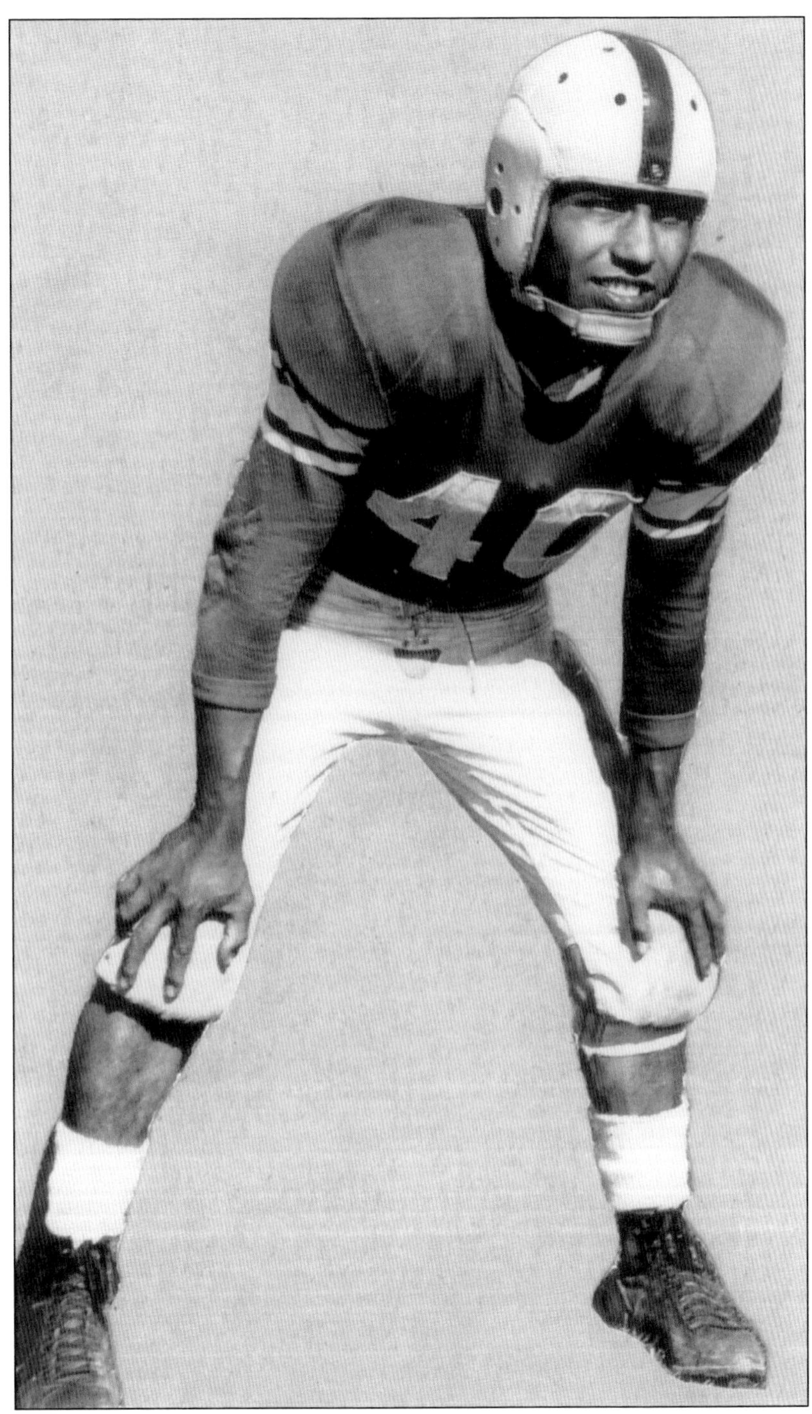

After an outstanding career at Redondo High School, "Socko" Torres played running back at El Camino College in 1949, earning the all Metropolitan Conference halfback award. He played at 120 pounds, and when he weighed in for the stadium announcer's statistical announcements, he put rocks in his pockets to boost his weight. He was later inducted into the El Camino College Sports Hall of Fame. (Courtesy "Socko" Torres.)

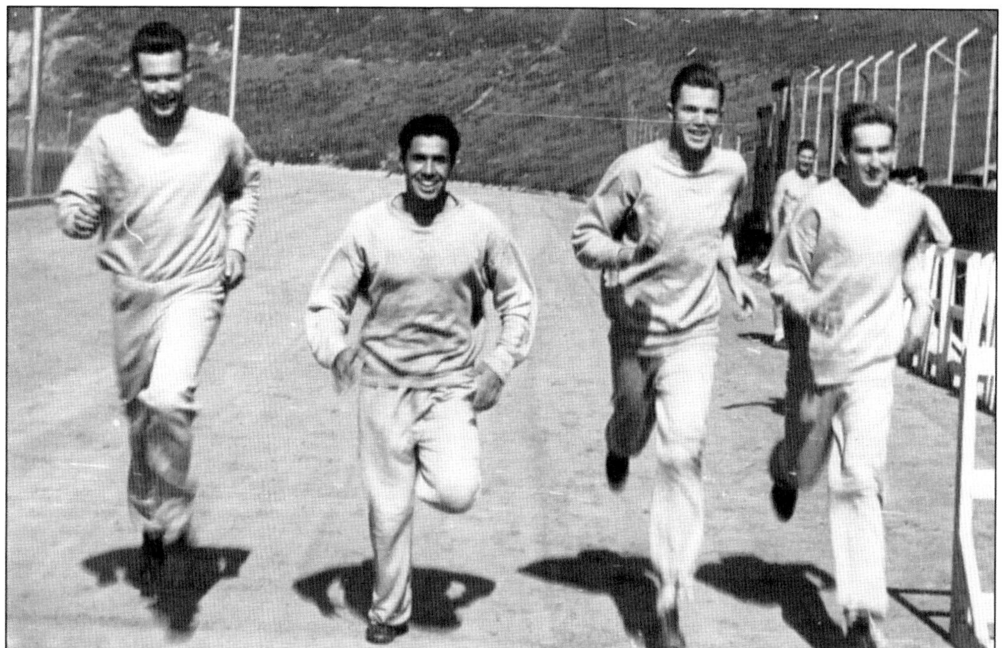

In addition to excelling in football, Nick Vargas was also an outstanding varsity track and field miler and ran the eight-eighty yard run, hurdles, and relays at Redondo High. Training together at Redondo's Seahawk Stadium are, from left to right, Ronnie Dixon, Vargas, Howard Bugbee, and Art Keely. In the 1940s, the stadium doubled as a baseball and football venue. (Courtesy Nick Vargas.)

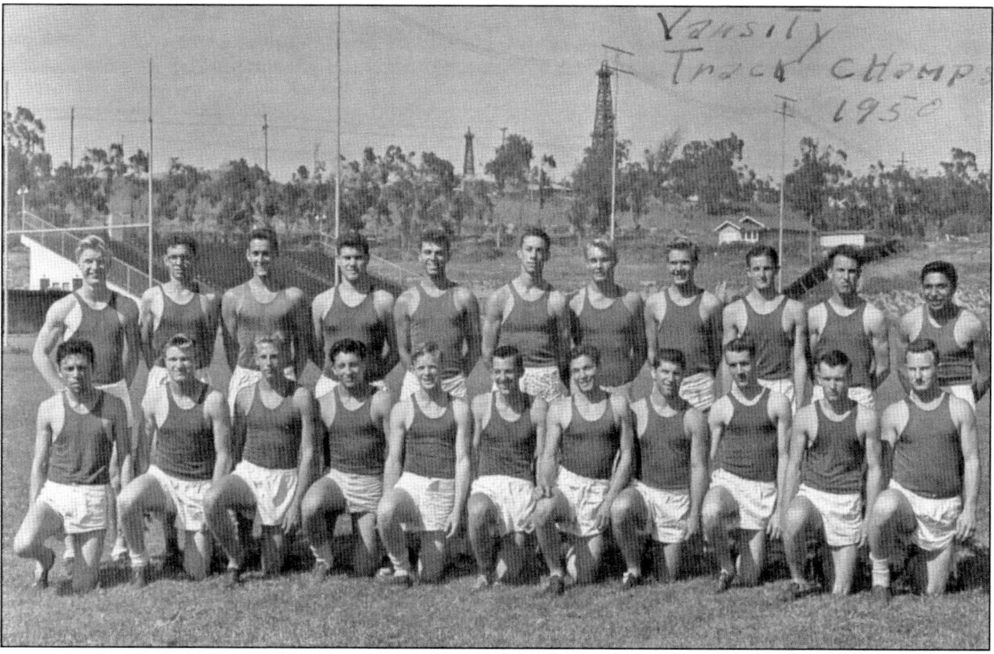

The 1950 varsity Bay League champions track team poses for this photograph at Redondo's Seahawk Stadium. Included in this image are Richard Castillon (first row, far left), Ricardo Real (first row, fourth from left), and Phillip Gonzalez (second row, far right). At extreme left behind the white bleachers is "Tightwad Hill," the locals' free spectator spot. (Courtesy Richard Castillon.)

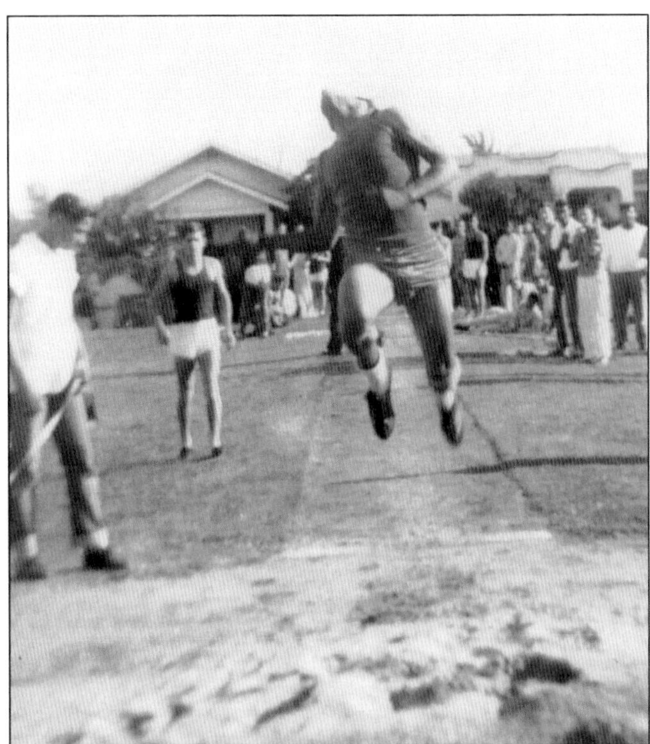

At the 1947 Inglewood High School relays, "Socko" Torres competes in the afternoon broad jump, after driving from Santa Monica High School, where he competed in another sport earlier that day. (Courtesy "Socko" Torres.)

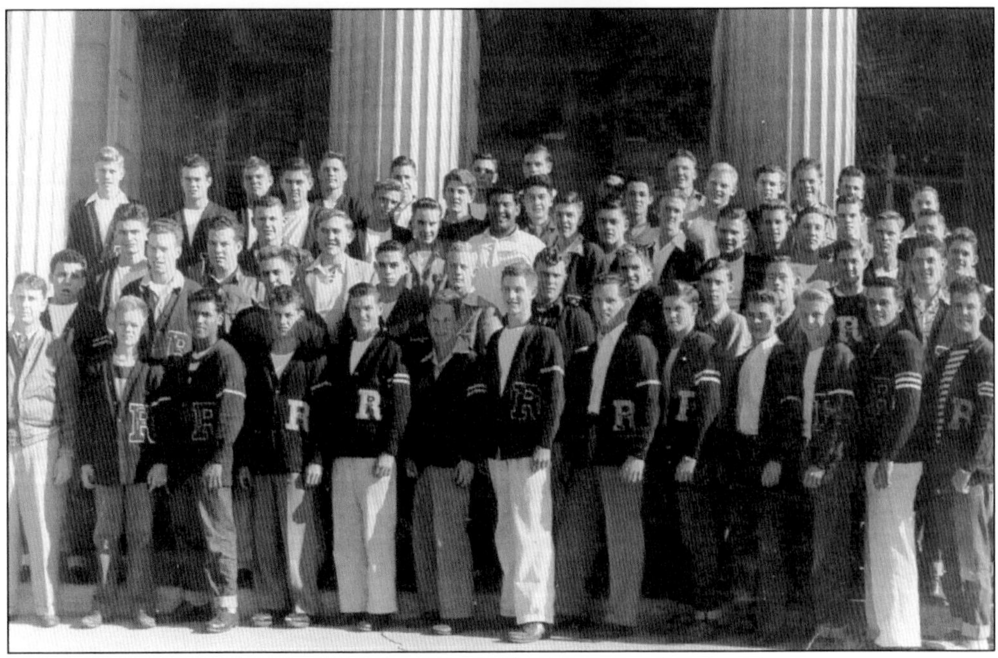

Fifty-eight members of the Redondo High's R club, the varsity lettermen's organization, pose in front of the old auditorium in 1946. Included in this photograph are Coach Harold Grant (first row, far left), "Socko" Torres (first row, third from left), Henry Burke (first row, sixth from left), and Emo Torres (third row center, white shirt). The rest are unidentified. Burke became the sports editor for the *Daily Breeze* newspaper in 1951. (Courtesy "Socko" Torres.)

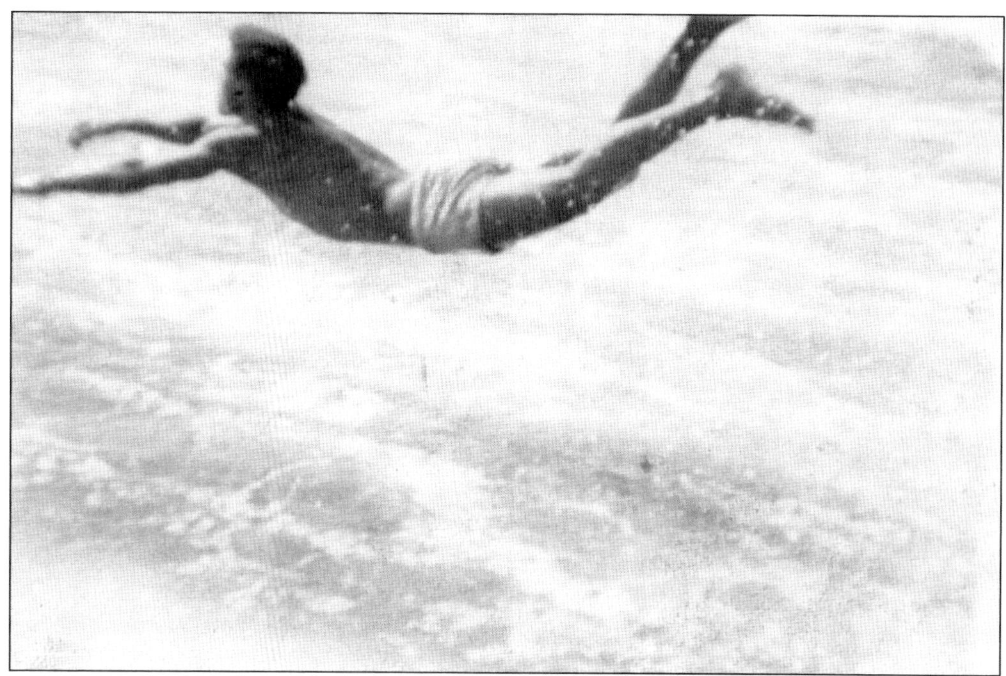

Beach activities like swimming and body surfing attracted many Mexican American youngsters to Hermosa Beach. In this 1945 photograph, "Socko" Torres is diving into the surf at Second Street. (Courtesy "Socko" Torres.)

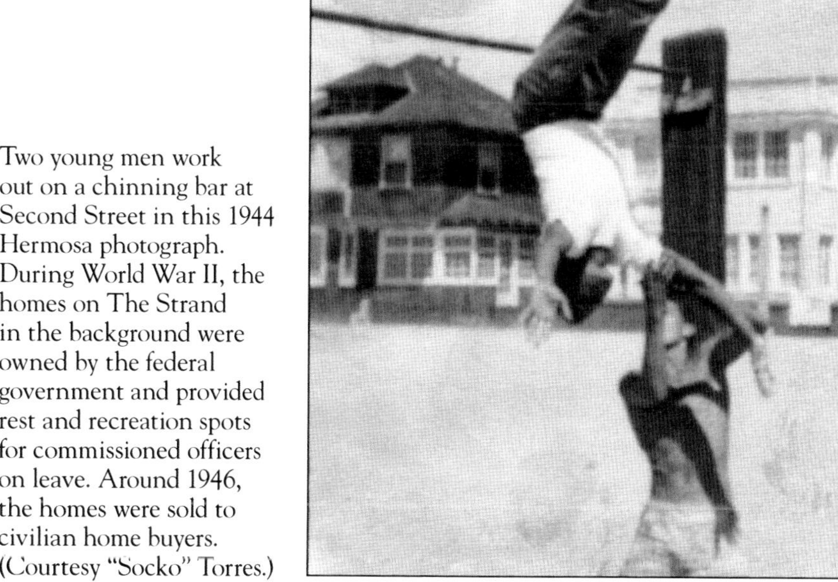

Two young men work out on a chinning bar at Second Street in this 1944 Hermosa photograph. During World War II, the homes on The Strand in the background were owned by the federal government and provided rest and recreation spots for commissioned officers on leave. Around 1946, the homes were sold to civilian home buyers. (Courtesy "Socko" Torres.)

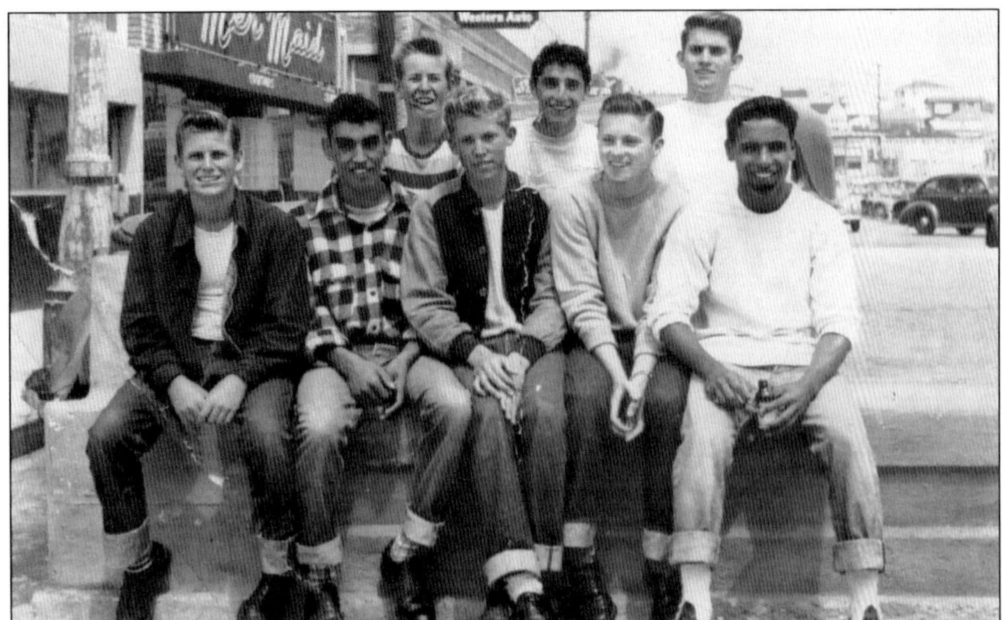

In this 1946 photograph of eight beach buddies, old downtown Hermosa is visible. Pictured are, from left to right, (first row) Bert Matthews, Danny Espinoza, unidentified, Bud Waller, and "Socko" Torres; (second row) Jim Foxworthy, Bert Ferris, and unidentified. Note the location of the Mermaid restaurant at that time. In later years, it moved to The Strand, to the left of where the boys are seated. (Courtesy "Socko" Torres.)

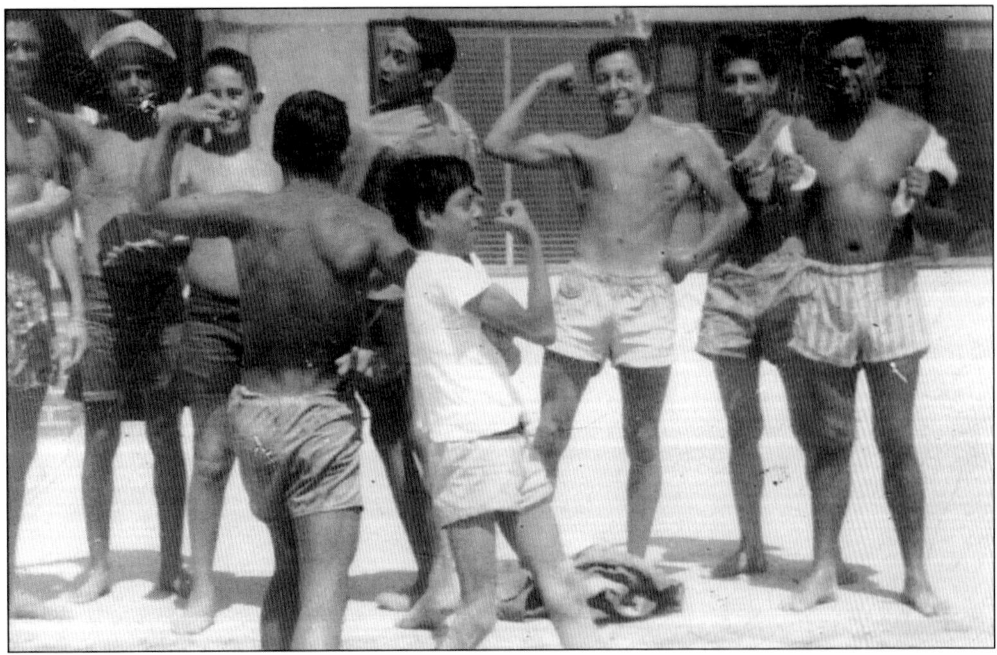

Second Street in Hermosa is again captured in this 1947 image of friends gathered at the beach. From left to right are (first row) Bobby Serrato (back exposed) and Ivan Marin; (second row) Richard Castillon, unidentified, Ernie Hernandez, "Chuey" Hernandez, Edward Marin, unidentified, and Marty Duarte. Second Street was the "in" beach at that time. (Courtesy "Chuey" Hernandez.)

This 1947 snapshot catches sunbathers on the beach in front of the old Southern California Edison electric plant located in Redondo Beach. At left is George Escobar, age 16, and his brother Andy, age 14. (Courtesy Henry Escobar.)

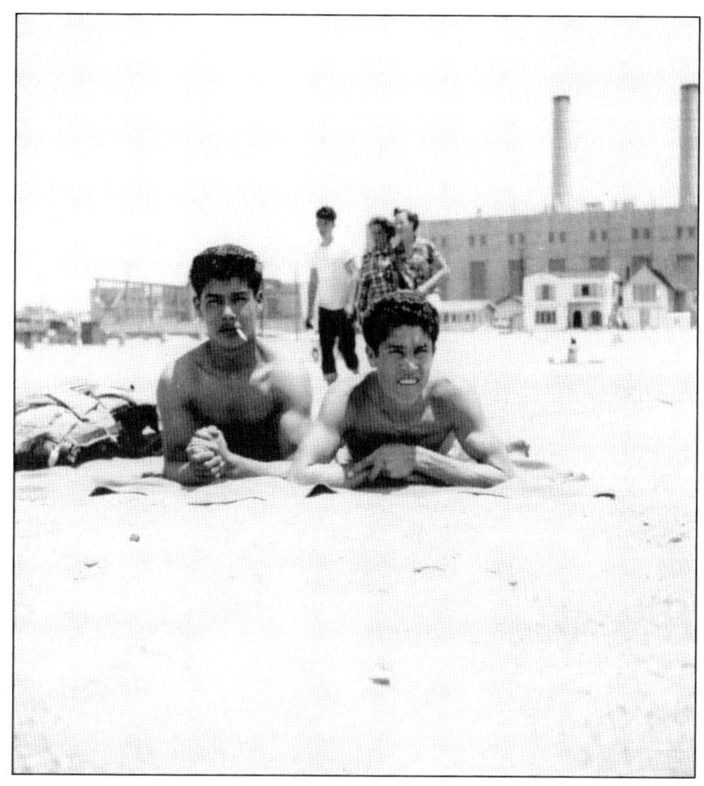

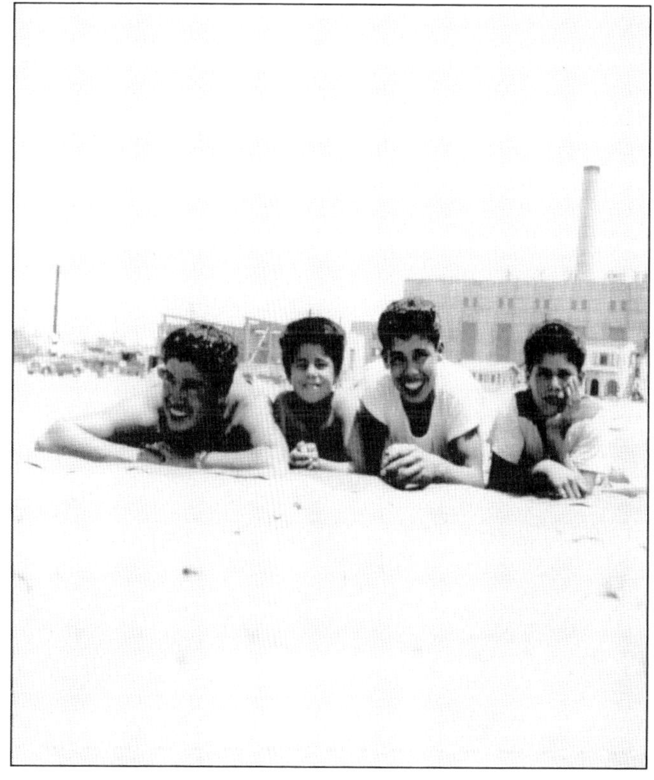

Three brothers and a friend enjoy the beach in 1946. From left to right are Robert Trevino and three Escobar brothers—Herman, Oscar, and Alfredo. All the Escobar brothers were taught to box by their father, German, who boxed professionally in Arizona before coming to California. (Courtesy Henry Escobar.)

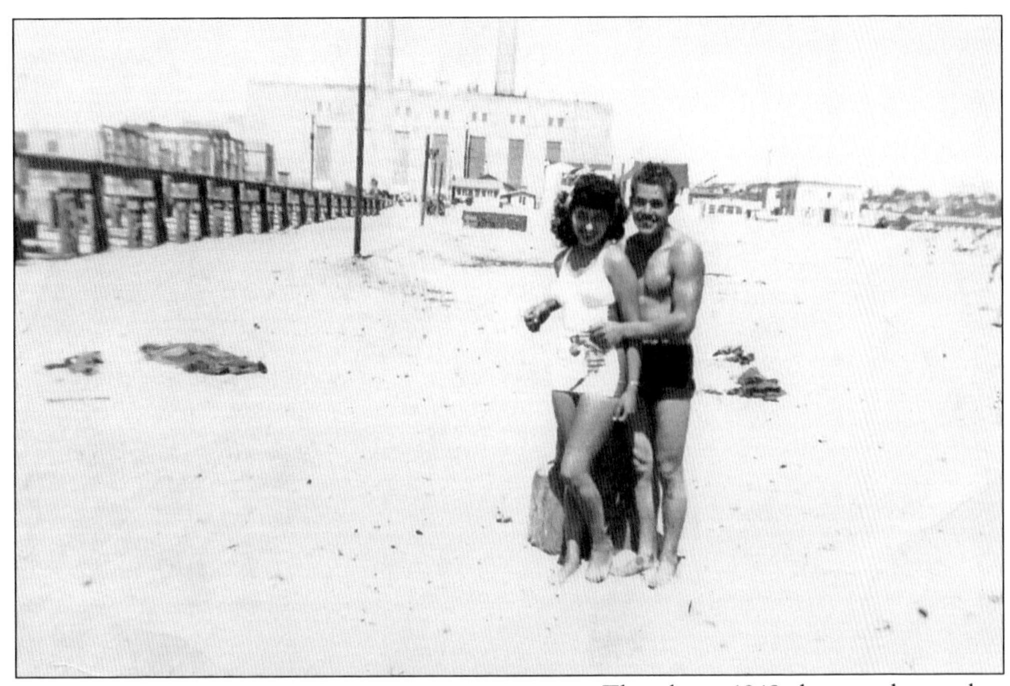

This classic 1948 photograph reveals Alice Lopez and an unidentified friend enjoying the summer in Redondo. The exposed pipeline on the left was buried in the 1950s. Today the Chart House restaurant is located approximately left of the pole. (Courtesy Alice Buffington.)

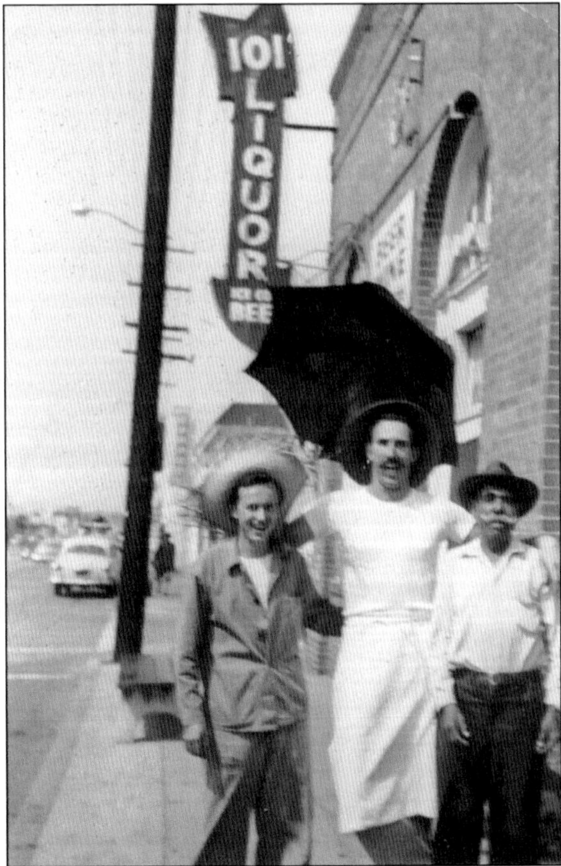

A form of adult recreation in Hermosa Beach was visiting the Pitcher House saloon. Here, pictured from left to right in this 1950s snapshot, an unidentified patron, owner "Big Mike" Bigo, and Jose Gomez pause for a photograph. Gomez was the greeter and goodwill ambassador and joined Bigo on trips to the Tijuana, Mexico, bullring. The saloon was a bank before the 1929 stock market crash and later a billiard parlor. (Courtesy Margaret Carillo.)

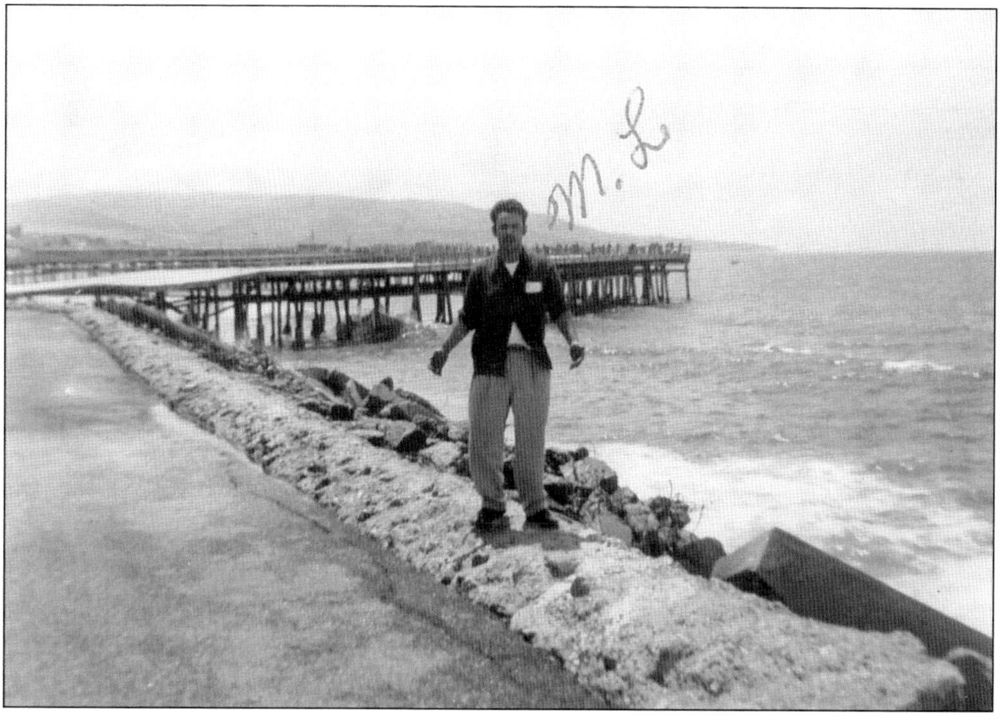

Reymundo Leon poses near the old Redondo horseshoe pier around 1950. Mexican American families enjoyed pier outings for sightseeing, visits to the fresh fish markets, and shrimp dinners. (Courtesy Ordie Fernandez.)

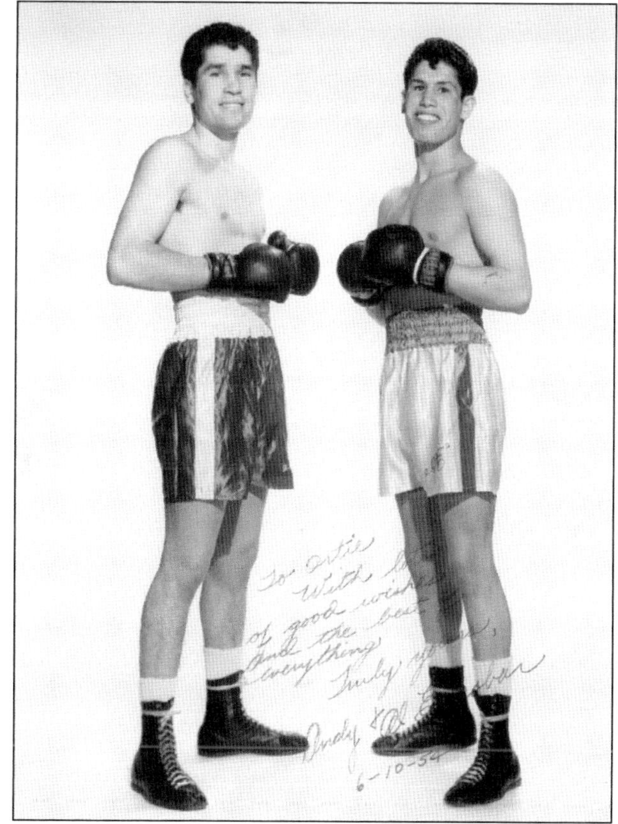

Andy, left, and Alfredo Escobar were both National Golden Gloves boxing champions from Redondo Beach—Andy won the 1953 lightweight championship; Alfredo the 1954 bantamweight title. Both won the championships in Chicago and were greeted by large crowds on their return to the South Bay. The brothers followed in their father's footsteps and went on to fight professionally. (Courtesy Henry Escobar.)

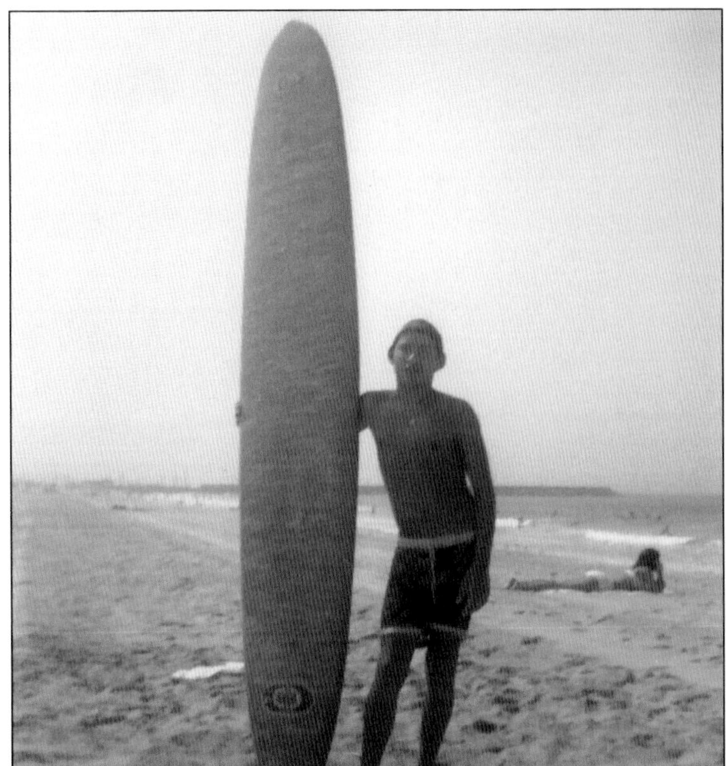

This view looks south from Hermosa Beach toward Palos Verdes. Pictured around 1963 on an overcast day is Luis "Luigi" Moreno. With wet hair, wet trunks, and wet surfboard, he ignores the scene on the sand behind him. (Courtesy Roberta Robles.)

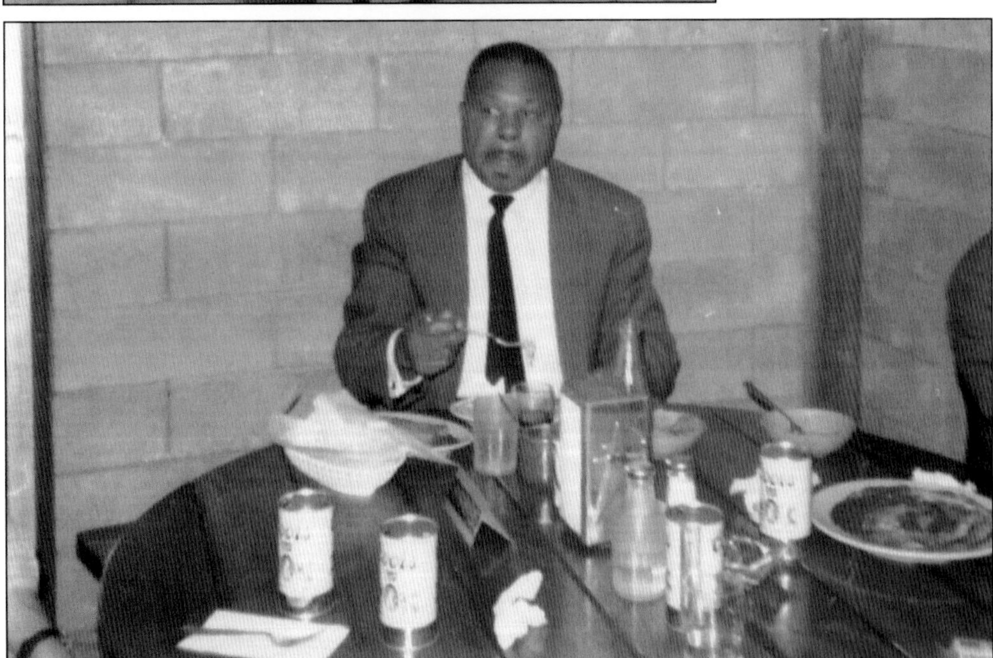

Archie Moore, the world light heavyweight boxing champion, dines at the original Leo's Mexican Food restaurant in the late 1960s. Moore was a friend of Ricardo Real, who played football at Redondo High in the mid-1940s and later competed in wrestling competition at the state level. (Courtesy Ricardo Real.)

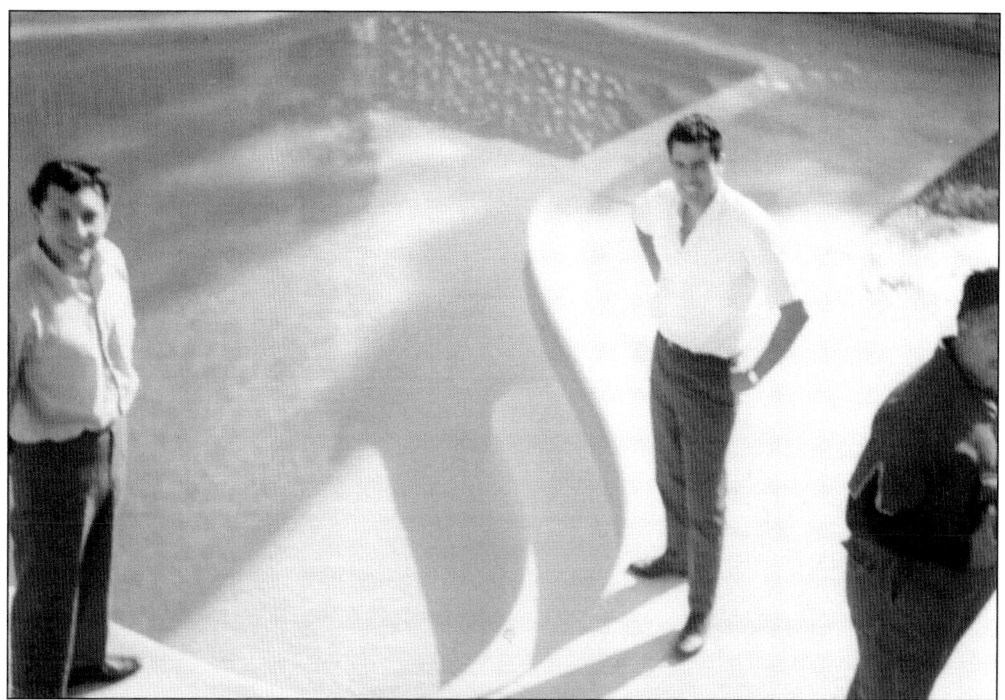

Standing near the boxing glove shaped pool at Archie Moore's home in San Diego, California, are, from left to right, Ricardo Real, Nick Vargas, and Moore (partially hidden). (Courtesy Ricardo Real.)

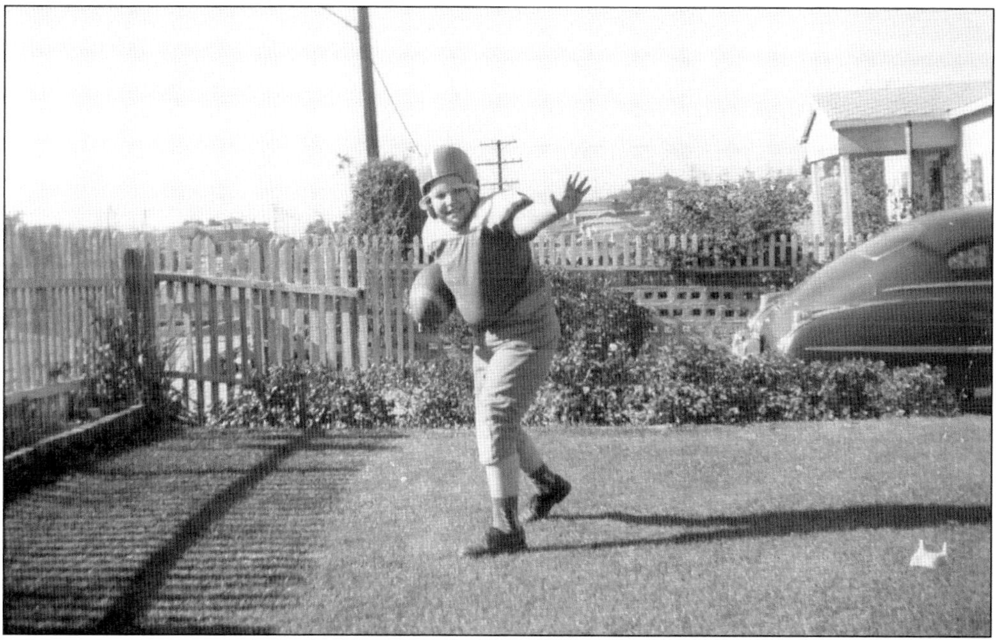

Aspiring athlete David Ortiz, who went on to earn a master's degree, poses in his football uniform on the front lawn of the family's Morgan Lane home in northern Redondo. His parents were Salvador and Socorro Ortiz. Behind him in this c. 1955 photograph are homes on Seventh Street in Hermosa Beach.

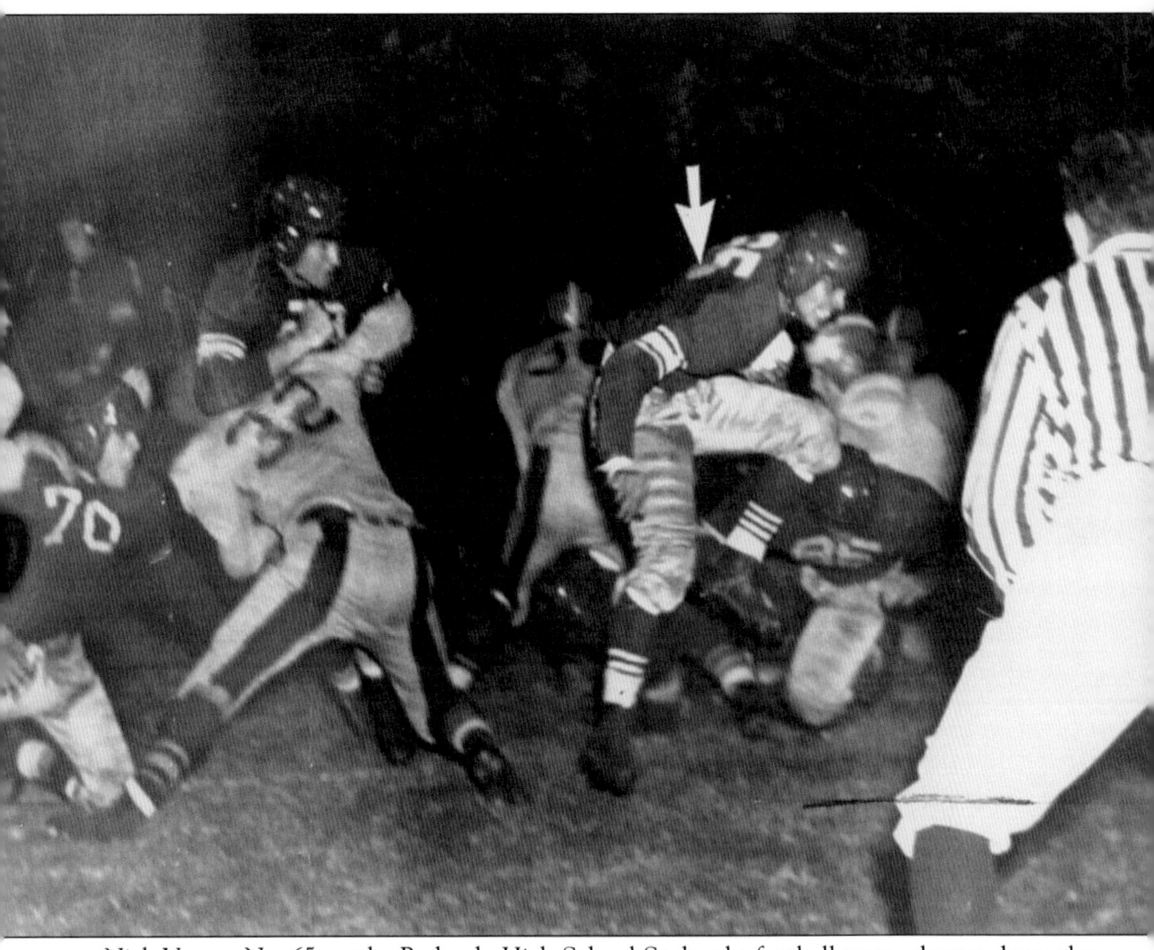

Nick Vargas, No. 65 on the Redondo High School Seahawks football team, charges down the field in this 1948 football game against Long Beach Wilson High School. His successful adult career as a musical artist and orchestra leader started at Redondo High School when he decided to play trombone while waiting for football season to begin. (Courtesy Nick Vargas.)

Six

Military Service

Mexican Americans represented less than two percent of Redondo Beach and Hermosa Beach during World War II and the Korean War, yet 85 men served with distinction and valor.

Johnny Gonzalez, the first local casualty and recipient of a Purple Heart, perished at the age of 19 when his ship was torpedoed by a submarine. Joel Rodriguez received his Purple Heart 30 years after being injured in World War II. He returned home to graduate from high school. The Mendez brothers served in the U.S. military in both wars. Manuel Mendez received several Purple Hearts and a Bronze and Silver Star for valor and gallantry, becoming one of the most highly decorated soldiers in the South Pacific. When he was discharged, Gen. Douglas MacArthur sent a personal letter of commendation to his mother, Josefa Mendez, on Spreckles Lane. By coincidence, Jesse Mendez, U.S. Army, and his brother Frank, an air force radio operator, met unexpectedly on an airfield in China as Jesse was refueling Frank's aircraft. Four Mendoza brothers served with distinction in three branches of the military. David Mendoza was an air force A-20 gunner and received the Air Medal. Amador Espinosa flew 30 combat missions as a B-24 waist gunner over Germany, returning home in 1948 to earn a college degree. He retired from the Redondo Beach Police Department in 1993 and continues working as a volunteer. Tony Vallejo, who spoke Spanish, Japanese, and Tagalog, was a Filipino and Japanese translator during the war. Paul Saldana spoke seven languages, including German, Japanese, and Russian, and was aboard the USS *Missouri* serving as a translator at the Japanese surrender in 1945. After his discharge, he attended the University of Southern California, earning a degree in foreign languages. Alfonso "Ponche" Gonzalez was at the Battle of Okinawa and, after his discharge, earned a degree in microbiology at the University of Southern California. Josie Mendez, sister of the Mendez brothers, recalls that the streets of Redondo Beach and Hermosa Beach seemed deserted of Mexican American men who had answered their country's call during its time of need.

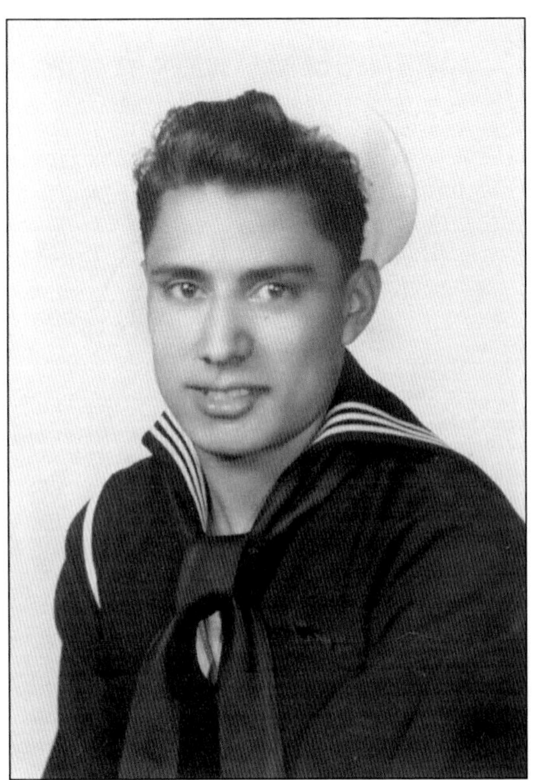

Johnny Gonzalez, U.S. Navy, was the first World War II casualty from Redondo Beach. His ship was torpedoed in the Atlantic, where he and several thousand perished. The sinking occurred three days after the war ended, and he was posthumously awarded a Purple Heart. (Courtesy John Luna Moreno.)

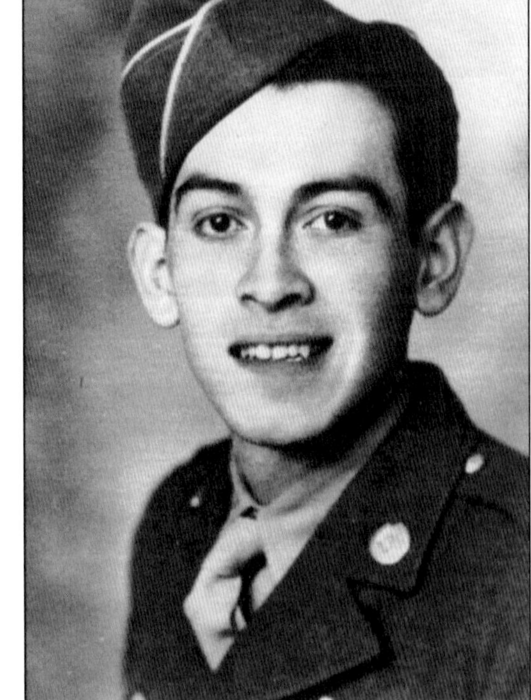

Another World War II casualty was Nestor Flores, U.S. Navy, from Redondo Beach. Little is known about Flores except that he died in the early years of the war, and his father may have resided in the city in the early 1930s. (Courtesy American Legion, Redondo Beach.)

Two photocopied pages of Staff Sgt. Manuel L. Mendez's U.S. Army discharge are all that remains of his exceptional military record. According to sister Josie Mendez, he was the first Mexican American from Redondo Beach to volunteer for military service. He served in the Aleutian Islands and the Pacific theater and, like many others, served with valor and distinction. (Courtesy Josie Pacheco.)

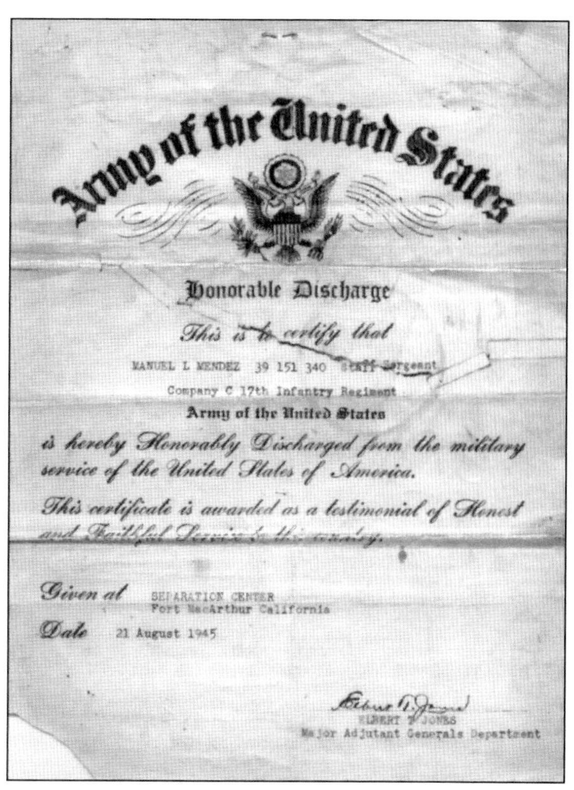

Army of the United States

Honorable Discharge

This is to certify that

MANUEL L MENDEZ 39 151 340 Staff Sergeant

Company C 17th Infantry Regiment

Army of the United States

is hereby Honorably Discharged from the military service of the United States of America.

This certificate is awarded as a testimonial of Honest and Faithful Service to this country.

Given at SEPARATION CENTER Fort MacArthur California

Date 21 August 1945

ELBERT T JONES
Major Adjutant Generals Department

ENLISTED RECORD AND REPORT OF SEPARATION
HONORABLE DISCHARGE

Mendez Manuel L | 39 151 340 | S Sgt | Inf | AUS
Company C 17th Infantry Regt | 21 Aug 45 | Sep Cen Ft MacArthur Calif
1820 Spreckles Lane Redondo Beach Cal | 25 Aug 15 | Gallinas New Mexico
See 9 | Brown | Black | 5' 7" | 140 lbs. | 2
Mexican x | x | Nurseryman II 3-39.10

MILITARY HISTORY

28 Jan 41 | 28 Jan 41 | Los Angeles California
x | 281 | Los Angeles Calif | Redondo Beach California
Squad Leader 745 | Combat Infantryman Badge 10 Jan 44
Aleutian Islands Eastern Mandates Southern Philippines GO 33 WD 45 Ryukyus GO 40 WD 45
Good Conduct Medal American Defense Service Medal Philippine Liberation Ribbon with 2 Bronze Stars Asiatic Pacific Campaign Medal (55)
Okinawa 2 May 45
Jul 44 | Apr 43 | Dec 43 | Cholera Feb 45 | 24 Apr 43 | Asiatic Pacific Theater | 11 May 43
2 | 0 | 13 | 0 | 3 | 23 | S Sgt | 6 Aug 45 | United States | 6 Aug 45
None
Convenience of the Government RR1-1 (Demobilization) AR 615-365 15 December 44
None | 8 | 0 | 0

PAY DATA

4 | 4 | 6 | 300 | 100 | None | .80 | $ 216.70 | F MURRAY Maj FD

INSURANCE NOTICE

x | x | 31 Jul 45 | 6.90 | 1000

Lapel Button Issued (33) Bronze Star Medal GO 49 7th Inf Div 29 Jul 44 with 1 Oak Leaf Cluster Purple Heart GO 9 374th Sta Hosp 15 May 45 Time lost under AW 107 78 days

R C LEES
2d Lt WAC

APPLICATION FOR READJUSTMENT ALLOWANCE

The second page of Sergeant Mendez's discharge shows he was the most highly decorated soldier in the South Pacific in World War II, receiving three Purple Hearts, a Bronze Star with one Oak Leaf Cluster, a Philippines liberation ribbon with two Bronze Stars, and a Silver Star. His mother, Josefina, received a personal letter of commendation from Gen. Douglas McArthur after Mendez's discharge. (Courtesy Josie Pacheco.)

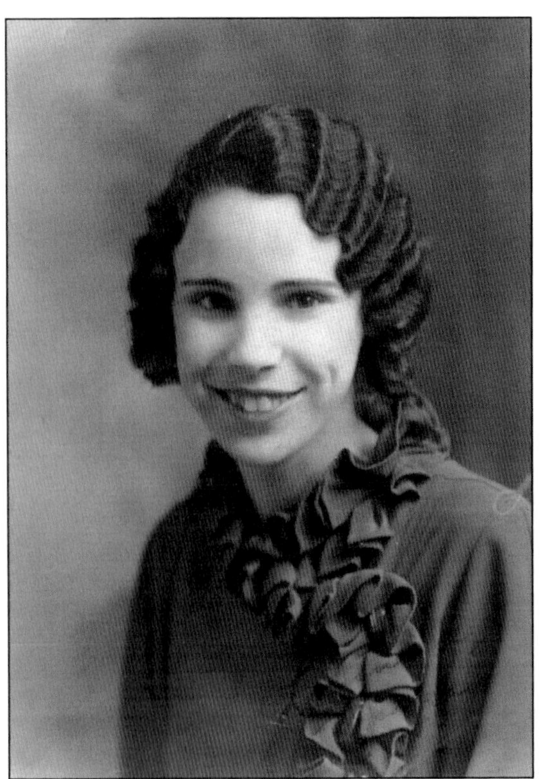

In June 1938, Joyce Devereux graduated from high school in Canada. She became Manuel Mendez's wife after his discharge from the U.S. Army in 1945. (Courtesy Pearl Vidal.)

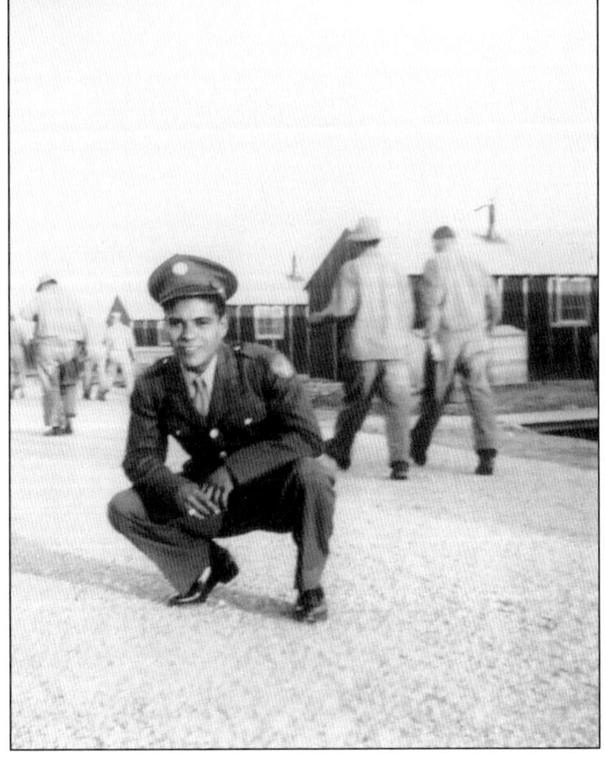

Frank Mendez, shown here as a U.S. Air Force radio operator, accidentally met his brother Jessie Mendez, U.S. Army, at an airfield in China in 1942, while Jessie was refueling Frank's aircraft. Brothers of Manuel Mendez, Frank and Jessie were both granted leave from their commanding officers to visit the Great Wall of China and the Taj Mahal in India together. (Courtesy Josie Pacheco.)

Pvt. Louis Saldana, U.S. Marine Corps, is pictured here *c.* 1945 wearing his Purple Heart, received for combat injuries sustained on Okinawa in July 1944. Paul Saldana, his brother, spoke seven languages and served as a Japanese translator on board the USS *Missouri* at the time of the surrender. (Courtesy Louis Saldana.)

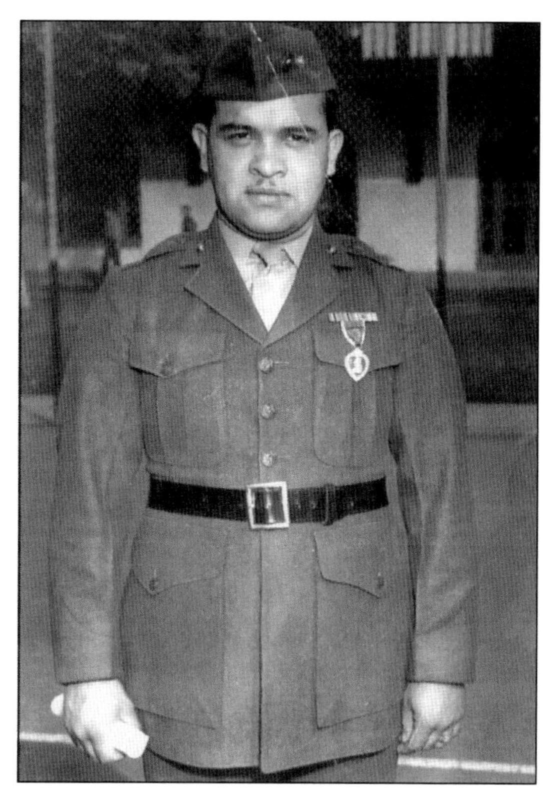

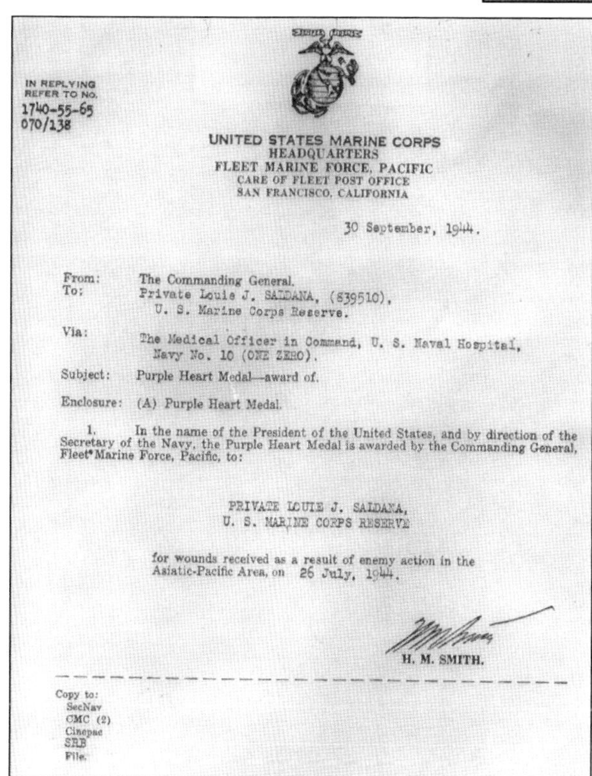

IN REPLYING REFER TO NO.
1740-55-65
070/138

UNITED STATES MARINE CORPS
HEADQUARTERS
FLEET MARINE FORCE, PACIFIC
CARE OF FLEET POST OFFICE
SAN FRANCISCO, CALIFORNIA

30 September, 1944.

From: The Commanding General.
To: Private Louie J. SALDANA, (839510), U. S. Marine Corps Reserve.

Via: The Medical Officer in Command, U. S. Naval Hospital, Navy No. 10 (ONE ZERO).

Subject: Purple Heart Medal—award of.

Enclosure: (A) Purple Heart Medal.

1. In the name of the President of the United States, and by direction of the Secretary of the Navy, the Purple Heart Medal is awarded by the Commanding General, Fleet Marine Force, Pacific, to:

PRIVATE LOUIE J. SALDANA,
U. S. MARINE CORPS RESERVE

for wounds received as a result of enemy action in the Asiatic-Pacific Area, on 26 July, 1944.

H. M. SMITH.

Copy to:
SecNav
CMC (2)
Cincpac
SRB
File.

Pictured here is a copy of the letter received by Private Saldana from Gen. H. M. Smith, U.S. Marine Corps, awarding him his Purple Heart on September 30, 1944. (Courtesy Louis Saldana.)

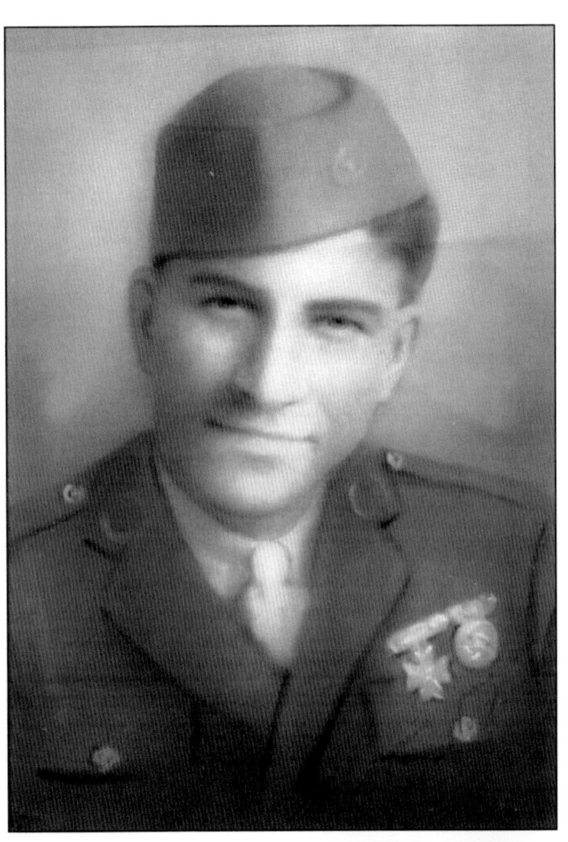

In addition to earning a Purple Heart, Pvt. Joel Rodriguez, U.S. Marine Corps, saved another Marine's life by providing emergency aid to him on Okinawa after more than seven days of continuous shelling, while disregarding his own injuries. The act was documented by a fellow Marine sharing Rodriguez's foxhole. (Courtesy Ordie Fernandez.)

Joel Rodriguez received this Purple Heart nearly 30 years after suffering combat injuries on Okinawa in 1945. The award came when he returned to school to complete his high school diploma. After sharing his experience, he was encouraged to apply for the medal. (Courtesy Ordie Fernandez.)

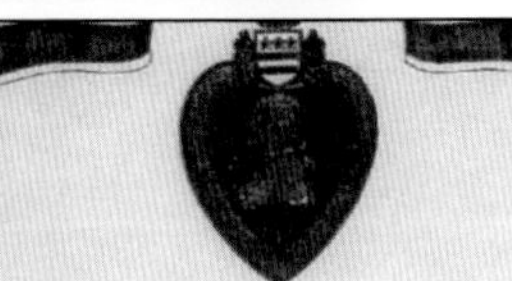

THE UNITED STATES OF AMERICA

TO ALL WHO SHALL SEE THESE PRESENTS, GREETING:

THIS IS TO CERTIFY THAT
THE PRESIDENT OF THE UNITED STATES OF AMERICA
HAS AWARDED THE

PURPLE HEART

ESTABLISHED BY GENERAL GEORGE WASHINGTON
AT NEWBURGH, NEW YORK, AUGUST 7, 1782
TO
MR. JOEL A. RODRIGUEZ
FORMER MEMBER UNITED STATES MARINE CORPS
FOR WOUNDS RECEIVED
IN ACTION
ON OKINAWA ON 13 MAY 1945

GIVEN UNDER MY HAND IN THE CITY OF WASHINGTON
THIS 17TH DAY OF APRIL 1980

GENERAL, U.S. MARINE CORPS
COMMANDANT OF THE MARINE CORPS

Joaquin "Jack" Mendoza, U.S. Navy, is pictured reading a newspaper at his parent's home in Redondo Beach, around 1945. He served as a Seabee in a naval construction battalion. (Courtesy Julian Mendoza.)

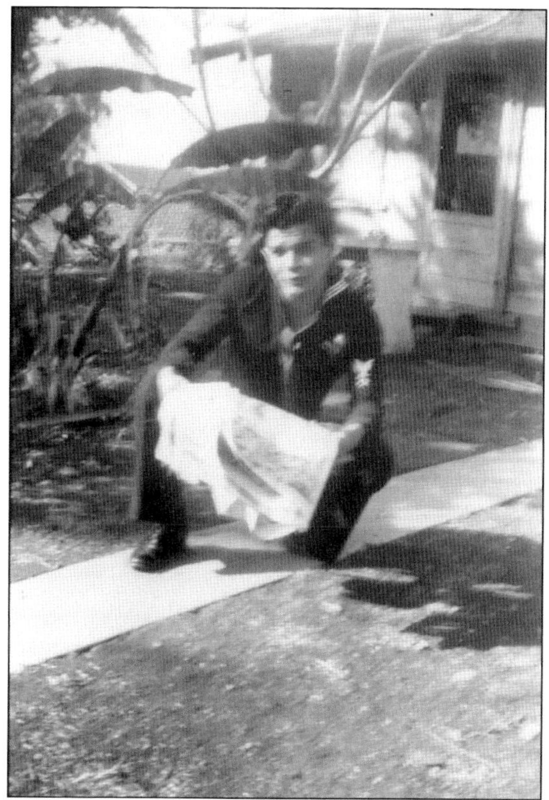

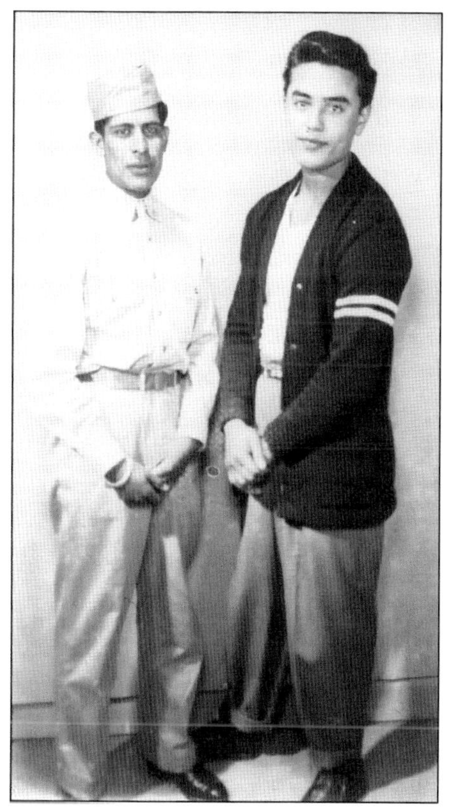

In this c. 1943 photograph, Calistro "Cal" Gonzalez, on leave, poses with his friend Peter Fernandez, who later operated a family Mexican restaurant in Gardena, California. (Courtesy Nieves Gonzalez.)

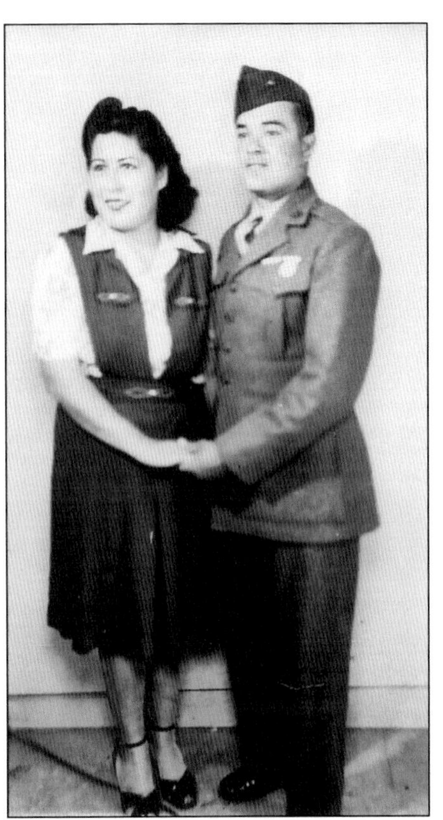

Alfonso Duarte, U.S. Marine Corps, pictured here with his wife, Rebecca, in 1943, initially enlisted in the navy but was transferred to the Marine Corps by the government. The Duartes settled in Hermosa Beach with their three children—Margaret, Rick, and Robin. (Courtesy Margaret Carillo.)

This photograph, taken by Alfonso Duarte from the top of a landing craft that he was operating, shows the invasion of Iwo Jima in World War II. Visible is the smoke from exploding enemy artillery rounds. At top left center (barely visible) are two parachutes dropping supplies to U.S. forces. (Courtesy Margaret Carillo.)

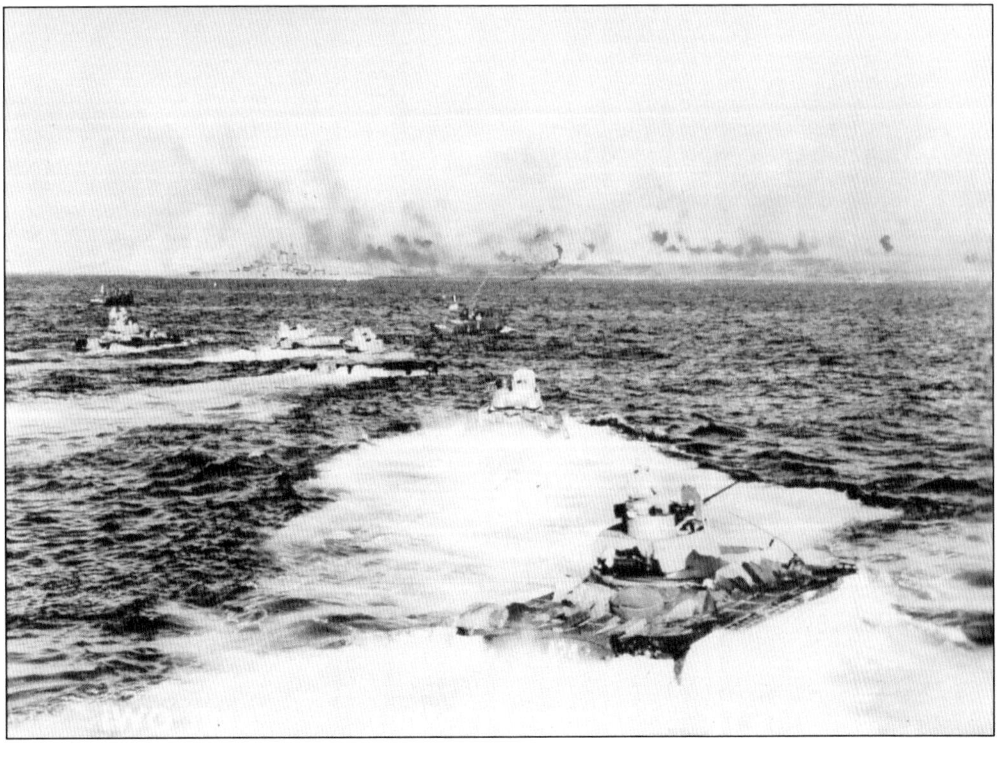

Salvador Ortiz, U.S. Army, married Socorro Leon in 1946, after his discharge. One of 10 families living on Morgan Lane in northern Redondo in the 1950s, they were parents to fraternal twins David and Rachel, also known as "Rocky," a nickname given to her by her father. (Courtesy "Rocky" Ortiz.)

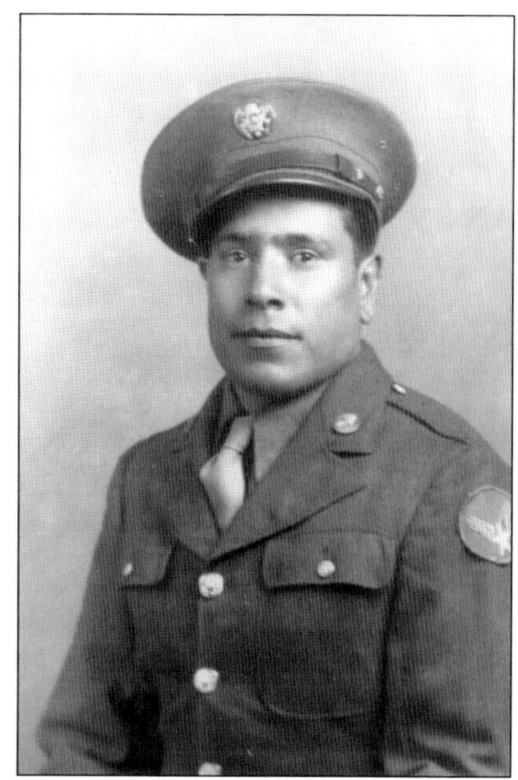

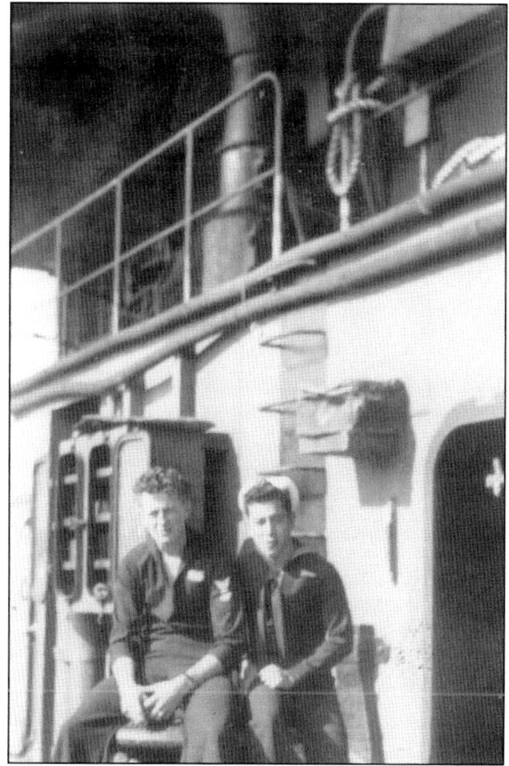

In this *c.* 1945 photograph, Julian Mendoza, right, U.S. Navy, is pictured aboard a ship off the coast of Saipan, one of the Mariana Islands. The other person is unidentified. (Courtesy Julian Mendoza.)

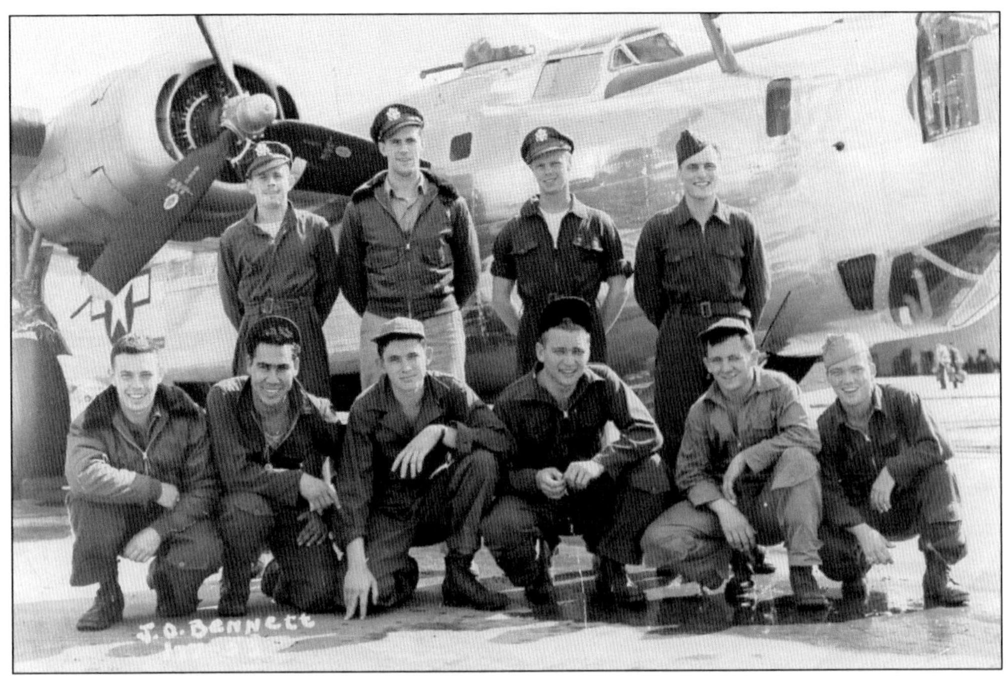

This 1948 photograph shows the crew of a B-24 bomber in Topeka, Kansas, before the ship was ferried to England for combat. Pictured here are, from left to right, (first row) Lee Garrison, Amador Espinosa, Robert Vest, Richard Hoyt, Coleman Pinkerton, and unidentified; (second row) Rodney Erxleven, Richard Dixon, John Bennett (pilot), and Frank Federrici. Espinosa flew as a waist gunner on 30 missions during the war. (Courtesy Amador Espinosa.)

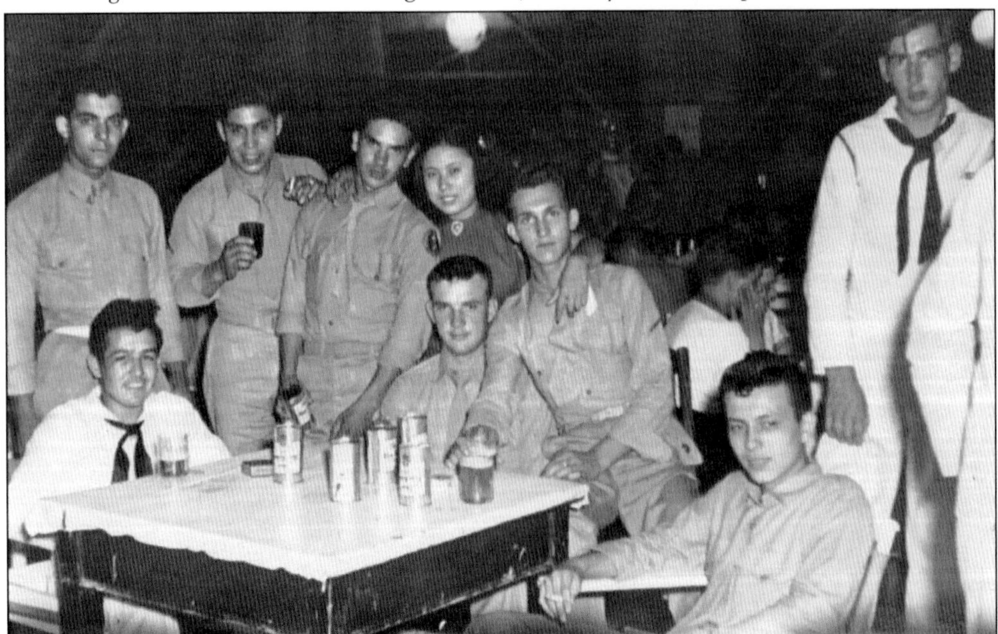

This 1947 photograph shows "Rom" Ordaz, U.S. Marine Corps (second row, second from left), off duty in Tsing Tao, China. The rest of the subjects in the photograph are unidentified. (Courtesy Ram Ordaz.)

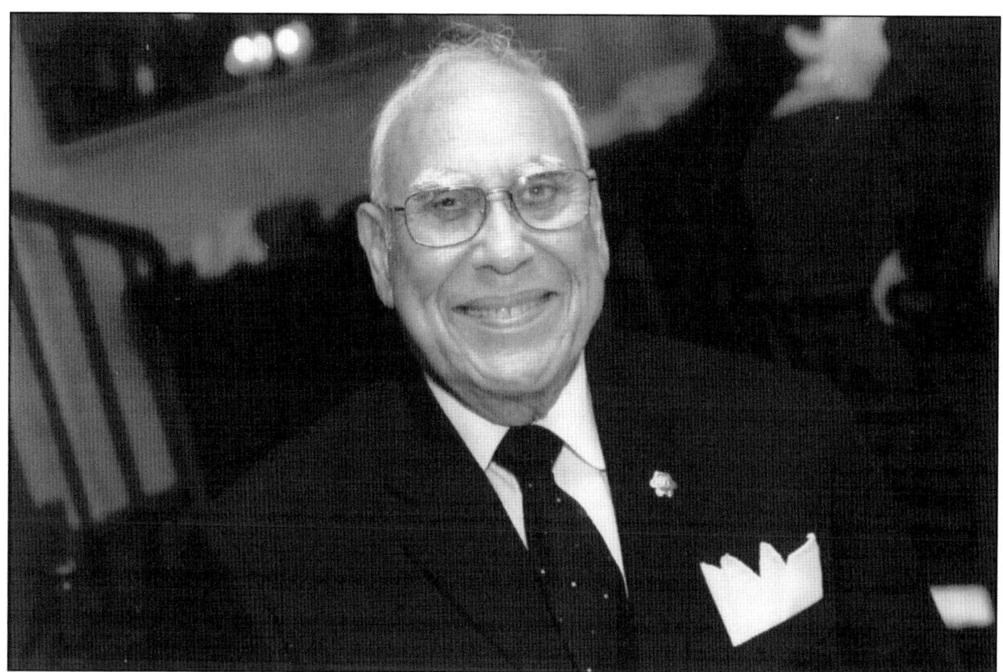

In 1993, Amador Espinosa is seen celebrating his retirement from the Redondo Beach Police Department after 50 years of service. His retirement party was attended by a multitude of colleagues, friends, and city officials attesting to his outstanding work record. (Courtesy Amador Espinosa.)

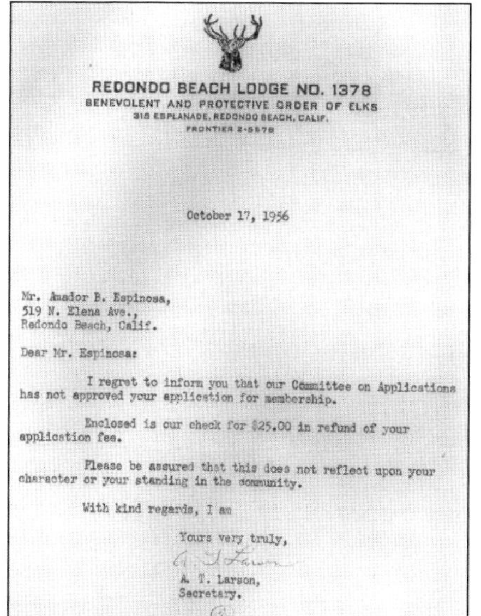

REDONDO BEACH LODGE NO. 1378
BENEVOLENT AND PROTECTIVE ORDER OF ELKS
318 ESPLANADE, REDONDO BEACH, CALIF.
FRONTIER 2-5578

October 17, 1956

Mr. Amador B. Espinosa,
519 N. Elena Ave.,
Redondo Beach, Calif.

Dear Mr. Espinosa:

I regret to inform you that our Committee on Applications has not approved your application for membership.

Enclosed is our check for $25.00 in refund of your application fee.

Please be assured that this does not reflect upon your character or your standing in the community.

With kind regards, I am

Yours very truly,

A. T. Larson,
Secretary.

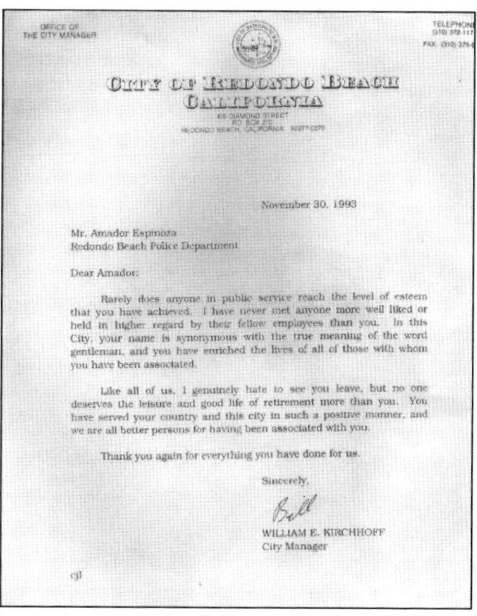

OFFICE OF THE CITY MANAGER

CITY OF REDONDO BEACH
CALIFORNIA

November 30, 1993

Mr. Amador Espinoza
Redondo Beach Police Department

Dear Amador:

Rarely does anyone in public service reach the level of esteem that you have achieved. I have never met anyone more well liked or held in higher regard by their fellow employees than you. In this City, your name is synonymous with the true meaning of the word gentleman, and you have enriched the lives of all of those with whom you have been associated.

Like all of us, I genuinely hate to see you leave, but no one deserves the leisure and good life of retirement more than you. You have served your country and this city in such a positive manner, and we are all better persons for having been associated with you.

Thank you again for everything you have done for us.

Sincerely,

Bill

WILLIAM E. KIRCHHOFF
City Manager

cjl

This 1956 letter, left, from the Redondo Beach Elks Lodge denied Amador Espinosa membership. He remembers when his mother, Ruth, purchased a home near Knob Hill in Redondo Beach in the 1950s, despite restrictive real estate covenants prohibiting the sale of homes to certain ethnic groups south of Torrance Boulevard. Thirty-seven years later, Amador Espinosa received the letter on the right from the Redondo Beach City Manager's office. Today he continues to serve as a volunteer in the Redondo Beach Police Department. (Both courtesy Amador Espinosa.)

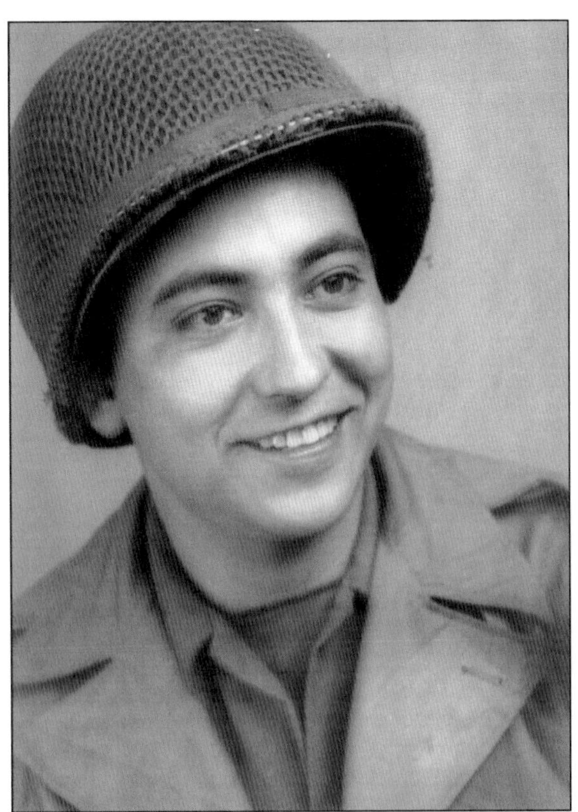

Pvt. Isaias "Chayo" Moreno, U.S. Army, served in four European theaters in World War II—Holland, Germany, Italy, and France. The Moreno family relates a story told by his deeply religious mother, Maria, that when Chayo returned home from the war, entered the house, and closed the living room door, a crucifix, which had been positioned over the door, fell. (Courtesy Roberta and "Luigi" Moreno.)

This German flag was captured by Chayo Moreno in an enemy bunker in Normandy, France, when he stormed the beach during the invasion. This photograph appears to have been taken at the Dicalite Mine in Walteria, where he worked before joining the army. The sign is held by Chayo's daughter Roberta, age three. (Courtesy Roberta and "Luigi" Moreno.)

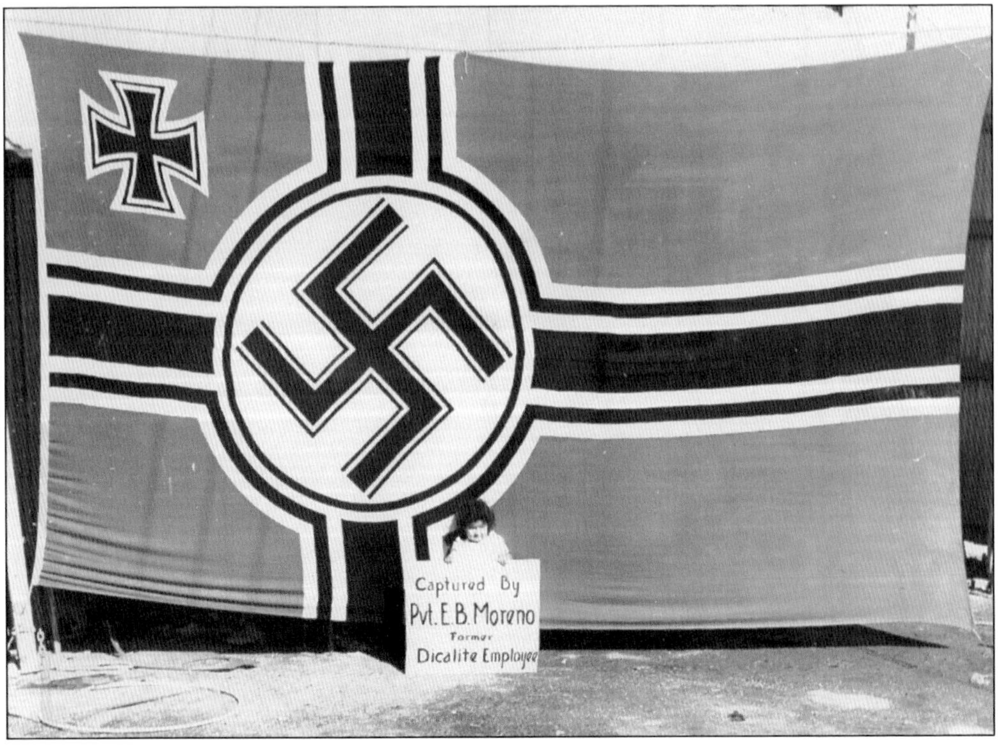

Bonifacio Moreno, U.S. Army, served in Korea after World War II. He was the son of Domingo Moreno, one of the early settlers of northern Redondo Beach, and brother of Chayo Moreno. (Courtesy Inez Areyan.)

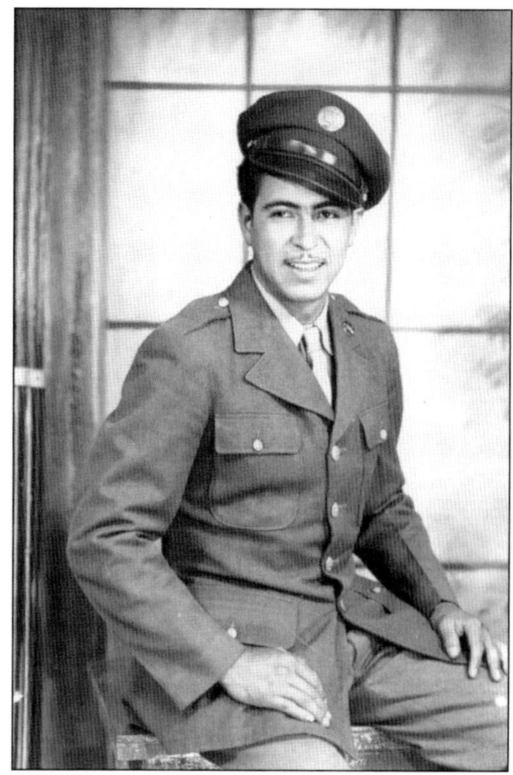

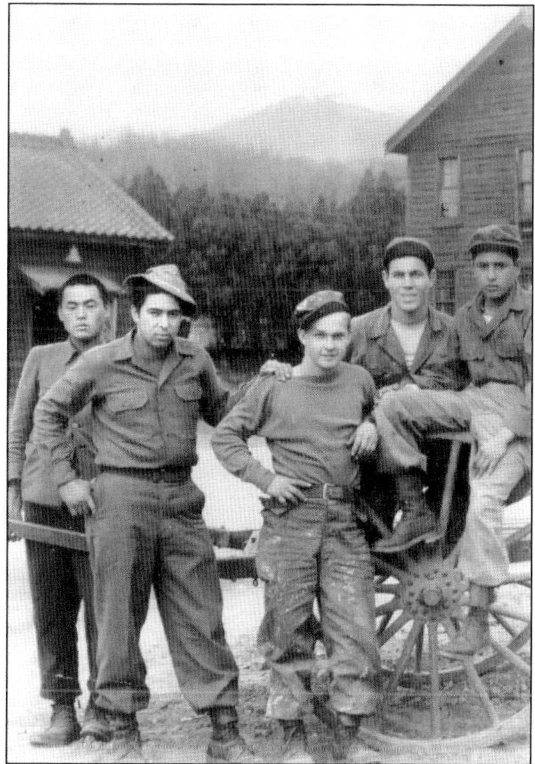

Somewhere in South Korea, Bonifacio Moreno (second from left) posed for this c. 1952 photograph with a Korean rickshaw and driver. The other three soldiers are unidentified. (Courtesy Porfiria Banda.)

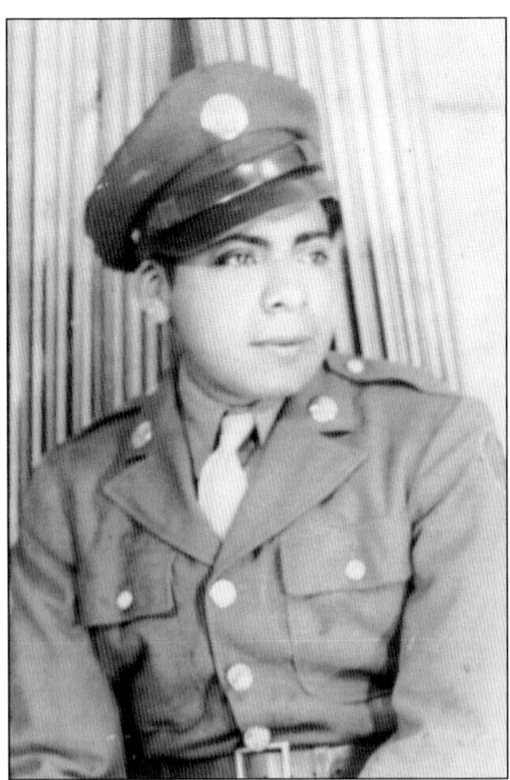

Cirilo Colin, U.S. Army, served in the Philippine Islands and occupied Japan after World War II. He was the son of Mauricio Colin, an early settler of northern Redondo Beach. (Courtesy Inez Areyan.)

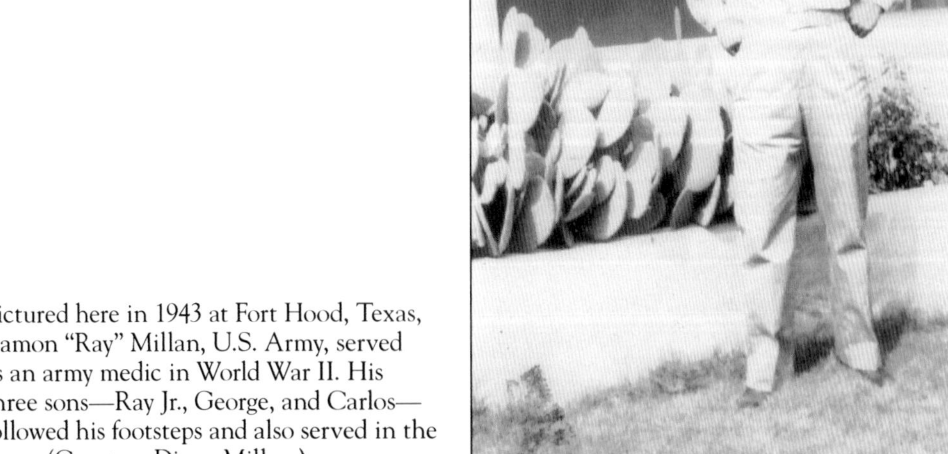

Pictured here in 1943 at Fort Hood, Texas, Ramon "Ray" Millan, U.S. Army, served as an army medic in World War II. His three sons—Ray Jr., George, and Carlos—followed his footsteps and also served in the army. (Courtesy Diana Millan.)

Carlos Millan, U.S. Army Airborne, served in North Carolina and became an airborne jump instructor. (Courtesy Candy Millan.)

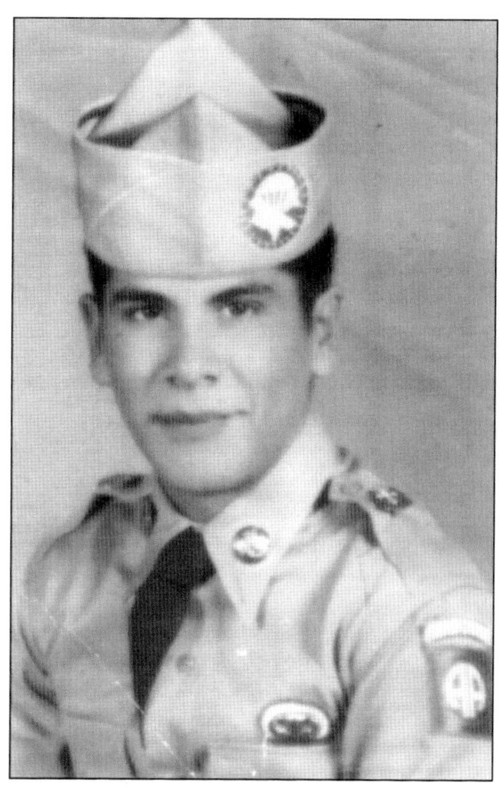

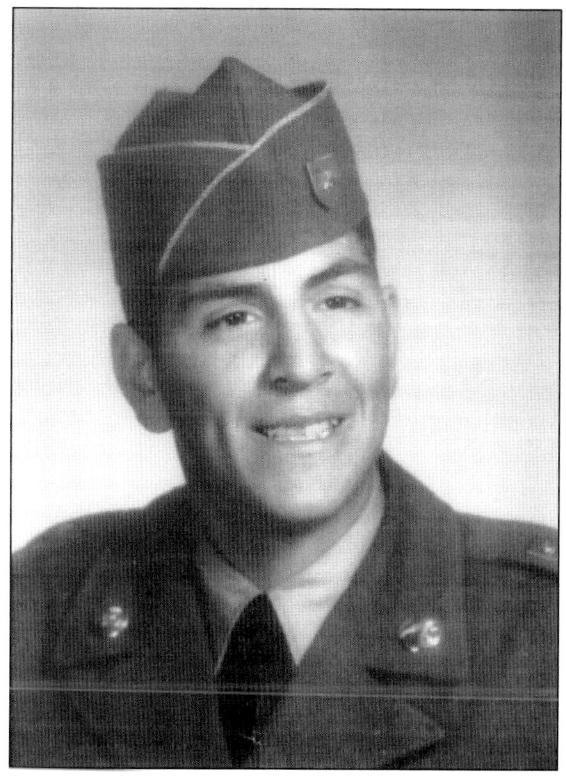

George Millan, U. S. Army Airborne, served in Korea from 1951 to 1953 and received a Purple Heart for combat injuries. (Courtesy Candy Millan.)

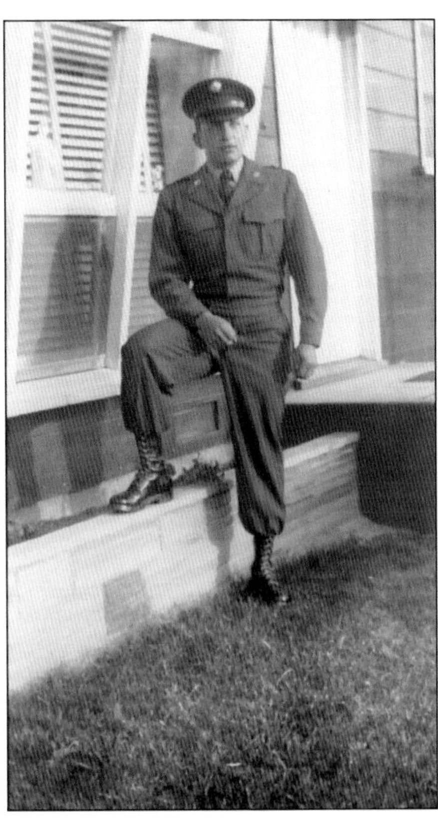

Ricardo Real, U.S. Army, posed for this 1952 photograph in Washington State. After his discharge, he successfully operated restaurants in Manhattan Beach and Redondo Beach. (Courtesy Ricardo Real.)

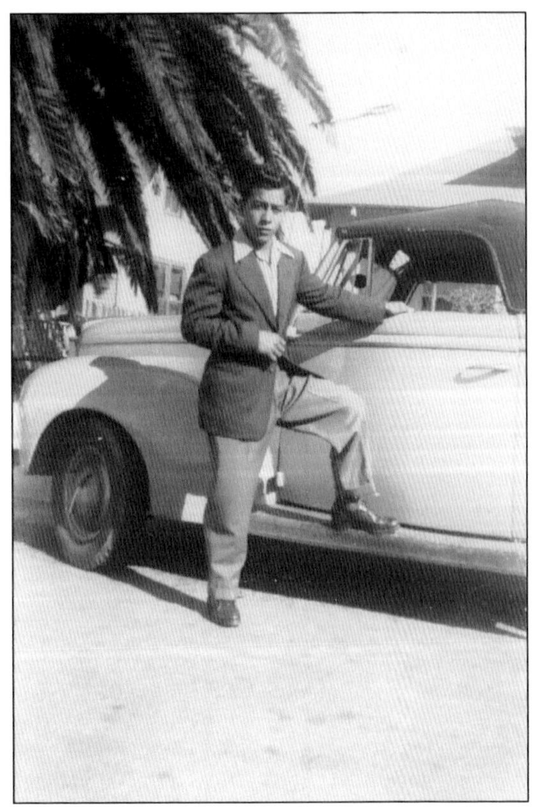

Julian Mendoza, seen here in 1944, sold his 1940 Ford convertible before joining the U.S. Navy and gave the proceeds to his mother to help provide for her while he served. (Courtesy Julian Mendoza.)

Paul Pacheco, U.S. Army, served as a military policeman in Colorado and Indiana and returned to Redondo Beach after his discharge in 1945. (Courtesy Tommy Pacheco.)

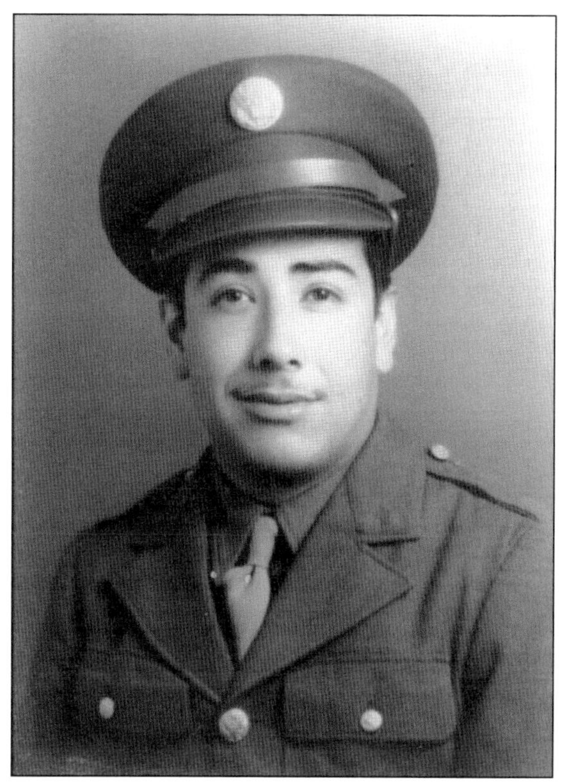

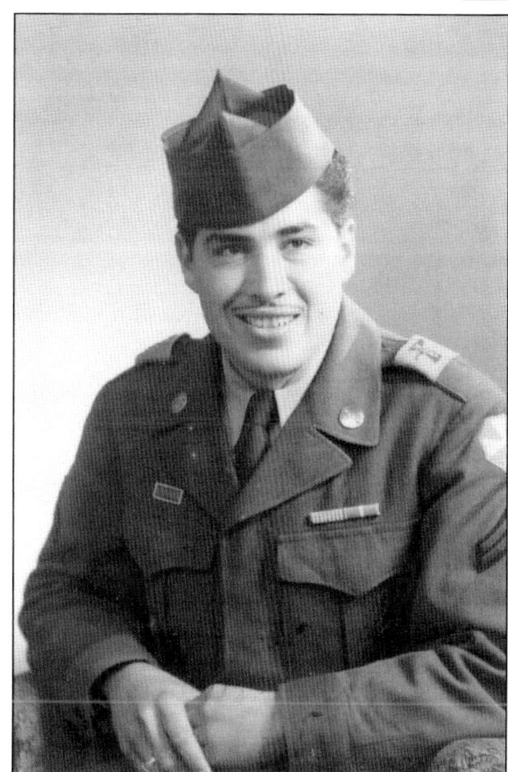

Robert Trevino, U.S. Army, served in Korea and Japan in 1953. After his discharge, he and his brother, Richard "Dick" Trevino, established the Trevino Brothers Plumbing Company. (Courtesy Lupe Trevino.)

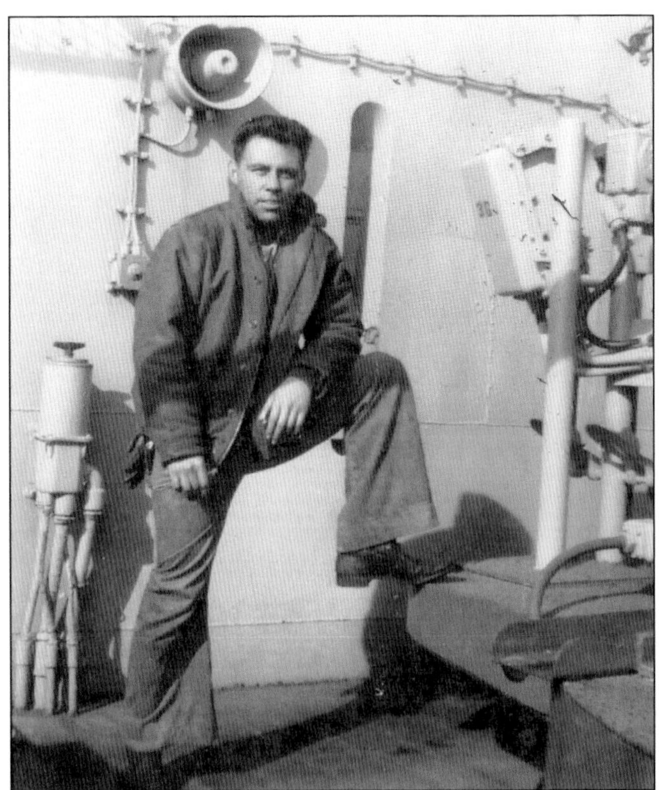

Richard Castillon, U.S. Navy, served aboard the USS *Essex*, a CVA9 aircraft carrier, from 1951 to 1954. This photograph was taken off the coast of Korea in 1954. (Courtesy Richard Castillon.)

In 1951, four friends enlisted in the U.S. Navy at the same time. From left to right are Herbert Madrid, Artie Espinoza, two unidentified friends, Richard Castillon, and "Chuey" Hernandez. This photograph was taken at the U.S. Naval Training Center in San Diego, California. (Courtesy "Chuey" Hernandez.)

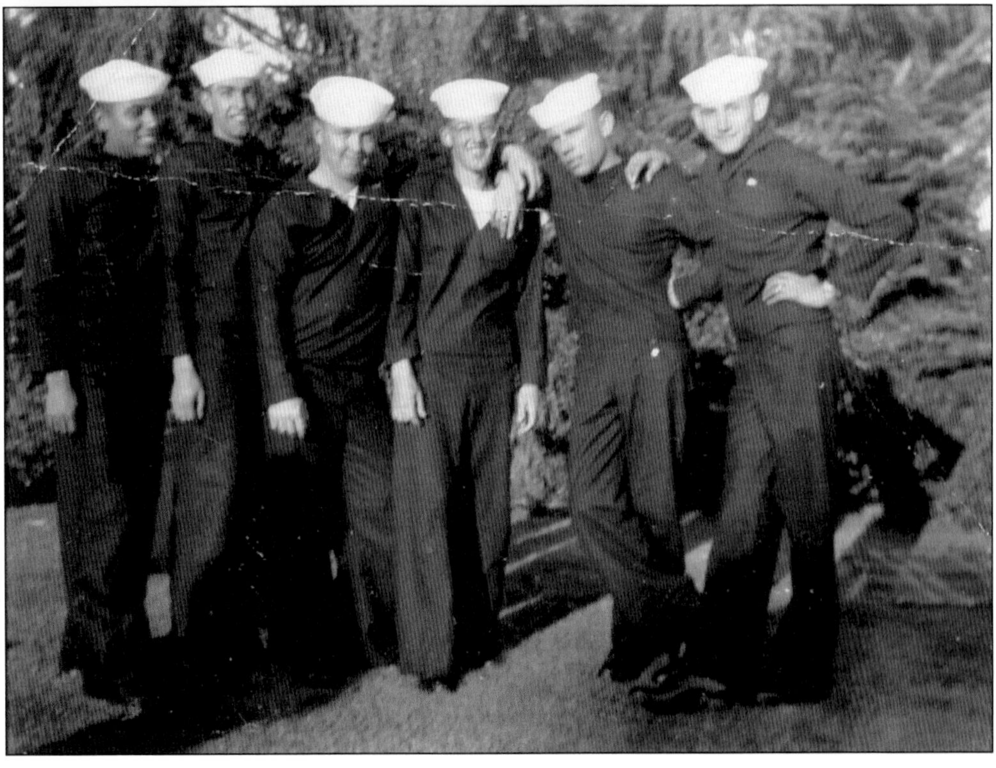

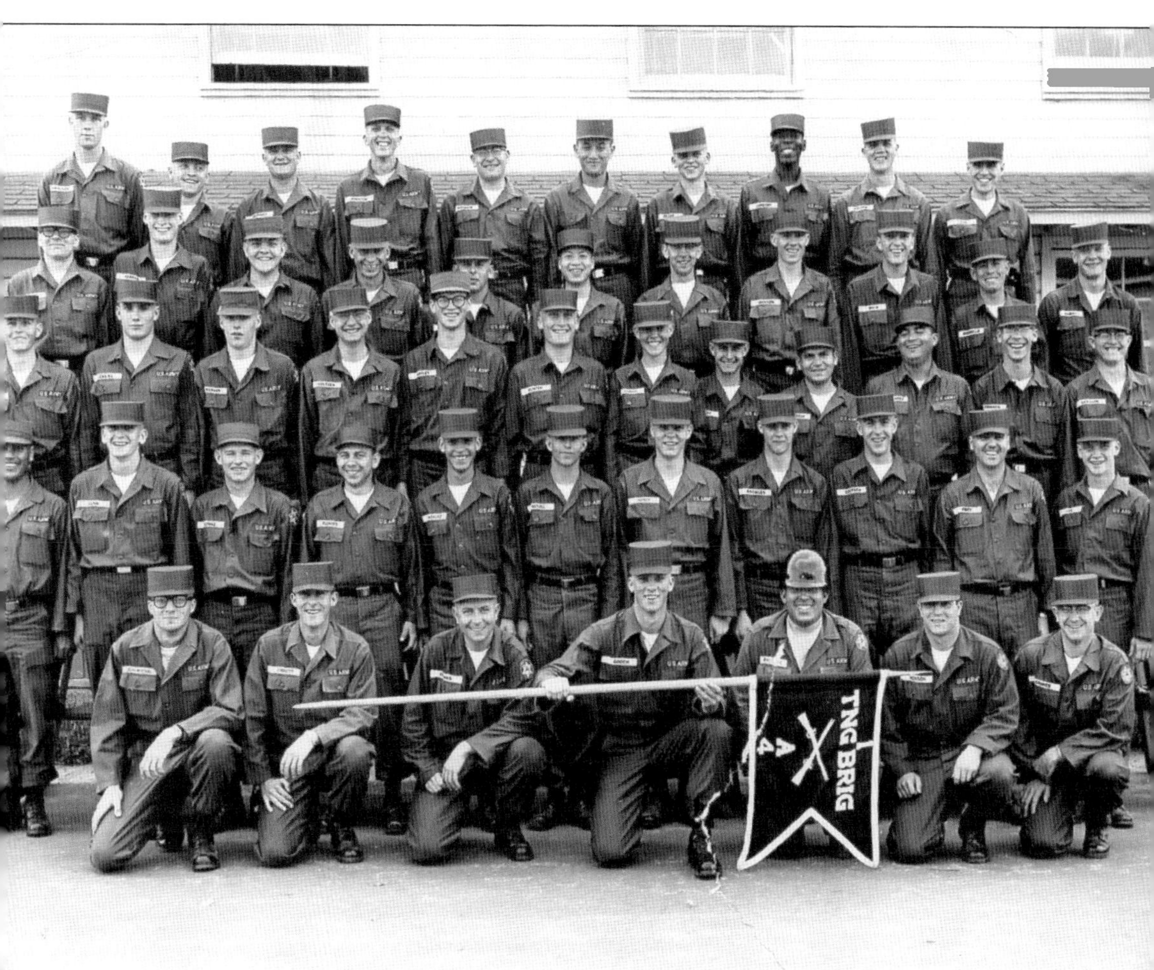

Fort Ord, California, was the setting for this U.S. Army A Battalion, 1st Brigade photograph, taken of the recruits just prior to graduation from basic training. Here Henry "P. C." Fernandez is pictured in the second row at far left. Before joining the army, he was a talented place kicker on the Redondo High football team. (Courtesy Ordie Fernandez.)

Consistent with our mission to preserve history on a local level, this book was printed in South Carolina on American-made paper and manufactured entirely in the United States. Products carrying the accredited Forest Stewardship Council (FSC) label are printed on 100 percent FSC-certified paper.